Interpreting Quantitative Data

David Byrne

SAGE Publications
London • Thousand Oaks • New Delhi

First published 2002

SAGE Publications Ltd
6 Bonhill Street
London EC2A 4PU

SAGE Publications Inc
2455 Teller Road
Thousand Oaks, California 91320

SAGE Publications India Pvt Ltd
32, M-Block Market
Greater Kailash - I
New Delhi 110 048

British Library Cataloguing in Publication data

A catalogue record for this book is available from the British Library

ISBN 0 7619 6261 1
     0 7619 6262 X

Library of Congress control number available

Typeset by SIVA Math Setters, Chennai, India
Printed in Great Britain by The Cromwell Press Ltd, Trowbridge, Wiltshire

Contents

Preface

I began this book because I wanted to write a text that reflected my own practice both as a social researcher and as someone who most years teaches two MA modules entitled 'Philosophy of Social Research' and 'Quantitative Research Methods'. In neither of these roles was I happy with the 'prevailing orthodoxies' that defined the nature of quantitative social research. Whenever I had come across a heresy I seemed to have signed up to it – to Tukey's programme of exploratory data analysis, to critical realist ontology and the consequent understanding of cause as complex and contingent, to complexity theory and its descriptions of complex evolutionary systems, to a commitment to social research as critical practice rather than neutral observation. It seemed time to synthesize all of these things and this book is the result.

Frankly, I think it is an opportune time for some loud heretical ranting. At a time when people are seriously proposing randomized controlled trials as an appropriate investigative strategy (other than in the clinical and educational contexts where this approach *might* – note the stress on might – be valid), the UK ESRC has just, I hope, been more or less warned off making the study of structural equation modelling compulsory for all research students funded by it whatever their discipline, and 'reductionist emergence' typified by rational choice theory is getting altogether too cocky in its claims to be the way to understand the social world, in my dialectical vernacular it is time to say 'Just hold on there a minute' very loudly indeed.

It would be tempting to write a philosophical critique of quantitative research practice, and there is plenty of such criticism here. However, I do believe not just in the validity of, but in the necessity for quantitative exploration of the social world. So I have tried to produce a book which rather than saying 'Don't do that', offers some suggestions about how, using the enormous resources we have as cyborgs whose cognitive capacities for handling numerical information are massively extended by our connections to data managing and processing computers, we might understand the world through combining quantitative and qualitative modes of investigation as the basis for social action.

A lot of people have helped on the way to producing this book. Malcolm Williams and Will Medd have read chapters and given me some very useful criticism. A lot of the ideas have been presented at the ESRC seminar series 'Making Realism Work' run by Caroline New and Bob Carter and I am grateful to them and to all the participants. Likewise Tim May and Malcolm Williams gave me the opportunity to present my views on measurement to their conference 'Knowing the Social World' and again I am grateful to them and to those who participated in discussion. I have also benefited from discussion with the Tufton group of clinical and other health researchers organized by Frances Griffiths. David L. Harvey and Paul Cilliers not only provided me with core ideas from their published work but have generously commented on pieces which I wrote in preparing this text and again have helped to clarify my approach and argument.

At Durham Wendy Dyer and Emma Uprichard have argued with me in the course of postgraduate supervision, a process from which I have learned at least as much as they have. Several waves of MA students have had complexity inflicted on them in ever increasing amounts and I am grateful for their forbearance, indeed active interest, and for ideas generated in discussion.

Finally, Sally Ruane kept me at this book in her own inimitable fashion and it is only appropriate to dedicate it to her.

Introduction

The title of this book is *Interpreting Quantitative Data*: I want to begin it by addressing the meaning of those words – interpreting – through comparing and contrasting it with another word, analysis. A more conventional title would have been 'Quantitative Analysis'. There are lots of books on quantitative methods with the word 'analysis' in the title and even plenty of books and software packages in which the expression 'qualitative analysis' is used in the description of their contents. Analysis is almost taken for granted as the systematic mode through which we understand the products of social research. The approach adopted here can be demonstrated by comparing and contrasting these two words – interpretation, which is what I am going to deal with, and analysis, which is the conventional approach.

Analysis is easily defined. Its literal meaning has to do with the breaking up of something into its component parts and explaining the whole in terms of the properties of the parts which make it up – the reductionist programme. The important statistical technique analysis of variance, the statistical basis of randomized controlled trials as a method of investigation, illustrates this rather well. The variance is the standardized sum of the squared deviations around the arithmetic mean of values on a continuous variable – squared to eliminate negative numbers and standardized so as to eliminate the influence of the absolute number of cases examined. Tautologically, but importantly, we can say that it is a measure of how a variable varies, which is what variables by definition do. It is analysed into two parts – the within sum of squares, which is considered to represent random variation within a set of categories, and the 'between' sum of squares, which is considered to represent variation among the categories. The bigger the latter is as compared with the former the more likely it is that membership of a given category has implications for the values on the continuous variable whose variance is being analysed.

The point of the analysis is to establish cause by seeing if 'between' differences as compared with 'within' differences are sufficiently large in relation to the sample size for us to *infer*, an important word, that they really exist in the world. On this basis we proceed, without any logical validation from the test itself,[1] to assert that the categorical variable has a causal influence on the continuous variable, the variance of which we have just analysed. We understand by breaking something up into bits and we see the world as understandable in terms of the properties of, and relations among, those very bits.

Indeed we have fragmented even before we begin to analyse because the very process of constructing variables detaches particular aspects of things from the thing as whole. Variables describe properties of cases but the real things are the cases, not the traces of them which we measure as variables. This is an extremely important point and we will discuss it at length subsequently. For now we should note that data 'analysis' is a process of double fragmentation – we fragment important social realities, both entities and relations, into aspects of them and then we fragment the aspects in order to establish 'causal' relations.

'Interpretation' is rather more difficult to define than analysis. The distinction between them is often asserted to lie in the purposes of the processes. The purpose of analysis is seen to be the establishing of cause whereas interpretation is considered to be about the elucidation of meaning. We must be careful to note that not only social scientists interpret. On the contrary, continuing interpretation by actors underpins the whole social constitution of the social world. With the exception of actions derived from habitus we interpret the world as we act in it. So we interpret in acting and we interpret to elucidate the meaning of those acts. Certainly interpretation is concerned with meaning but it is also concerned with cause. Max Weber's assertion of the necessity for social scientists to engage in a process of *verstehen*, of interpretative understanding, was directed just as much at ensuring that the explanations were adequate at the level of cause as at achieving adequacy at the level of meaning. For Weber structures of meaning could be causal to social transformation – the general theme of his discussion of the relationship between the character of Protestantism and the rise of capitalism. We must examine meanings because we think structures of meaning are causal to social actions and social structures.

So far the idea of 'cause' has been taken for granted, but this word is perhaps the most contentious in the philosophy of science. Most of the arguments about the nature of causes have been epistemological – about how we can know what causes what – and generally derive from Hume's original argument about observed constant conjunction. The realist position, to which this text adheres, takes an ontological rather than epistemological view of cause. It specifies the nature of causes as complex and contingent and we will examine the implications of that in great detail in subsequent chapters. However, there is something rather fundamental which needs spelling out here. To say that causes are real is to say that something generates something else. The something can be a complex generative mechanism rather than any single factor but something does have generative capacity. When we look for causes we are seeking to identify and to understand the nature of that generative capacity, to know the nature and potential of the something we call 'cause'.

It is perhaps fruitful to consider whether there is such a radical difference between cause and meaning as tradition has held in relation to these important terms. The rise of 'Cultural Studies' has led to the assertion of a relativism based on unique interpretation – meaning alone and meaning which may be different for every interpreter. Note that the point here is the unique.

The major traditions of qualitative empirical research are by no means to be understood in terms of this kind of ultimately solipsist perspectivism. Pawson and Tilley have made a crucial distinction between 'Hermeneutics I', the original programme of social constructionism, and the postmodernist perspective which they describe as 'Hermeneutics II'. Hermeneutics I is based on a research programme in which:

> by being witness to the day-to-day reasoning of their research subjects, by engaging in their life world, by participating in their decision making, the researcher would be that much closer to reality. The hermeneutic approach, it was assumed, almost literally placed one in touch with the truth ... (Pawson and Tilley, 1997: 21)

This is a description of interpretative ethnography but it can be extended to cover any interpretative programme, including qualitative interviewing and documentary work in which there is no direct experience by the researcher. In this tradition there is a social world to be known and accounts of that social world can be ranked in terms of the degree of accuracy of their representation of it. Hermeneutics I is entirely compatible with a realist programme, the programme endorsed in this book. For realists the world does exist and, ahead of a lot of discussion of this issue in Chapter 1, we can know it, although the process of knowing is a social process with social content. The key phrase here for the quantitative programme is 'data construction'. Our measures are not given, the literal meaning of data, but made, but for realists they are made from something rather than nothing. They are not merely reifications.

In contrast, fully fledged 'phenomenologicalism', which also operates under the trade name of 'post-structuralism', Pawson and Tilley's Hermeneutics II,

> starts from the point of view that all beliefs are 'constructions' *but* adds the twist that we cannot, therefore, get beyond constructions. It insists, in other words, that there are no neutral/factual/definitive accounts to be made of the social world. (1997: 21; original emphasis)

This is not the position of either classical hermeneutics or realism. The object of hermeneutic examination is always a text, although that word has a very wide range of potential meanings. However, not only does classical hermeneutics assert that texts can be understood, but as Crotty puts it:

> Included in much hermeneutic theory is the prospect of gaining an understanding of the text that is deeper or goes further into the author's own understanding. This aim derives from the view that in large measure authors' meanings and intentions remain implicit and go unrecognized by the authors themselves. Because in the writing of the text so much is simply taken for granted, skilled hermeneutic inquiry has the potential to uncover meanings that are, in this sense, hidden in the text. Interpreters may end up with an explicit awareness of meanings, and especially assumptions, that the authors themselves would have been unable to articulate. (1998: 91)

Note the similarity between the positivist social scientist and the hermeneutic interpreter. Both assert a special privilege of understanding which goes beyond the understanding of those whose world or work is being understood. This issue will be considered subsequently by reference to the ideas of Paulo Freire (1998) and his very different conception of research as a participatory process.

This book is a realist text and Banai explains the implications of this commitment for our consideration of meaning and cause:

> Although critical realism accepts a place for hermeneutics, it differs from hermeneutic philosophies in insisting that there is also causation in society. It posits a hermeneutic which is 'historically' situated and a social science which allows for interpretative, critical, systematic, and practical inquiry of the concepts and activities of how we constitute our social world. (1995: 466–7)

In this book the approach will be to try to understand the complex causal processes of the social world and of the interactions between the social and natural worlds, through a process of measurement but not through a process of analysis. I suppose the crucial meta-theoretical credo of this text can be put like this. Of course our observations are social acts and are conditioned by the social contexts we occupy when we make them. This applies absolutely to measurement as much as to any other process of observation. Nevertheless the social world is there to be observed. It is real. The perspective of our observation matters but then so does the local character of that which we observe. As so often, Raymond Williams put his finger right on the core of the matter:

> it is necessary to recall an absolutely founding presumption of materialism: that the natural world exists whether anyone signifies it or not. (1979: 167)

And so does the social world, in both its material and immaterial aspects, so long as we realize that processes of assigning meaning, of signifying, are part of our everyday social existence. This is not just a programme of realism – it is a process of construction.

Kritzer's observation is most helpful here:

> That interpretation is important in quantitative social science should not be surprising because interpretation is central to analysis of human phenomena. In literary analysis, one is typically presented with a text for interpretation. In qualitative social science the analyst must construct the text for interpretation. In quantitative social science, the analyst constructs both a first order text (in assembling the data) and a second order text (in the form of statistical results). With each additional step in the process, the role of interpretation increases, as do the technical elements that must be considered part of the integrative process. Thus, rather than being more divorced from the human process of interpretation, quantitative social science probably involves more levels of interpretation than does qualitative social science. (1996: 2–3)

There is an oxymoron in the idea that analysts construct, but if for analyst we read researcher throughout this passage, then it is absolutely right.

We have to recognize that there is more to interpretation than abstract contemplation. Desrosières (1998) argues that processes of measurement have actually played a crucial role in constructing our world as it is today. Daston's review of Desrosières's important text summarizes things for us very well:

> As an insider [Administrator of France's Institut National de la Statisque et des Etudes Economiques], Desrosières is all too aware of the fragility of statistical categories and the contingencies of statistical techniques. There is nothing inevitable about either, as his book shows in considerable detail. But he is not an apostate. Statistics works in and on the world, simultaneously describing and remaking. It straddles the chasm between the invented and the discovered, the real and the constructed – oppositions that have structured an increasingly sterile debate about the nature of science among historians, philosophers, sociologists and scientists. The great merit of Desrosières' study is that it points the way beyond this impasse by showing how statistical entities are simultaneously real and constructed, invented and discovered. (2000: 36)

We will keep coming back to these themes and the first three chapters of the book will take the form of a development of them. Here I am engaged in a process of 'seeing off'. Pawson and Tilley and Desrosières have been drawn on to see off the absolutely relativist forms of postmodernism. Now I want to turn to beginning to see off the major form of contemporary statistical reasoning, the testing of hypotheses based on probability theory as applied to sampling distributions. Let me moderate my argument just a little. I do not want to drown this dog, just put it back in its kennel. The use of statistical inference has an important place in quantitative work in the social sciences in informing us when we use data derived from samples, when we speak about the whole in terms of the properties of part of that whole. And that is it. If we look at works written within the framework of 'social statistics', particularly in the British if rather less in the US tradition, we find that this important set of methods has taken over practically everything. The use of statistical inference is considered to be the basis of explanation, despite the inherent problem of the fallacy of affirming the consequent, the statistical version of Popper's contention that we can never prove, only fail to falsify. This book will follow the lead given by Tukey when it comes to statistical methods. It endorses exploration and description. As Tukey put it:

> Once upon a time, statisticians only explored. Then they learned to confirm exactly – to confirm a few things exactly, each under very specific circumstances. As they emphasized exact confirmation, their techniques inevitably became less flexible. The connection of the most used techniques with past insights was weakened. Anything to which a confirmatory procedure was not explicitly attached was decried as 'mere descriptive statistics', no matter how much we had learned from it. (1977: vii)

Actually, I want to go somewhat further. I want to praise classification and endorse stamp collecting as the proper form of science.[2] Indeed, I am going to argue that classification is perhaps the most important way in which we can understand a complex non-linear world.

This book is not simply realist – it is 'complex realist'. That is to say, it follows the proposal made by Reed and Harvey (1992), who argue that it is by combining 'complexity' as a scientific ontology and critical realism as a philosophical ontology that we can understand the social world and use our understanding to act within the social world. I hope and expect that within the first decade of the new millennium it will become unnecessary to outline the general principles of complexity in this sort of text. However, we are not there yet so I will begin to do so here.

The crucial point is that we are dealing with systems, not with atomistic objects. Most of the language of causality in science draws on the Newtonian programme in which objects move under the influence of forces. Newton's system of mechanics is a mathematical representation, re-presentation, of the way in which the objects move. If we know all of the laws of motion, the initial position of objects and the forces applied to them, then we can say what will happen to them over a given time period. The forces are the causes of motion.

In the social sciences variables are seen as equivalent to forces. Traditionally, quantitative social scientists have tried to construct a social mechanics that can generate predictions of future states on the basis of the measurement of variables in the same way in which Newtonian mechanics predicts through the measurement of forces.

The Newtonian programme is:

- analytical/reductionist – it breaks up the mechanical system into its component parts and explains the trajectory, that is, the movement through time of the system as whole in terms of the properties of the parts – the forces and objects – that compose it.
- linear – changes in what is caused are proportionate to changes in what in causes. Small changes in causes produce small changes in what is caused. Newton's calculus is a mathematical system which works exactly by dealing with small proportionate changes.
- based on additionality – the combined effect of two or more causes is the sum of the causes taken separately.

In the nineteenth century physicists encountered a new kind of real pheno-menon which they wanted to model. The heat engines of the industrial revolution could not be described mathematically by Newton's mechanics. The new approach of thermo-dynamics, intended to describe systems in which both heat and motion were in play, required not an analytical/reductionist account of the components of the systems, but rather a descrip-tion in terms of the properties of the systems taken as wholes. This was not, just, a turn from analysis to holism – from explanation in terms of parts to explanation in terms of the properties of the whole system. Rather it required an explanation in terms of the whole system and of the parts of the system and of the interactions among the parts and of the parts with the whole. Systems of this kind are complex. Rosen distinguishes complex from simple in a particularly clear fashion:

a simple system is one to which a notion of state can be assigned once and for all, or more generally, one in which Aristotelian causal categories can be independently segregated from one another. Any system for which such a description cannot be provided I will call *complex*. Thus, in a complex system, the causal categories become intertwined in such a way that no dualistic language of state plus dynamic laws can completely describe it. Complex systems must then process mathematical images different from, and irreducible to, the generalized dynamic systems which have been considered universal. (1987: 324)

Complex systems have emergent properties – they have properties that cannot be explained in terms of the properties of their components. Given that they display emergence, they can and do change in non-linear ways. Small changes in 'causes' can produce radical transformations of the state of the system as a whole – phase shifts. This means that these sorts of systems are neither equilibric or homeostatic. They do not stay in one state – equilibrium. They do not return towards equilibrium if they are disturbed from equilibrium, unlike homeostatic systems in which changes generate negative feedback moving them back towards equilibrium. They are instead far from equilibric. This is very important but what matters for the moment is the implication of this approach for the idea of variable. Variables describing complex systems are descriptions of properties of the system as a whole. We can consider them as the dimensions of a multidimensional state space with the actual character of the system at any given point in time being represented by the set of values on measured variables considered as co-ordinates in that state space. However, the co-ordinates are more of an address than a description of causes. They tell where – not why. We describe changes in the character of the system in terms of its trajectory through the multidimensional state space – that is by plotting a graph of its co-ordinates through time. This approach is inherently dynamic. Our measures are indicators of condition. The trajectory is the path which describes how condition changes.

There are several important implications of this understanding of complex systems. These are:

- We describe the system as a whole rather than in terms of parts.
- We plot the way the system changes – systems are temporal and dynamic. They exist in time and they change through time.
- We are particularly interested in changes of kind – in phase shifts in which systems undergo radical transformations.
- We are as much and usually more interested in the ways in which things interact as in the way in which they operate separately.

A central thrust of the approach adopted in this book is that we can re-interpret, understand in a different way, traditional multivariate statistical methods. This argument does not apply to regression analysis and its derivatives which seem irredeemably linear and analytical, but it does apply to contingency tables and methods of inferring cause from them. Above all else, it applies to the much neglected techniques (at least in sociology) of numerical taxonomy typified by cluster analysis. I am going to argue that it also applies to neural net approaches and might apply to some sorts of simulation procedures.

The preceding paragraph is saying something implicitly which now needs to be said explicitly. If we think of the world as complex and real we are thinking about it in a very different way from the ontological programme that underpins conventional statistical reasoning about cause. Moreover, our ability to explore this complex and real world in a quantitative way depends on the availability of instruments that allow us to deal with very large numbers of measurements and to relate these measurements to each other for very large numbers of cases and all at the same time. In other words, we can only do what I am going to propose we should do because we have electronic computers to do the number crunching for us. But we can do and we are doing things now which would have been impossible quite recently.

Conventionally, expository quantitative texts start with simple and traditional approaches and work towards radical and innovative ones. The advanced procedures are seen as founded on the simpler ones. There is something to be said for this sometimes, but in relation to numerical taxonomy and neural network techniques this 'build it up from the beginning' approach doesn't work. The new approaches are very different things and have to be understood as such. We certainly will pay attention to simple descriptive methods – they, alongside graphical representations made much easier by computing technology but available to us before – are very good ways of seeing the patterns in data. They are always a good place to start. However, they are not foundational to more advanced classification approaches. They belong in the same toolbox of exploratory methods but they are another set of tools.

Actually belonging in the same toolbox does matter because there is something about the simple exploratory devices, graphical representations and heavy number crunching taxonomy-making which is the same and which is very different from traditional causal approaches. They all pay more attention to cases than to variables. This is crucial. By thinking about cases as primary, we can construct connections between individual cases and collectivities in which the collectivities are understood as something more than mere aggregates of individuals. We can not only get beyond simple mechanics – we can get beyond statistical mechanics as well.[3]

I want to conclude the arguments in this introduction by spelling out the nature of the proposed quantitative programme founded on the basis of an ontological programme which we might call complex realism. The easiest, and at this stage best, way of doing this is by saying what such a programme can do which traditional approaches cannot do.

1   A realist approach recognizes the social nature of measurement as a process whilst still allowing that measurements can be descriptions of the real. Traditional approaches, as we shall see in Chapter 1, either assert a

crude positivism in which measurements are taken to be brute facts or fall back on a conventionalism in which measurements are not understood as having any necessary correspondence with the world at all. This latter is always merely an epistemological apology. In traditional approaches measurements are in practice always taken as brute facts.

2   Complex realism provides us with a way of handling what is really important in the social world – the changes in kind – transformations that can be understood as phase shifts.

3   Complex realism does not reify the aspects of real systems which we measure and call variables. Instead these aspects are understood as indicators of the character of the real systems rather than as things that have a real existence outside them.

4   Complex realism enables us to cope with the problem of levels. Conventional statistical reasoning in the social sciences is incapable of dealing with relationships among levels – of relating individuals to social collectivities – other than by regarding social collectivities as mere aggregates of individuals with no emergent properties. In general it falls back on the individual level, with social structures reduced to variate properties of individuals – the nominalist fallacy. Indeed, attempts to understand relationships among levels in a quantitative way are often dismissed by reference to 'the ecological fallacy'. Such references are usually misconceived because they confuse inferring individual properties from measurements of aggregates/collectivities[4] with discussion of relationships at the level of collectivity.

5   Complex realism allows us to work other than in an analytical way. We can explore interaction as a guide to the character of systems understood as complex products of parts, wholes, part–part interactions, part–whole interactions and part–part–whole interactions.

Finally, and at a kind of meta level in which all the previously specified elements are contained, complex realism allows us to understand our scientific practice as interpretation rather than as analysis. Moreover, there is the necessary predicate of interpretation specified by Marx in Thesis XI on Feuerbach: 'The Philosophers have described the world – the point however is to change it.' Interpretation is necessarily critical. The inevitable consequence of criticism is action. We understand the world by changing it but understanding is part of the process of changing.

The organization of the book

There are lots of books on how to get quantitative data, on the design and execution of surveys and secondary analysis, even more on how to carry out statistical operations on data, and even some on the new non-statistical methods of exploring and modelling based on numerical taxonomy, simulation and the use of neural nets. In this text I want to cover all of these topics whilst arguing for a radically different way of understanding the nature both what is being measured and of the measurements themselves. The book begins with two chapters that lay out the fundamental argument. Chapter 1 is about the nature of the things we are measuring. Chapter 2 is about the nature of measurement as a process.

The next three chapters deal with issues about how we get our data in the first place and how we understand it as generating a representative account of the social world. In Chapter 3 we will deal with the interpretation and use of measurements created by others, particularly the measurements created by agencies of the state, statistics in the most conventional meaning of that word. Chapter 4 deals with the nature of social surveys as exercises in data construction and develops arguments originally formulated by Marsh (1982) and Bateson (1984). In Chapter 5 the whole use of probabilistic reasoning in quantitative research is tackled head on.

The last four substantive chapters of the book deal with the actual processes of interpreting data. Chapter 6 outlines a programme of exploration, description and classification. Chapter 7 takes on the General Linear Model and extracts from that dominant approach those procedures which can be reinterpreted as exploratory and used in an exploratory way. Chapter 8 deals with the new procedures of simulation and neural net approaches. In Chapter 9 the issues of the relationship between quantitative and qualitative data are tackled through an examination of computer based qualitative data 'analysis'. Finally, in the Conclusion, the implications of the arguments here for quantitative social research as an active social practice are laid out as the basis for future work.

Notes

1 This means that we ignore Popper's assertion that a hypothesis can only be disproved but never proved. We commit the fallacy of affirming the consequent. It is worth noting that when analysis of variance is employed as part of an experimental design there is at least temporal ordering to justify assertions of causality because the variation is introduced by the experimenter and precedes any possible dependent change. The causal proposition is represented by the experimental design and its plausability is assessed by the test. However, control can never be complete, the essential basis of Popper's position. This means that all we can ever do is reject the null hypothesis and say that things *might* work as the research design proposes.

2 Rutherford is said to have divided science into physics and stamp collecting – a reductionist programme of cause in which everything can ultimately be explained in terms of a general theory of matter and energy, and mere classification as indulged in by biologists. We will classify here as a way of understanding causes.

3 We have to be careful with the words mechanics and mechanism. Newtonian mechanics is the description of motion under laws and depends on the analytical programme. The word 'mechanism' is used to describe the generative complexes which realism understands to be the complex and contingent causes of the actual world. Frankly this similarity is unfortunate because the ideas are fundamentally different but we are pretty well stuck with the expression 'generative mechanism' when something like 'generative complex' would be better.

4 Aggregates are mere agglomerations for counting purposes with no emergent properties. Collectivities are real social entities composed of individual social actors or some lower level aggregate of individual actors such as households but with emergent properties which are not reducible to the properties of the collectivities' components. Developments of traditional statistical techniques, and in particular multi-level modelling, have attempted to resolve these issues, but I will argue in Chapter 7 that such approaches are fundamentally flawed.

1

Interpreting the Real and Describing the Complex: Why We Have to Measure

> It is very striking that the classic technique developed in response to the impossibility of understanding contemporary society from experience, the statistical mode of analysis, had its precise origins within the period (early nineteenth century) of which you are speaking. For without the combination of statistical theory, which in a sense was already mathematically present, and arrangements for the collection of statistical data, symbolised by the founding of the Manchester Statistical Society, the society that was emerging out of the industrial revolution was literally unknowable. (Williams, 1979: 170)

Why does Williams consider that without statistical measurement 'the society that was emerging out of the industrial revolution was literally unknowable'? The simple answer is that the society was complex. Let us begin by trying to understand what that important word 'complex' really means. We can do this by making two comparisons. One is with the kind of society traditionally studied by anthropologists, using the techniques of ethnography. The other is with the artificial and constructed domain of the laboratory experiment.

The traditional locales of anthropological fieldwork are certainly not occupied by 'simple' societies, nor are they, as contemporary anthropology recognizes, occupied by societies without a history and therefore without change. However, the typical locale of fieldwork has always been small scale and open to being known through direct observation. The classic collection of the 1960s, Frankenberg's *Communities in Britain* (1966), contains summaries of studies in which social scientists came to know that complex combination of place and way of life which we call 'community' through living in and among people and observing what those people did – participant observation. Note that in these community studies, observation alone was never enough. The reportage was always contextualized by the use of quantitative measures which both described the places as they were *and* how they were changing.

Urban industrial society cannot be known by direct observation alone (although direct observation is one of the set of ways through which it can be known when these are used in combination) because it is too big and it is changing too fast. It is a matter of both scale and dynamism. Dynamism is not just a matter of change in the sense of incremental differences. Williams wrote about a society that was 'emerging' out of the industrial revolution. Emergence means that something new and different comes into being. We have change of kind rather than just change of degree. In Marx's terms we see a transformation of quantity into quality. In the language of complexity theory we have a phase shift. Let me illustrate by an example which is of the greatest importance for the mid-term future of Western industrial societies. One of the oldest statistical processes is the measurement of 'vital statistics' through the registration of births and deaths. The flows into and out of the human population are counted. In all Western industrial societies the last quarter of the twentieth century saw an enormous reduction in achieved human fertility – women are having far fewer children. The maintenance of a stable human population requires that the mean number of children women should have by the completion of the fertile part of their life is 2.1.[1] In almost all Western industrial societies this is not being achieved. The figure is well less than 2 and in many countries, especially in Latin Europe, is as low as 1.4. The implications of this over the next fifty years for population sizes and dependency ratios, the ratios of working adults to dependent pensioners, are profound. This pattern of reproduction will change our societies in important ways, most probably by mass immigration of people from societies with demographic surpluses. The implications for culture and society are enormous. This will generate a phase shift.

We cannot know this without measurement. We may have an impression that families are smaller, but that could just be the people we know directly – and most of us know directly at most a couple of hundred households. We have to measure to know the big picture and we have to keep measuring to see how the picture is changing. Size matters. Change matters. Without measurement we can describe neither current condition nor the history of current condition – we cannot say what the social world is like and we cannot construct a narrative of how it got to be like it is. Moreover, we have to measure in an effort to have some grasp on the way things are likely to develop. These changes in family size have profound implications for our society. We do not yet necessarily know what they are. Changes in family size will not operate alone. Other things will matter. However, knowing about changes in family size is important.

So we measure, and have measured these vital statistics in England and Wales since 1837. Now we have to ask how we measure and what we are measuring. Let us deal first with 'how' in a very general sense. The detail of the processes of measurement will be addressed in Chapter 2 but here we need to think about the contexts or frames of those measurements. There are two frames for measurement in science – a word which in this book should be translated from English into a Slav language – *Nauk* – or German – *Wissenschaft* – and then translated back again. In other words, here science means all organized knowledge gathered/created by any systematic means and does not mean just that organized knowledge created by methods which privilege a particular way of understanding what the world is and how we can know it. The two frames of measurement in science are the survey and the experiment. The experiment carries out measurement in a world created by the experimenter by abstraction from the world as it is – what Hayles (1999: 12) calls 'the platonic backhand'. The variation in the world of the experiment – traditionally a world set on the laboratory bench – is created by the experimenter. Measurements are made in an ideal world which exists nowhere in reality and inferences are drawn about reality from the organization of those measurements.

The survey measures the world as it is. It records, however imperfectly and incompletely, and through a process of social construction, covariation as it happens without the intervention of an experimenter who creates variation. There is an important distinction between the words variation and covariation. Variation describes what happens for one aspect of the world. Covariation describes what happens for lots of aspects of the world all at the same time or through the same time period. In an experiment there is control – things are held constant. Surveys examine the world as it covaries with no constants. Experiment abstracts and constrains. Surveys deal with things as they are without intervention by the scientist.

We have made an important move here and now we need to identify what that move is. We have moved from thinking about how we can describe to thinking about how we can reason about cause. Experiments describe nothing. They are artificial constructs. We make those constructs in order to establish causes. Much of our survey work is about description but we are also interested in causes – the plural is very important. To understand the issues here we have to address questions of ontology and epistemology. We have to think about the nature of the world and think about how we can understand the world.

Positivism, realism and complexity

Conventionally, books that deal with issues of methodology – a word frequently misused by those who wish to impress as a synonym for method but one which should be confined to its proper meaning, which refers to questions about the ontological and epistemological status of our research procedures, questions of philosophical justification – begin with a discussion of positivism. The time for that is past. We do have to know what positivism is because it matters in the history of quantitative research and because most social research that uses data to generate stories about cause is still positivist, but we don't have to take it seriously as something that might inform the way we work. Here what we have to do with positivism is get it out of the way so that we can get on with our task of quantitative interpretation. I am going to do that by comparing positivism with realism.

As always in this book there are two intellectual gangs against whom we are working. One of those gangs we will call the reductionists and the other we will call the innumerates. The first gang can count but don't know what they are counting, why they are counting, or what to do with what they have counted when they have counted it. The second can't count, won't count, and assert that counting is a vile and perverse activity which ought not to be allowed. The reductionists are positivists but don't use the term all that much. The innumerates use positivism as a pejorative label for all quantitative work, including both descriptive measurement, which is not necessarily positivist, and realist quantitative causal work, which explicitly rejects central tenets of the positivist position.

There are full discussions of positivism in a range of texts – that in Williams (2000) is particularly clear. All we need to do here is spell out the essentials of the position, whilst recognizing that there is no single positivism and that the position has been laid out with widely varying degrees of sophistication. However, what matters is brute positivism – the lowest common denominator, since that is how the reductionists work in practice and it is that against which the innumerates rail.

Brute positivism deals with brute facts. In this account the things we measure exist and measurements of them describe them as they are regardless of the context or character of the measurement process. Sophisticated positivism as a philosophy of science is much more subtle and does not necessarily assert this sort of brute realism but brute realism is the basis of positivist scientific practice. We have to be careful here because I have asserted that this book is a realist text and that realism is not positivism but have just described positivism as informed by brute realism. This word 'realism' requires close attention. In its simplest sense it just means that the world exists separate from our consciousness of it. This does not mean that the world exists separate from our actions – the social constructionist account in which human social actions are crucial to the construction of the social world is perfectly compatible with realism – the social world is made by us and is real having been made and as it continues to be made. However, realism has now come to be used as a label for a meta-theoretical position, meta because it is a theory about the nature of theory, which is different from brute positivism in other important ways although both realism and brute positivism (although not necessarily sophisticated positivism) are realist.

The first important way in which realism in this modern sense differs from brute positivist reductionism is that it recognizes that measurement is a social process which occurs in social contexts. However, realism differs from relativist innumeracy in that whilst recognizing and asserting the importance of the social processes involved in measurement, it does not regard measurement as mere reification. For realists we measure socially and that matters a lot. We construct as opposed to find our data, but we make it out of something, not out of nothing.

Brute positivism asserts that the objects of scientific study are grasped by human beings through direct sensory perception. This principle is one of the great weaknesses of positivism. In much of science, including most laboratory science, we sense nothing directly. Instead we use instruments which are supposed to be dealing with things we cannot sense for ourselves. Physics became instrument based once electricity mattered. Even GCSE students measure current flow with ammeters but there is no direct perception of electrons involved. Indeed our models – a crucial word – of both the electron and of perception assert that we cannot sense electrons because we sense through them. Realism is happy with indirect observation – in important respects, as we shall see, the realist approach insists upon it. All forms of positivism are reductionist. Positivism insists that we can explain complex things in terms of simple things and simple things alone. Ultimately it argues that we can, in principle if not in practice, derive the properties of everything from the basic physics of energy and matter (although information is starting to appear as well in this story, which disrupts it completely). Positivism denies emergence. It absolutely cannot accept that wholes can be greater than the sum of their parts. Realism is not reductionist and readily accepts emergence.

This takes us back to complexity. The essentials of complexity have been outlined in the Introduction but I want here to emphasize the anti-reductionist implications of complexity as a general account. Complex systems are to be understood not in terms of their parts, the analytical error, nor in terms of their wholes, the reverse holistic error, but in terms of parts, interactions among parts, the whole, and the interaction of the whole with the parts. The word 'interaction' is vitally important. In reality things work together and what they produce is not predictable from the inherent character of the things themselves. Emergent properties contradict reductionism.

Finally, brute positivism has a unitary conception of cause. All effects have a cause – one cause, and the mechanism of cause is understood in Galileo's terms. If the cause is present the effect always follows. If the cause is absent then the effect never occurs. This is an ontological statement. Galileo was saying that is what the world is like. The medical doctrine of specific aetiology – one cause for each disease – reiterates Galileo's account. Hume's constant conjunction account of cause in which we know what the cause of an effect is because they are always found together is an epistemological statement. Hume was saying that is how we know what the cause of something is. Meta-theories always combine epistemological and ontological accounts and generally the character of each side derives from the other. This is a recursive relationship – ontological positions have epistemological consequences and epistemological positions have ontological consequences.

Realism in contrast sees causes as complex and contingent. The best illustration I know of this relates to infectious disease and comes from the work of Bradbury (1933) on the causes of tuberculosis on Tyneside in the 1930s. Bradbury began his book by pointing out that in one sense people might think it was stupid to ask what caused TB. The TB bacillus caused TB. However, the issue he was facing was that in the 1930s on Tyneside everybody was exposed to TB but only some people developed the clinical disease. Exposure to the TB bacillus was a necessary condition for the clinical disease but it was not a sufficient condition. Bradbury did some very impressive statistical work and concluded that the causes of TB on Tyneside as a clinical disease were to be found, for each individual case, in the diet of that case, the housing conditions of that case, and the ethnic origins of that case – for Bradbury being Irish, but the Arab seamen in South Shields demonstrated his argument even more clearly. The pattern of poverty – housing conditions and diet – is not surprising. The ethnicity mattered as a biological component because the Irish had two generations less of urban industrial life and hence of natural selection for resistance. The Arab seamen who came straight from rural Yemen had neither resistance nor early exposure and died like flies from TB despite their extreme general physical fitness – they worked as firemen (stokers) in the merchant navy, not a job for a weakling.

In the 1960s I was exposed to an active case of TB as a teenager. When tested for antibodies I had an extreme reaction but when examined, very thoroughly, I had no sign of the clinical disease. By one possible classification I have tuberculosis but nobody, least of all myself, would know it. I will never forget the explanation for my robust good health offered by the chest physician who examined me. He said that, like all my generation, I was fed like a fighting cock and housed like a racehorse, and since my parents, both of whom had siblings who died of TB as young adults, had never had the disease, I had been bred for resistance. So the cause of TB was actually a complex interaction of social *and* natural processes in an ecology in which both mattered.

This illustrates the basic account of realism rather well. For Bhaskar (1979), there are three levels which we have to think about in the world. The first is what Bhaskar calls the real – the level of complex mechanisms like the urban ecology which generated TB in a specific spatial and temporal context. This was contingent – even in the 1930s good diet, good housing and genetic propensity for resistance blocked the effects of exposure to the disease. Not all exposed got it. By the 1960s the mechanism itself had changed – the urban ecology had been transformed by the achievements of welfarist labourism.

The second level is precisely that of the individual case of TB and the general prevalence of the disease – the level at which effects come to happen. Bhaskar calls this the actual. Real mechanisms may, or may not, cause actual effects. Finally, we have the level of the empirical, the actual recording by science of an event. In 1964 in Sunderland I was not recorded as a case of TB whilst my school fellow who had the clinical disease was, but some classifiers using another set of administrative principles would have recorded me as a case. The empirical is social but also, in this bio-social context, natural.

Naturalism – a soft foundationalist argument

A dangerous word has just been inserted into this text – natural. This opens up the possibility of arguments about the relationship between the social world, which is the product of human actions, and the natural world, which exists independently of them, or so it used to be said. In a world subject to the threat of global warming and profound ecological transformation as the product of human industrial activity, we really do need a story which links the natural and the social.

Traditionally, accounts which link the natural and the social have been reductionist and scientistic. By reductionist I mean that they have sought to explain social relations in terms of biological predilections – the current fad for evolutionary psychology is merely the latest and most sophisticated version of this game. It would be absurd to deny the biological character of human beings and equally ridiculous to ignore the role of evolutionary processes in the emergence of human consciousness and society – an emergence which was necessarily a single process. However, the key word is emergence. Emergent phenomena are not explicable in terms of that from which they emerge. The biological substrate is part of the story but by no means all, or even the most important part, of it.

The scientistic component of naturalism, or as Khalil (1996) puts it, 'crude naturalism', is methodological. It asserts that the methods and meta-theory of the natural sciences can and should be employed both to understand the social world and to inform public policies directed at achieving changes in that social world. The description of randomized control trials as the 'gold standard' in evaluation is an example of considerable contemporary significance. The ontological programme of social constructionism which asserts the role of social action in the production of a variant social world is essentially a defence mechanism against the methodological imperialism of crude naturalism.

Khalil (1996) turns this whole game around. He puts it like this:

> most social scientists (the orthodox as well as the heterodox) uncouple most human phenomena from nature. They assume that natural forms are commanded by external and given forces which do not allow intentionality, the role of habits, and the relevance of context. Such an assumption leads, put simply, to the presentation of nonhuman natural phenomena as no different from the artificial realm which includes tools and machines. Boulding and I agreed that the dichotomy should not be pencilled along the social realm on the one hand, and the natural realm understood as artificial on the other. Rather the dichotomy should be drawn along the social and natural realms, on the one side, and the artificial on the other. (1996: xi)

I want to take this somewhat further. It seems to me that Khalil's artificial includes not only the real machines of the world, although even here boundaries are imprecise in the case particularly of the 'built environment', but also the mechanistic models of much of science. All models, a term to which we shall be paying a great deal of attention in due course, are artificial, but mechanistic models constructed from the abstract conceptions of force and the social and ecological analogy of force, variable, are essentially artificial. Here essentially is meant literally – mechanistic models are artificial in their very essence. This is not to say that they are not, sometimes, 'true' in the sense of being representations which correspond to what they are supposed to represent. Even more importantly they often work – people can do things by using them – and the idea that what we require is practical knowledge – knowledge that works – is one to which we will return. None the less, they belong in the artificial domain in that the things from which they are made are abstract reifications, components of Hayles's (1999) platonic backhand and forehand – the experiment and the simulation.

Hanneman and Patrick explicitly assert the 'artificiality' of scientific models, describing them as 'artificial objects that are used by researchers to provide representations of social structures and processes' (1997: 2.2).[2] They repeat this mechanistic imagery in phrases which include: '... the construction of the machine' (1997: 3.3); 'Having built a machine ...' (1997: 3.6); 'Simulation models are highly artificial ...' (1997: 3.8). It is important to quarrel here seriously with the assertion made by these authors that observation of 'natural experiments' is the least artificial of model based methods (1997: 2.3). This is based on a fundamental misconception of the distinction between natural and artificial. The natural is that which exists separate from the actions of the scientist as scientist. The artificial is that which is created for the purposes of scientific inquiry. Note that the products of human action, including the material products, can be natural in this frame of reference.

Khalil argues for a non-crude naturalism founded on the redrawing of the epistemic boundary as proposed above. From this he derives a 'soft foundationalism' (1996: 7), which for me is essentially identical to Cilliers's (1998) specification of the necessarily local character of knowledge in a world composed of nested and intersecting complex systems. Let us turn to the essential argument of localism which Cilliers presents in a particularly clear way.

There are no universals but, nevertheless, we can know

The most obvious conclusion drawn from this perspective is that there is no over-arching theory of complexity that allows us to ignore the contingent aspects of complex systems. If something is really complex, it cannot be adequately described by means of a simple theory. Engaging with complexity entails engaging with specific complex systems. Despite this we can, at a very basic level, make general remarks concerning the conditions for complex behaviour and the dynamics of complex systems. Furthermore, I suggest that complex systems can be modelled. ...

To think in terms of relationships rather than in terms of deterministic rules, is not a novelty for science but it has always been seen as part of qualitative descriptions and not as part of the quantitative descriptions and calculations deemed necessary ever since Kepler's insistence that 'to measure is to know'. (Cilliers, 1998: ix)

We must recognize localism/context for what it is. Statistical reasoning proceeds in principle, although not as we shall see always in practice, by testing probabilistic hypotheses. However, the implications of localism/context as expressed in interaction, mean that no single hypothesis can be generalized beyond the exact conditions under which it is tested. If there is any non-linearity then no covering law is ever possible. In this frame of reference experiments merely describe local and unique conjunctions. Hypotheses cannot be somehow summed into a general overarching account.

Cilliers is careful to distinguish his position from complete relativism (1998: 112–13) and his insistence on the possibility of modelling complexity is extremely important. Indeed, I want to argue that modelling must have measurement as a crucial but not absolutely necessary foundation. In other words, most modelling will derive from measurement but we can also model on the basis of language form accounts of reality as well. Here the driving force is the technology. As Cilliers puts it: 'Modelling techniques on powerful computers allow us to do with technology what we cannot do with science' (1998: 2).

Unpleasant though this is for the contemplative ideal of the philosophical tradition, the implications of local knowledge are that we can use knowledge, in context, within its limits, as part of the foundations of our actions. In other words, we can be like engineers rather than scientists. Crutchfield put it like this:

> the epistemological problem of nonlinear modelling can be crudely summarized as the dichotomy between engineering and science. As long as a representation is effective for a task, an engineer does not care what it implies about underlying mechanisms; to the scientist though the implication makes all the difference in the world. The engineer is certainly concerned with minimizing implementation cost ... but the scientist presumes, at least, to be focused on what the model means *vis-à-vis* natural laws. The engineering view of science is that it is mere data compression; scientists seem to be motivated by more than this. (1992: 68)

Halfpenny (1997) considers that the above passage illustrates the difference between empiricist – that is, law-seeking – and conventionalist – what works works. It does but there is more to it than that. The engineering view is dominated by the idea of things working and it can cope, happily, with the notion that rules hold only in particular contexts – that there are no universal laws that hold always and everywhere, laws of nature. Instead, we have rules of place and time. As Ursula le Guin says of magic somewhere in her *Earthsea* books, 'Rules change in the reaches'. The traditional conception of science with its programme of reduction to universal and fundamental causes finds this localism deeply disturbing, although it is wholly compatible with the realist programme and with Sayer's view that

> truth might better be understood as 'practical adequacy', that is in terms of the extent to which it generates expectations about the world and about the results of our actions which are realized. Just how practically adequate different parts of our knowledge are will vary according to where and to what they are applied. (2000: 43)

Let me return to the quotation from Cilliers (1998) which provides the epigraph for this section, and in particular to the passage that reads 'we can, at a very basic level, make general remarks concerning the conditions for complex behaviour and the dynamics of complex systems. Furthermore, I suggest that complex systems can be modelled.' This permits representation, although always distributed representation rather than a description of complex systems by any set of non-linear equations or rules for a game.[3] Cilliers opposes the view that algorithms can describe significant natural complex systems. His theory of representation is, I think, essentially one of heterologous analogy as that term is defined by Khalil who distinguishes superficial, heterologous (or analogous), homologous and unificational metaphors 'by the criterion of the *kind* of resemblance which a metatheoretical statement is supposed to inform' (1996: 4). Superficial metaphors are simply similes. Heterologous metaphors described similarity of function without necessarily common origin – the wings of a butterfly and a bat. Homologous metaphors are based on common context or origin – the forelimbs of a mouse and the wings of a bat. Unificational metaphors 'express similarities when they arise from the same common law' (Khalil, 1996: 6).

Cilliers understands modelling in this way:

> It bears repetition that an argument against representation is not anti-scientific at all. It is merely an argument against a particular scientific strategy that assumes complexity can be reduced to specific features and then represented in a machine. Instead it is an argument for the appreciation of the nature of complexity, something that can perhaps be 'repeated' in a machine, should the machine itself be complex enough to cope with the distributed character of complexity. (1998: 86)

For me, this is a matter of heterologous analogy – things work in the same way although we might consider that the general character of complex systems might be understood as a kind of meta-law which covers all systems that work in this way. The behaviour of any particular complex system cannot be derived from that meta-law because it is only a guide to general character. This is not like the local initial conditions which have to be put into a universal law in order to see the outcome in a specific context. Context in complex systems is more than a matter of initial conditions. It extends to the way the system actually works. And yet complex systems, in the most general sense, work like complex systems. Let us turn to the issue of how we might think about modelling them in real instances.

Models and measures: a first pass

> [T]he characteristic of models that causes difficulties with regard to deriving an acceptable definition, is precisely the attribute that marks them out as useful tools both in conceptual and practical terms. They are a representation of the real world and *not* the real thing. It is important, however, to remember that while models are devices to help us understand the real world more clearly, they are also part of that world both through their physical – or cognitive – presence and

more significantly through the impacts which arise from their development and use. (Jeffrey et al., 1999: 76)

Jeffrey et al.'s description of models as 'representations', re-presentations, of the world, is entirely acceptable. A model is something which stands for the world because we argue that it works in the same way as the world, or at least as that part of the world in which we are interested. Note that in this very minimalist specification there is no reduction. Contrast this with Gilbert and Troitzsch's assertion in a discussion of simulation: 'Every model will be a simplification – sometimes a drastic simplification – of the target to be modelled' (1999: 18). Cilliers will not have that. His account of complex systems says that any models of them can only be considered useful if they work in the same way – if they too are complex systems. It may well be that such models are not as complex complex systems (it seems wrong to write simpler complex systems!) but actually we don't necessarily know that because we don't know the internal form of any system characterized by emergence from connectionism. However, the models are things we can play with, just so long as we recognize that playing with models is part of the process of socially constructing the social world and the intersection of the social and natural worlds. The models are, if not outside the world, then at least enough apart from it for us to do things with them which help us to grasp the world, certainly the world as it has been although there are much more profound difficulties in grasping the world as it might become.

The issue of how we can use anything other than a complete representation of a complex system to say anything about the potential behaviour of a complex system is of crucial importance. There are two related solutions to this problem. One is to turn to the idea of essential features – control parameters in the language of dynamic systems. We have lots of components of description of a complex system but at any given time point, some of these in interaction are what determines the set of potential trajectories of the system. Note the usage of 'determine' here not as exact specification, but as setting limits to possibilities, with the limits understood not as boundaries to one state space but rather as a limited set of possible state spaces. The other is to use the idea of near neighbour – to say like behaves like like. This issue is fundamental and we will keep returning to it.

There is one very important set of models which the above discussion implies are of very limited use to us in dealing with a complex world, at least so long as they are used in the way in which they have traditionally been employed. These are the various aspects of the General Linear Model. Davies and Dale describe what they consider to be the essential features of 'statistical modelling' which, given the context of their discussion, can be considered to be a specification of the character of linear models:

Statistical modelling is important because it enables researchers to make informed judgements about the systematic relationships in complex[4] survey data. The problem is, of course, that empirical associations in survey data may be misleading without allowing for the effects of control variables, the sampling scheme used, and variation due to other, possibly unsuspected, features of the process of interest. This is precisely the issue that statistical modelling addresses by permitting many interrelationships to be considered simultaneously within a single analysis together with an error structure to represent unmeasured effects. The researcher is therefore able to distinguish systematic relationships from each other and obscuring detail. (1994: 5)

Davies and Dale go on to to endorse the software package GLIM (an acronym for General Linear Model) and to specify a range of linear techniques. The very language of their description with its use of terms like analysis, control, distinguishing relationships, should illustrate the character of this approach. Brown tells us why people do this and what is wrong with it:

More complicated models quickly become mathematically intractable in the probabilistic setting, forcing researchers to compromise their specifications by using simpler and less substantively satisfying approaches to theory building. Anyone familiar with modelling from a probabilistic perspective will state that the worst error that can be made with any model is a specification error. In the presence of misspecification no estimate is reliable. Yet it is precisely because of the convenience of linear models (because of their mathematical simplicity and the ease with which probabilistic assumptions may be inserted into them) that researchers often depart from isomorphic parallels between social theory and nonlinear algebraic formalisms, leading them into the most dangerous of terrains. (1995: 5–6)

There are arguments to be had with Brown about his recourse to specified deterministic models, precisely the approach which Cilliers dismisses as a way of representing complex systems. However, Brown does describe the basic and essential inadequacy of linear modelling, however complicated it gets.[5]

The quotation from Brown introduces the issue of probabilistic reasoning, which is often described by use of the word stochastic. I want to return to the whole probabilistic issue in Chapter 5, but it is necessary to say something about it here. First, a careful distinction should be made between the idea of probabilistic reasoning and stochastic processes. Both are tied to the notion of randomness but the role of randomness is rather different. The word stochastic has an etymology which derives from the process of aiming an arrow. Aimed arrows generally get somewhere close to what they are aimed at. However, there is variation, 'randomness'[6] between the discharge of the arrow from the bow and its arrival at the target. The process has direction but a random component – hence the use of stochastic processes as mathematical formulations for queuing. Queues have a random duration but a directional outcome. In a queue one gets to the end, however random waits and queue lengths may be. Stochastic models typically work by adding a noise, that is, a random term, to an otherwise deterministic process. Most things are fixed but one thing is random and that is taken to be the randomness in the stochastic world.

In probabilistic reasoning the randomness has to do with inferring from samples to populations, using the mathematical laws of probability theory. Of particular significance here is the estimation of variance, of the degree to which a variable varies. Since this book's argument is founded, among other things, on a sustained attack on the priority of variables, this objective is not prime. And yet, despite long-standing and fundamental criticism, it is prime in statistical reasoning. Desrosières quotes Vining in the late 1940s referring to a comment of Yule's in 1942:

> The initial problem of the statistician is simply the description of the data presented; to tell us what the data themselves show. To this initial problem the function of sampling theory is in general entirely secondary ... (quoted by Desrosières, 1998: 321)

Although the contemporary use of stochastic implies that the term is essentially synonymous with random, recourse to the *Oxford English Dictionary* shows that the older 'Now rare or obsolete' meaning of the word does retain the directional implications of its etymology and that the stochastic faculty was distinguished from prophecy, in which foreknowledge comes from outwith the world because the stochastic ability to predict was based on knowledge of the world. This resonates far more, as we shall see, with Bayesian approaches than with traditional statistical reasoning. There is a great deal more to be said about the implications of this but it is worth bringing the issue up here in relation to modelling. Linear models of a probabilistic form are just so taken for granted that we have to get in every kick at them we can.

Let us say what models of a complex world are not – in other words we can begin to move forward by throwing out a deal of the baggage:

- Models of a complex world are seldom something we can represent through linear mathematical description. If there is emergence that approach does not work.
- Real and significant complex systems can seldom be represented even by non-linear mathematical formalisms, that is, by sets of non-linear equations. There is just too much going on for any such approach to be particularly useful.
- We have to be very careful about the probabilistic element in models. We cannot simply take this aspect for granted. There are different conceptions of probability in play and different uses being made of these different conceptions.

The title given to this section included the phrase 'a first pass'. Modelling is crucial to the whole quantitative enterprise in social science. We will return to the issue of what models are constantly in this book. Here we have first encountered the fundamentals of that discussion. It has deliberately been an 'in at the deep end' approach, at least in terms of the mounting of a challenge to things about quantitative models which are so often taken for granted. There is more of this to come.

Contingency and method – retroduction and retrodiction

> I am not speaking of randomness ... but of a central principle of all history – *contingency*. A historical explanation does not rest on direct deductions from laws of nature, but on an unpredictable set of antecedent states, where any major change in any step of the sequence would have altered the final result. This final result is therefore dependent on, contingent on, everything that came before – the uneraseable and determining signature of history. (Gould, 1991: 283; original emphasis)

Gould in *Wonderful Life* (1991) argues for the validity of history, of the narratives of how what is came to be what is, as crucial to the scientific project. What he describes is a process of interpretation of the past so as to construct a model of development towards the present in which the actual form of that development is often the product of contingent factors at key points of transition/transformation. This account is very close to that of bifurcation in mathematical processes which have a chaotic component. In chaotic processes it is a matter of Poincaré's very small causes which we cannot measure and choose to call random, although in real contingent history the cause may be large – in palaeontology the effects of the impact of an asteroid's collision with the Earth. The introduction of noise in stochastic simulations involves the use of random perturbations in a repeated fashion in order to mimic the effect of real contingent, and necessarily deterministic, causes. In other words, randomness is used as a substitute for small deterministic cause – the world itself is not random.

Gould's approach might be called retrodiction – the explanation of what has happened by the use of models that fit the data. Prediction extrapolates from such retrodiction to assert that what has happened will happen in the future – a very chancy process if our retrodictive story is contextual and local. In other words, what has happened might not happen again because context might change. This is not a postmodernist epistemological point – we can know what has happened – we can construct a valid history. It is rather an ontological point – contingency and context mean that the ability to extrapolate on the basis of that history cannot be taken for granted. We might be able to do so, but not necessarily.

There is a relationship between retrodiction and retroduction but they are not the same. Blaikie suggests that retroduction

> be restricted to the process of building models of structures and mechanisms which characterizes the Realist approach. ... The Retroductive research strategy involves the construction of hypothetical models as a way of uncovering the real structures and mechanisms which are assumed to produce empirical phenomena. (1993: 168)

This is fine, but Blaikie then proceeds to quote Harré to confirm this approach and there is something important to argue with in Harré's stipulation:

When a non-random pattern is identified, the first step is to undertake a series of experiments to determine the range of conditions under which it appears. Then the processes which generate the pattern are to be looked for in the natures of the things and materials involved. It is the fact that these are usually not known that brings into action the model building process. The creative task is to invent a plausible analogue of the mechanism which is really producing the phenomenon. (Harré, 1976: 21, quoted by Blaikie, 1993: 169)

The issue in that passage is the use of the word 'experiment' and the idea that we can know the world by constructing a series of experiments which determine, in the sense of establish the co-ordinates of, the boundaries of our knowledge. This is of course a localist story, which is entirely compatible with the inherently local, and thereby contingent, character of complex systems. The dispute is methodological, not ontological. I have no problem with the idea that the description of the world does consist essentially of the combined specification of mechanisms and the delimitation of the boundaries of operation of those mechanisms, but would assert very vigorously that experiments are not the way to go about this. Blaikie summarizes Bhaskar's general realist programme very clearly as 'a process of description, explanation and redescription, in which layers of reality are continually exposed' (1993: 169). Quantitative retrodiction seems essential to this but quantitative retrodiction is not experiment.

Hayles's specification of the platonic tennis game of forehands and backhands has been mentioned before in this chapter. Let us return to what she says about this and see her full specification:

Abstraction is of course an essential component in all theorizing, for no theory can account for the infinite multiplicity of our interactions with the real. But when we make moves that erase the world's multiplicity, we risk losing sight of the variegated leaves, fractal branchings, and particular bark textures that make up the forest. In the pages that follow, I will identify two moves in particular that played important roles in constructing the information/materiality hierarchy. Irreverently, I think of them as the Platonic backhand and forehand.

The Platonic backhand works by inferring from the world's noisy multiplicity, a simplified abstraction. So far so good: this is what theorizing should do. The problem comes when the move circles around to constitute the abstraction as the originary form from which the world's multiplicity derives. Then complexity appears as a 'fuzzing up' of essential reality rather than as a manifestation of the world's holistic nature. Whereas the Platonic backhand has a history dating back to the Greeks, the Platonic forehand is more recent. To reach fully developed form, it required the assistance of powerful computers. This move starts from simplified abstractions and, using simulation techniques such as genetic algorithms, *evolves* a multiplicity sufficiently complex that it can be seen as a world of its own. The two moves thus make their play in opposite directions. The backhand goes from noisy multiplicity to reductive simplicity, whereas the forehand swings from simplicity to multiplicity. They share a common ideology – privileging the abstract as the Real and downplaying the importance of material instantiation. When they work together, they lay the groundwork for a new variation on an ancient game in which disembodied information becomes the ultimate Platonic Form. (1999: 12–13)

The approach to the generation of knowledge through measurement which is being asserted in this book is explicitly one which, in general, forswears either of the above platonic strokes. To continue with Hayles's form of metaphor we can transfer from tennis to badminton and argue for the Aristotelian smash. In other words, we will work with measurements of the world as it is. In Chapter 6 I will propose how we can use computer based classificatory procedures to do this and explain the nature of the Aristotelian smash understood as systematic and dynamic relational classification.

Conclusion

The purpose of this chapter has been to spell out some meta-theoretical princi-ples and to begin to say what those principles imply for quantitative social research. The principles can be summarized simply by saying that what we have to deal with are complex systems – non-linear, far from equilibric and evolutionary complex systems – and that we can understand such systems in a realist frame of reference. This means that positivist and linear approaches will not work as ways of describing and understanding the world. We must proceed differently. This means that in modelling – the fundamental process of describing how social systems might work, with might here understood both in terms of tentative current description *and* as a way of grasping the possible futures of social systems, we have to not simplify, but essentialize. We have to find some way of grasping the essentials of complex systems without reducing those systems to simplistic, and hence non-isomorphic, representations. Practically, as we shall see in Chapter 7, this means that linear modelling is pushed from its pedestal as *the* mode of quantitative representa-tion, to being at best a possible exploratory device to be used in limited circum-stances. This does not mean that we abandon quantitative representation – far from it – but we need to understand just how our measurement might permit us to represent. To do that we need to replace the reified idea of variables with a complex realist approach to measurement which does not abstract from real complex systems; we need to understand what we measure as variate traces rather than variables. This is the subject matter of Chapter 2.

Notes

1 It is 2.1 rather than 2 to allow for the failure of some female children themselves to live through the fertile years of adult life.

2 Hanneman and Patrick consider the survey to be experimental in form, thereby making the fundamental error of failing to distinguish between variation observed in the world as it is – the survey – and variation created in an artificial world – the experiment. We will consider the implications of this further in our discussion of simulation in Chapter 8.

3 Here Cilliers's approach is absolutely different from that of Holland (1998), which typifies that of those adherents of complexity and emergence who nevertheless want some 'simple' mathematical representation which is supposed to represent a simple foundation for complexity and emergent properties. This nostalgia for the simple is quite misplaced. Cilliers turns to the unanalysable and connected – typified by neural nets, of which more in Chapter 8.

4 The word 'complex' does not carry here the burden which we have placed upon it in previous discussion. Davies and Dale mean that the data sets they are dealing with are multi-level/hierarchical in that they include measurements at different levels of reality, e.g. of children in classes in schools.

5 Regrettably the Chief Executive of the UK's Economic and Social Research Council seemed to be endorsing these kinds of linear approaches when in 2001 he identified a skills deficit in quantitative *analysis* as a key issue for UK social science. Context suggests an endorsement of Dale and Davies's conception of what makes complex data complex, and an agreement with the linear approaches to analysing such data sets suggested by them.

6 Poincaré would not accept that this is randomness; rather it is the determined outcome of a set of non-measured small causes.

2

The Nature of Measurement: What We Measure and How We Measure

If auto/biographies are stories about people, then perhaps statistical models are best understood as stories about variables. ... Taking this analogy a step further, while auto/biography may be understood as textual means of establishing identities for individuals, quantitative analysis might be read as establishing identity for a social group defined by variables such as gender and class. In other words, although variables are treated as individual attributes during the data collection phase of survey research, analyses and texts will subsequently be produced by the researcher which offer insights about the determining power of those variables as a social and narrative construction.

... it is important not to lose sight of the individuals whose lives provide the data for the models. Although variables rather than individual people may become the subjects of the statistician's narrative, it is individuals rather than variables who have the capacity to act and reflect on society. (Elliott, 1999: 101–2)

... class is not this or that part of the machine, but *the way the machine works* once it is set in motion – not this interest and that interest, but the *friction* of interests – the movement itself, the heat, the thundering noise. Class is a social and cultural formation (often finding institutional expression) which cannot be defined abstractly, or in isolation, but only in terms of relationship with other classes; and, ultimately, the definition can only be made in the medium of *time* – that is, action and reaction, change and conflict. When we speak of *a* class we are thinking of a very loosely defined body of people who share the same categories of interests, social experiences, traditions and value-system, who have a *disposition* to *behave* as a class, to define themselves in their actions an in their consciousness in relation to other groups of people in class ways. But class itself is not a thing, it is a happening. (Thompson, 1978: 85; original emphasis)

Death to the variable

In quantitative social science the things which we measure are usually called variables. This use of variable as a noun is a modern product of the mathematical representation of the world through scientific modelling. The *Oxford English Dictionary* defines a variable in maths and physics as: A quantity or force, which, throughout a mathematical calculation or investigation, is assumed to vary or be capable of varying in value. The *OED* dates the first use to the early nineteenth century. This specifically scientific usage seems to predate the more general application of the idea to describe anything that can vary. It is worth unpacking the *OED* definition because it actually contains two very different conceptions of the nature of 'variable' and two different conceptions of the processes in which variables occur. The idea of variable as quantity simply implies that a measurement can and has been made. The idea of variable as force implies that something real exists and can be measured. The process of mathematical calculation is abstract. The process of investigation involves empirical engagement with the world.

The *Encyclopaedia of Statistical Sciences* (1999) describes variables as 'features', although it does not say of what variables are features. It then distinguishes between 'hidden' or 'latent' variables on the one hand and 'observed' or 'manifest' on the other. This distinction derives from the process of measurement, with 'observed' or 'manifest' variables being directly measurable and 'hidden' or 'latent' variables being divided into two further classes of those that could be measured, were good enough instruments available, and those that are 'idealized constructs at best only indirectly measurable' (1999: 772). This is essentially an argument about the 'reality' of variables, with the degree of commitment to the reality of any given variable being a function of the ease of its measurement. However, the question we have to ask is whether variables as such really exist at all in the social systems and in the intersections among social and natural systems with which we as social scientists are concerned?

The first of the two quotations which open this chapter is from one of the relatively few chapters in a collection of nearly forty produced by members of the UK Radical Statistics Group dealing with *Statistics in Society* (Dorling and Simpson, 1999) which addresses issues of statistical method. On the whole the primary interest of Radical Statistics[1] has been in the use of statistical measures as a way of challenging social arrangements and its secondary interest has been in the social character of the production of those statistical measures. These are extremely important activities, to which we will pay considerable attention. However, Radical Statistics has tended to neglect the character of statistics as social science. Elliott's chapter is an important exception and of particular interest because she identifies the issue but doesn't quite bite the bullet in resolving it. Plainly Elliott is rather uneasy about variables. She recognizes that the world is constructed by the actions of people, not of variables. And yet she still sees variables as 'real' enough to define the nature of the collectivities which are the basis of so much of significant social action.

Compare Elliott with E.P. Thompson, who was arguing specifically with the use of the idea of class by sociologists as a static attribute. Thompson, a historian to his boots, was arguing for a specifically historical logic, an argument he developed in detail in *The Poverty of Theory* (1978), and by which he meant an approach to reality which understood it exactly as dynamic and relational. Class, the ultimate category which employs the foundational term of categorization, class, to describe systemic economic relations, is a process in a historical system and it is the historical system which is real. It is worth noting that the specifically social notion of class actually is the source of the use of the term in general taxonomy. Class had to do with economic and social hierarchy before it had any other meaning and it was the social distinction which provided the word for general scientific taxonomy. The important implication of this is that classification is not merely a matter of assignation to category. The categories are inherently relational. They are constructed by reference to other categories. Even if the relation is merely one of distinction, the relation matters at least as much as the actual name of the category. Classification is a process of relating as well as a process of naming.

Emirbayer has recently asserted a 'Manifesto for a Relational Sociology':

> Sociologists today are faced with a fundamental dilemma: whether to conceive of the social world as consisting primarily in substances or in processes, in static 'things' or in dynamic, unfolding relations. Large segments of the sociological community continue implicitly or explicitly to prefer the former point of view. Rational-actor and norm-based models, diverse holisms and structuralisms, and statistical 'variable' analyses – all of the beholden to the idea that it is entities that come first and relations among them only subsequently – hold sway throughout much of the discipline. But increasingly, researchers are searching for viable analytic alternatives, approaches that reverse these basic assumptions and depict social reality instead in dynamic, continuous, and processual terms. (1997: 281)

He draws on Dewey and Bentley (1949) and on Abbott (1988, 1992) to unpack the idea of 'interaction' as this is understood in variable centred analysis. In the variable centred approach the entities of the world remain fixed and unchanging whilst interaction occurs among 'variables' postulated as real and outwith the entities themselves. For variable centred analysis, Abbott (1992) argues, causality is established when variables do something. Abbott has summed this up by postulating the observation made by a scholar of the future about this approach:

> The people who called themselves sociologists believed that society looked the way it did because social forces and properties did things to other social forces and properties. Sometimes the forces and properties were individual characteristics like race and gender, sometimes they were true social properties like population density or social disorganization. Sociologists called these forces and properties 'variable'. Hypothesizing which of these variables affected which others was called 'causal analysis'. The relation between variables (what these sociologists called the 'model') was taken as forcible, determining. In this view, narratives of human actions might provide 'mechanisms' that justified proposing a model, but what made social science *science* was the discovery of these 'causal relationships'. (1998: 148–9)

So, death to the variable – or rather let us understand clearly, once and for all, that variables don't exist. They are not real. What exists are complex systems, which systems are nested, intersecting, which involve both the social and the natural, and which are subject to modification on the basis of human action, both individual and social.

So what is it then that we measure when we measure what we used to call variables? (I initially wrote 'the things we used to call variables' and then cut the phrase 'the things' – there are no such things as variables.) My argument is that we measure traces of the systems which make up reality. To understand what these traces are we need to think first about the idea of 'phase' or 'state' space, and secondly develop our understanding of the process of classification.

State space

The origins of the complexity approach to science derive in large, but not exclusive, part from thermo-dynamics, the branch of physics developed in the nineteenth century as a way of understanding the operation of the heat engines which were the mechanical basis of the industrial revolution. There is an interesting contradiction here. Heat engines are mechanical and the trade of mechanic is practised by those who make and repair them but these machines cannot be understood through the use of classical Newtonian mechanics. Newtonian mechanics deals with entities and forces. Heat engines are systems in which the parts interact with each other and with the system and with its environment. A heat engine has to be described in some way that takes account of this. The technique developed to do this was plainly derived from Newtonian mechanics, but it has rather different implications.

In Newtonian mechanics the position of an entity is specified by locating it through specifying the value of four co-ordinates. Three of these are dimensional co-ordinates which specify where it is in three-dimensional space. The fourth is a specification of the time point at which the entity can be located at that spatial point. An apparently similar system of co-ordinates can be used to describe a complex system but something rather different is going on when such a complex description is generated. The specification of the state of a complex system is done by identifying values on a range of parameters which do not necessarily include the three dimensions of space but will always include the specification of the time instant at which the system is in the given state. There can be as many parameters as are considered appropriate. We can, by analogy, think of the parameters as separate dimensions and consider the value of any given parameter at a given time point as a co-ordinate on that dimension at that time. The set of dimensions are considered to describe the 'state space' of the system and the location of the system in terms of its co-ordinates in the state space is the current state of the system.

The value of this approach is that it permits an examination of the dynamics of the system because measuring the parameters at successive time points enables the production of an account of the trajectory of the system, that is, of the path the system takes through the state space. The alternative term 'phase space' indicates that what is interesting is the conditions under which the system radically changes its state and hence its position in the state space – it changes phase. It is important to note that such phase changes are non-linear. In other words a small change in one or more of the parameters can produce a large change in the state of the system. This is essentially a product of interaction. Physical scientists call this a failure of superposition. In Newtonian systems effects are additive. The resultant of two forces is the sum of them acting separately. Bring in a third force and the sum is now the sum of the three acting separately. Superposition holds. In a non-linear system interaction means that things don't happen like this. Traditionally interaction is defined by saying that the relationship between two variables is modified by the value of a third, but this approach reifies the variables – it makes the variables the things. The things are not the variables but the systems, the cases, and what is happening is that aspects of the cases work together in the case – and as we shall see in relation to other cases – to change the state of the system/case in radical ways.

There are two other aspects to the idea of state space which I want to consider before we turn to the process of classification. The first relates to considering the condition not of single systems but of lots of systems – of, to borrow a useful term from the physical sciences, ensembles of systems. I am going to propose a method of classification which is based on ensembles of systems that have similar trajectories – in other words, a dynamic approach to classification rather than a nominalist approach. The other thing we need to think about is what Reed and Harvey (1992) describe, after Prigogine, as nested systems. It is very important to recognize that the idea of 'nested' implies neither hierarchy nor impermeable boundaries. In other words, systems that 'contain' other systems are as potentially liable to be influenced by those contained, as the contained are to be influenced by the container. Moreover, system boundaries are not exact. Cilliers (1998) goes so far as to say they are essentially momentary products of measurement/examination. I would go further but would still see the reality of boundaries as essentially temporal and contextual. Combining the idea of 'nested' systems and 'ensembles' of systems gives us a method of examining historical change – another way of expressing the idea of dynamism – both for social orders as a whole and for elements within those social orders, including both individuals and households and the social collectivities typified by class as defined by Thompson above. (See Byrne, 1999 for an illustration of this approach.)

There is something which has to be said very clearly before moving on from the discussion of state space. I have deliberately used the word 'parameter' rather than 'variable' as the name for the co-ordinate dimensions of state space. Here the term parameter means a measure of an aspect of the system as a means of describing the condition of that system and as a means for comparing it with other systems. But the system, not the parameter, is the thing.

Classification

I want to begin this section by a diversion back to the bad old days, which ended yesterday. It was conventional in discussions of measurement in methods textbooks to classify variables into three (sometimes four but the fourth didn't really matter) kinds. There were ratio scale variables, measured in such a way that all the operations of arithmetic could be applied to them. Of these money *seems* to be the most obvious. An income of a million pounds a year is twenty-five times as much as an income of forty thousand pounds a year, obviously.[2] Variables measured at this level were the best variables because they could be fed into models that used the full panoply of mathematical formalism. Subject to establishment of validity and reliability, of which more in our discussion of measurement which will conclude this chapter, they were almost, if never quite absolutely, as good as physicists' measurement of forces.

Then (if we omit interval scales, which only figure because early physicists didn't know about absolute zero in measuring heat) there were ordinal variables. Here we could rank things in order but that was all. We employed the ordering of numbers but not their comparative size. Things were bigger or smaller but we didn't know by how much. Obviously[3] we could always convert a ratio scale variable into an ordinal scale variable but not the other way around.

Finally, although not in all the mathematical statistics texts, we had nominal variables. Here the only property of numbers that we could apply was that they were different. We used them as names to distinguish things. We could in principle have as well used Chinese characters but in practice it was useful to use numbers, whole numbers, integers, because computers find it much easy to manipulate numbers, even when employed just in this symbolic way, than any other form of coding. Obviously we could convert ordinal ranks into nominal categories – and actually here this is not an ironic statement – we could and can. Nominal measurement was something we had to do but were rather ashamed of. Indeed Pearson, the inventor of many of the statistical methods that rely on ratio scale measurement, so disliked mere nominal classification that he proposed that categories were merely expressions of underlying real continuous (another name for ratio scale) variables which were expressed in this categorical way – the tetrachoric principle. So for example the difference between blue eyes and brown eyes, which was very important for Pearson who was interested in inheritable characteristics, was not really an absolute but an expression of an underlying scalar difference which was expressed only in these extreme values.

According to this conception of measurement, classification is a process of assigning a value to a case for a single nominal variable. It is a unidimensional process. However, if we look at philosophical discussion of classification we find that there is a great deal more going on. Bowker and Star (1999: 62) outline the distinction between Aristotelian and prototypical theories of classification. Aristotelian classification can be subdivided into two forms – monothetic if the classification depends on the presence or absence of a single property, or polythetic if multiple properties are considered. In prototypical classification, which originates from experimental psychology,[4] classification starts from an original broad picture and works by comparing that which is to be classified with the sets of prototypes available. In this approach we might classify things into the same class or category, even if they have no two binary properties in common. Bowker and Star (1999: 62) note that the distinction between Aristotelian and prototypical classification is useful but is not itself absolute, which is an important point.

The process of nominal measurement is exactly Aristotelian monothetic classification but it is a very partial and fragmented version because the cases/systems are classified by the assignation of a particular value for a nominal variable and only in relation to that specific nominal variable. We might consider the resulting classification to be important, for example into a gender, but it is never a full account of the case. Aristotelian polythetic classification takes things further because we add dimensions. For example, we now think of the person not just as a woman but as a woman who is a young adult (ordinal used as nominal), black, British, lower middle class (ordinal used as nominal), employed working full time (apparent ratio scale used as nominal), with two children, and a car owner. Here we have arrived at a class which has eight nominal scales to frame it. This class is actually generated in practice as a cell in an eight-dimension contingency table. The members of the class are those who have the appropriate value on all eight nominal, or used as nominal, variables.

However, as we shall see in Chapter 6, there other computer based ways of classifying cases. If we use either the set of numerical taxonomic techniques called cluster analyses or neural net methods, we don't use all the measures in an Aristotelian polythetic fashion but neither do we start with an explicit set of prototypes. Rather, we[5] make up a set of prototypes in a relational way in the process of doing the classification. Certainly cluster members may not have everything in common but we still think of them as members of the same class.

To my mind there is a clear relationship between the ideas of ensembles of systems in state space and classes. That is to say, systems whose trajectories belong in the same ensemble at any given time point are members of the same class. Note that this does not mean that such systems have identical co-ordinates in state space at any given time, nor that they stay in the same ensemble/class through time. The establishment of appropriate – which means meaningful and useful – boundary conditions for classes in terms of specifying domains of state space which contain classes, is a crucial task for 'complex classification'. The movement of systems from classes and indeed, even more importantly, changes in classification systems over time, is exactly what should interest us most.

We have reached a very important point because I am now going to specify what we measure and what that measurement means. Given that we must avoid reifying 'variables' and abstracting from real systems/cases, then we have to measure the systems/cases. However, whilst there are iconic ways in which we can represent systems/cases as wholes, we cannot measure them all at once other than through pure intuition. We can, however, measure aspects of them which can be thought of as the traces which they offer to us. I use the word traces because it implies both incompleteness and that something dynamic is going on. Things are changing and leave marks of those changes.

The dynamic systems which are our cases leave traces for us, which we can pick up. We can, as it were, track them, and we can infer from the traces what it was that left them. From the traces we can reconstruct a version of the real entities *and* of the relationships among those entities *and* of the emergent forms which are the product of and producers of the relationships among those entities. We can glimpse the entities and the systemic relationships among the entities.

Let me illustrate by returning to the idea of 'class' in its originary form. Marx, in *The Eighteenth Brumaire of Louis Napoleon*, distinguished between classes in themselves and classes for themselves. Classes in themselves were aggregates defined by the same relationship to the relations of production and with a common set of experiences in consequence of that relationship, but with no conscious collective sense or propensity to act on their common position. Classes for themselves were characterized by collective consciousness and propensity to act – they were E.P. Thompson's machine in motion with all the smoke, noise and fury. The method proposed here for classifying identifies classes in themselves – entities that have much in common. Note that it does not just identify the class of any individual entity – assign the nominal property – although it can do that. It also allows us to see the shape and scale of the ensemble – the class as a whole – and, more importantly, the relation of that class to other classes and, even more importantly, how those relations change over time. Indeed, in the event that we can 'measure' components of consciousness – which is a real issue – we might even say something about classes for themselves or about any other conscious and active collectivity.

So what we measure are the systems/cases and we do so by measuring traces with a view to classifying and establishing the trajectories of all of the individual cases, ensembles and classificatory sets. No small order, but in fact something I think has a long history, being neither Platonic backhand nor forehand but enhanced Aristotelian smash. Badminton is a far more subtle and interesting game than tennis.

It is worth noting here that there is a substantial philosophical debate about classification represented by the contributions to the collection edited by Douglas and Hull (1992). A central issue is whether or not we can talk of natural kinds, of things that exist separate from our processes of classifying them. Hull takes on this in relation to the classification of biological species, the original taxonomic programme, and asserts in a concluding and deliberately emphasized passage that 'if species are taken to be things that evolve, then they are not kinds at all and have no special implications for any of the issues relating to induction' (1992: 66). The problem with this is that plainly evolution is understood by Hull as a continuous and ongoing process, the biological parallel of Archer's ideas about social morphogenesis (1998). Complexity theory suggests that evolution does not take this form at all. Rather we find phase shifts, changes of state, precisely changes of kind. Far from change being a challenge to the existence of natural kinds, it is in the nature of natural kinds that they do change, by changing kind. Our taxonomies are local and contextual, not nomothetic universalism – but none the less they are real.

The process of exploring data so as to generate an account of the dynamic development both of individual systems and the dynamic transformation of social categories, that is, of ensembles/attractors and of movement of cases among ensembles/attractors, seems to me to be an instrument assisted form of Aristotle's intuitive induction. Losee describes this thus:

> Intuitive induction is a matter of insight. It is an ability to see that which is 'essential' in the data of sense experience. ... The operation of intuitive induction is analogous to the operation of the 'vision' of the taxonomist. The taxonomist is a scientist who has learned to 'see' the general attributes and *differentiae* of a specimen. There is a sense in which the taxonomist 'sees more than' the untrained observer of the same specimen. The taxonomist knows what to look for. This is an ability which is achieved, if at all, only after extensive experience. (1993: 8)

My argument is that the computing technologies we will examine subsequently enable us to do something which we have always done, by means of a more systematic intuitive process – one which maintains the Aristotelian principle of engagement with the world as it is. And so to measurement.

Sensible and useful measuring

Traditionally, discussions of measurement as process begin by considering how 'concepts' are translated into variables through the process of operationalization. Despite the extermination of the variable proposed earlier in this chapter, I am going to proceed in much the same way with the crucial distinction made that we must think about traces rather than variables and always have a relational frame of reference. I want to propose a distinction between two types of traces that can be measured. One type is a trace of the system that constitutes our case, whether that system is an individual, household, city, nation, bloc or whatever. The other type is a trace of the relations that system has with other systems both at its own level and at all other significant levels. Even this distinction is really heuristic. It is not an absolute but rather describes the ends of a continuum. Moreover, the location of particular traces on that continuum can change over time. However, heuristic is useful.

The social category of gender illustrates this point. Biologically, sex is pretty well absolutely a characteristic of individual organisms, at least in its elemental form. We can see how this works by considering parthogenesis as elemental. Parthogenetic organisms define the norm in sex as female because they can reproduce clones without any other genetic contribution being made. Males in biological terms are simply an externalized and 'othered' element in the reproductive process. The 'otherness' matters because the advantages of sexual reproduction derive from genetic diversity. Otherness is the origin of a relational element even at the biological level.

Plainly, the biological base forms the substrate of the social category of gender, which is embodied in individual people, but gender is far more relational than biological sex because its characteristics are constituted by the interaction of apparent biological sex with other human systems and with all the social systems within which people – the human systems – live their lives. However, gender is embodied and available. The ease with which the overwhelming majority of human beings can specify their own gender demonstrates this. We can work with gender, both as scientists and as people, by thinking of it as at least in very large part an aspect of the unique self.

Class is very different. Sure, administrative statistical systems and social science, usually working together, try to generate an individual label which will serve descriptive analytical purposes in the same way as gender. There is a sustained effort to construct class as an attribute of individual systems. Rose and O'Reilly have expressed this very clearly in relation to the recent project of redefining 'official' class in the UK:

> Why do we need an SEC (Socio-Economic Class) conceived and constructed in the manner set out here? One of the strengths of the approach we have taken in the review, indeed its underlying principle, is that the revised SEC offers not necessarily improved statistical association over the current SECs, but that it lends itself to the possibility of *explaining* the associations we find. Because we know what our proposed SEC is measuring – employment relations and conditions, i.e. aspects of the work situation and the labour contract – we can construct *causal narratives* which specify how the SEC links to a range of outcomes via a variety of intervening variables. ... The revised SEC defines *structural* positions which can be seen conceptually to exist independently of the individuals who occupy those positions at any particular time. The positions condition and shape the lives and life-chances of their occupants. (1997: 12; original emphasis)

The conceptual foundation of SEC in this frame is the combination of employment conditions and relations which constitute the occupation of a single individual. This enables the construction through an appropriate algorithm – rule for measuring – of an ordinal variable which can be attached to each individual. Rose and O'Reilly argue that this variable can then be considered as causal to other things, for example health states, even if the causes are indirect.

Of course this approach is remote from any relational and structural conception of class as described by Thompson or indeed from the main approaches to class of classical social theorists in general. And yet Rose and O'Reilly are rather eager that the SEC should have relational significance – it should enable a unidimensional assignation of the case to a category defined by structural relations. This will be done without any assessment of the relation of the cases to each other – the ranked typology is given, not in any way generated from information about the cases. The slots are there already and the cases fit into them, and then on the basis of this we can explore lives and life chances – we can establish individual trajectories which fit our scheme but not if the scheme itself has changed.

The problem this approach raises can be illustrated by considering exactly the classic function of class measurements in UK official statistics, as a means of organizing data about health which provides some information about the causes of differences in health states – in reality in mortality rates – among groups categorized by class. Individuals have a range of social relations which interact in crucial ways with SEC's foundational field – the combination of employment relations and conditions – and it is the interaction of these things in the individual system which matters. For example people live in households and the composition of these households affects the way their individual health is expressed. Feminist principles have led to the classification of individual female adults by their own occupation rather than by that of a male 'head of household' but the real issue in a society in which household life chances are a function of multiple earnings for most 'middle' people is the way in which the actual sum of incomes and work relations measured by SEC interact with wealth, tenure, location and a range of other factors to produce the generative mechanisms for life chances as these mechanisms are embodied both in individual people and in the households (which may of course consist of just one person) of which those individual people are part. The whole point of measuring class is to say something about relations and we cannot assert that one component, always expressed in real people in terms of multiple interactions, which include cross level interactions, has any causal properties whatsoever. Class is always relational, even when considered as an attribute.

Of course, it is perfectly appropriate to consider that employment relations and conditions, or rather the trajectory of what is in reality at least a bivariate trace, matter as a component of individual human beings. It is quite inappropriate to attempt to generate an algorithm on the basis of which knowing someone's occupation forms part of the process of tracing class relations as embodied within that person. We should not be making variables.

The preceding discussion has introduced a fundamental issue which has to be dealt with in line with the general principle informing this text to the effect that if the world is complex it is a pointless exercise to try to deal with understanding it on a foundation of abstracted and unreal simplification. This is the issue usually described as that of hierarchical data which in traditional quantitative reasoning creates real problems because of the difficulties of inferring causal relations among variables measured at the different levels. The issue of the relations between individuals and the households of which they are part illustrates this exactly. The problem was identified in commentary on the ESRC funded programme dealing with 'large and complex data sets' (ALCD):

> Most social science data are structured hierarchically. Examples are the clustering of students within schools, individuals within households with neighbourhoods, and repeated measurements within individual subjects. … Researchers dealing with large and complex structures, such as longitudinal panel surveys or studies of educational performance, require modelling techniques which respect the hierarchical and cross-classified structures in their data. (ALCD, 1997b)

The point I want to make is that the large and complex structures are real and that when we think about traces we have to think of systems at all these levels and see the traces in relation to them. In the case of 'class' this means that we have to think not of a single measure but about the product of classifications. I can see ways, through any method of numerical taxonomy, by which we can classify on a relational basis at any given level – for individuals, for households. I can see ways, through the use of relational data bases, by which we can relate levels to each other. This seems to me to take us some way towards a glimpse of the real dynamic structures of the social world.

So, back to operationalization: an operational definition is something defined by rules for measuring it – we might now say by the algorithm which defines the measurement process. A fundamental issue in measurement has always been that of validity which, in essence, means the issue of whether the thing which we measure using our measurement algorithm corresponds to the real thing we think we are measuring. Discussions of validity have always accepted that we can reify through the measurement process – make something out of nothing. An excellent example is provided by the concept of general intelligence reified through measurement into IQ. I want to be even more radical and argue that measurement to the extent that it has seen variables as real, has always reified.

The implication of this is not that we stop measuring. Far from it! It is rather that we recognize that the things we measure are not real in themselves but rather are expressions of the relationships among things which are real. This is not a licence for license. We still have to pay very careful attention to how we operationalize – generate a measurement rule which produces something we think corresponds to a trace of a real system as expressed in that system's relations. However, it means that we get more from reality than classical discussions of measurement have generally allowed.

It is useful to think about measurement as a process which is in some ways analogous to both hermeneutic modes of understanding and grounded theory, which in any event have much in common with each other. The point is that those modes involve a constant engagement of interpretation with the research material, which requires a return to the material in the light of each phase of interpretation and further refinement and development of the interpretative account. The material – text for hermeneutics, research products for grounded theory – has a constitutive role in the whole exercise. So it is with measurement. Given a generally exploratory view of measurement, then we can see measurements as provisional versions of reality which can be improved by re-engagement with the account they give.[6]

In the general complexity account a key word is 'emergence'. I don't want to overdo the argument, but we might consider that descriptions of complex systems and their trajectories emerge from our measurements, understood as traces of those systems, particularly in the form of multidimensional products of classifications. It bears repeating that this is not a licence for some sort of postmodernist perspectivism on issues of operationalization but rather an assertion that operationalization is provisional and reflexive. In some ways it is an iterative process rather like that of artillery spotting. The spotter suggests co-ordinates for the target, observes the fall of the shell, moves the co-ordinates iteratively on the basis of that observation, and eventually the shell hits the intended target.

If we start from this position then the traditional litanies around measurement become less important. Validity resides in the whole iterative process rather than in the original formulation of a specific algorithm, a method which could never logically achieve anything more than measurement by fiat – we declare that we are measuring what we say we are measuring – because there was no re-engagement of the definition with the observations of the world made using the original definition.

Certainly the idea that there is a hierarchy of measurement in which ratio scale measurement is the ideal and ordinal and nominal measurement are mere approximations to it, makes little sense if we adopt this approach. The view of ratio scale measurement as the ideal is a product precisely of the linear, Newtonian mechanistic, account of reality. Changes for that perspective are always proportionate so we need to measure exactly in order to be able to represent that exact proportionality. If interesting and important changes are changes of kind rather than degree, then what we need to be able to measure is instead the occurrence of changes that are categorical. It is important to recognize the implications of this approach. Although we can agree with Marx that quantity can become transformed into quality, the interactive effect of changes in quantitative aspects is not the only source of qualitative change. There can be gross qualitative origins for qualitative transformation, often in the form of interventions from outside the system.

Conclusion

This has been a rather radical chapter. It has followed Emirbayer's and Abbott's dismissal of the idea of 'variable' and argued instead for attention to be paid to both the entities of the social world and the relations among them. It has followed the logic of the relational position by recognizing that relations exist among the complex entities that constitute the social world, both at the micro level of real people and at the macro level of real social collectivities. It has stolen – a theft now freely acknowledged – the common term 'embodied' to describe the way in which relations are part of people and to do with the intersections of the systems that are people, both with other people and with the real entities of the social world, and with the real entities of the natural world. This account is absolutely anti-reductionist. However, it is not simply holistic. In the tradition of complexity, it is about both parts and wholes.

The argument has been that the things we can measure are not 'variables' but traces – the expression of the real systems that compose the world. If we are measuring traces in a dynamic world and if what interests us most are changes of kind, the phase shifts, in that dynamic world and in components of that world, then we have a very different understanding of the process of measurement itself. It becomes a much more provisional and interactive process – hence the analogy with hermeneutic and grounded theory approaches. Classification, sorting things out, becomes primary. I am very pleased that we can line up with Aristotle against Plato here. The adulation of the formalized mathematical model, the assertion that the abstract representation of the world through establishing a causal model based on variables and isomorphic with an algebra – the construction of interpreted axiomatic systems – is precisely what Hayles identifies as the privileging of abstraction over the real. We absolutely need a down and dirty empiricism in which understanding is grounded in the real and constantly returns to the real.

The issue of validation illustrates this rather well. Conventional discussions of validation have a platonic aesthetic quality to them. Measurements are good to the extent that they correspond to the platonic ideal form but will never quite get there. Validation procedures are all about the aesthetic construction of an approximation of that ideal form. Systematic and reflexive categorization is something different. Actually it fits with Williams's (1965) second definition of culture, not as the effort to replicate the platonic ideal form, but rather as documentary, as the description of what is. We are documenters when we measure.

But we don't just document – we change – we make. And measurement in modernity is a crucial process by which we make. Statistics are tools and tools are used as well as regarded. With tools things are made. 'By Hammer and Hand do All Things Stand' was the motto of the Blacksmiths' Guild of Newcastle. We might consider that statistics have played a crucial role in making things stand as well. They do describe – document – the world, but they also constitute it. To that process we now turn.

Notes

1 I recently joined this organization, not before time! I should have joined years ago.

2 Or not, if we think of income in relation not just to simple purchasing power but as a demarcating trace of lifestyle/social group membership.

3 Or not – because establishing the 'right' cut-off point for converting ratio scale measurements into a system of ranks is a far from obvious procedure.

4 Lakoff and Johnson argue that: 'Categorization is … a consequence of how we are embodied. We have evolved to categorize: if we hadn't we would not have survived. … a small percentage of our categories have been formed by conscious acts of categorization, but most are formed automatically and unconsciously as a result of functioning in the world. … Even when we think we are deliberately forming new categories, our unconscious categories enter into our choice of possible categories. … it is not just that our bodies and brains determine *that* we will categorize; they also determine what kinds of categories we will have and what their structure will be' (1999: 18; original emphasis). This approach to the 'embodied mind' is extremely important and will almost certainly have a profound influence on theories of measurement in the future.

5 We, the researchers, do this because we specify, at least in cluster analyses, the components of the algorithms that do the classifying. These components are the actual measured traces which are used to classify and the actual mathematical procedures selected. In neural nets the net works with us so the plural is still appropriate but there is much less, if any, specification of algorithms.

6 This means that the traditional concern of measurement with reliability becomes redundant. Reliability is the quality of repeated constancy of the measurement instrument – when it measures the same thing more than once you get the same measurement on every occasion. Given an iterative conception of the measurement process reliability is neither possible nor desirable. Of course, the whole conception of reliability is dependent on a reification of variables.

3

The State's Measurements: The Construction and Use of Official Statistics

Statistics is a word with two meanings. It is used generally to refer to specific measurements – lies, damned lies and statistics – of the kind presented in the Guinness advert which asserted that 99 per cent of Manchester United fans have never been to Old Trafford. The 'early use' (*Oxford English Dictionary*) was specifically social but the word has been extended to cover all: 'collection and arrangement of numerical facts or data'. This chapter is about the products of this process and in particular about the measurements generated by states and similar organizations either deliberately in order 'to know' their social and economic environments or as by-products of administrative activity or as both together.

The other meaning of the word describes that branch of mathematics concerned with the relationships among sets of numbers. Interestingly, the *OED* does not cite this meaning and all variations of the word there are defined empirically with reference to specific sciences. However, the *Encyclopaedia of Statistical Sciences*, naturally, prioritizes 'the branch of mathematics devoted to the study of mathematical methods for the organization, processing and utilization of data for scientific and practical conclusions', although this definition too is intrinsically empirical and emphasizes application rather than abstract use. The *Encyclopaedia* does mark out statistics as a general set of procedures which can be abstracted from specific investigative contexts: 'This formal mathematical side of statistical research method is indifferent to the specific nature of the objects being studied and comprises the topic of mathematical statistics.'

These two sorts of definitions illustrate an important point made by Desrosières. Statistics has a particular authority among forms of knowledge because of 'an unusual interaction, brought about by history, between two forms of authority that are clearly separate: that of science and that of the state' (1998: 17). A general characteristic of modernity has been the separation of authority in knowledge from political authority. The first has claimed independence of the second and the subordination of knowledge to political power is regarded as a sign of backwardness and ignorance, whether in the case of the relationship between Galileo and the Inquisition or the assertion of Lysenko's views under Stalinism.[1] What is interesting is that statistics represent the extreme case of a reversal of the pre-modern order of political power and knowledge. In the modern world political power is supposed to 'accept' knowledge as 'objective' and 'true'. Statistics is the extreme case because the given 'data' relates to the activities of the state within society. It is true that 'mere' description would not suffice for this authority and that the development of techniques founded on probability theory is an essential component of the authority claims made by this particular branch of knowledge. We will return to that aspect in Chapter 5. Here we will deal with the 'data' and the uses that we might make of it.

The history of statistics as measures

In the history of the development of statistics

> the real action takes place circa 1835–1935, when governments in Europe and the US established official statistical bureaux, when there was quantitative data gathering on an unprecedented scale, when social reformers looked to statistics to diagnose and even cure the ills of industrial cities, and when descriptive statistics met and eventually married with mathematical probability. (Daston, 2000: 35)

There were certainly important developments before these dates. Whatever status we give to revenue audits like Domesday Book, the UK has had a census since 1801, although in the middle of the eighteenth century the British parliament rejected efforts to introduce either a census or civil registration. Civil registration of births, deaths and marriages was actually introduced in 1837, almost exactly in accord with Daston's dating. What did precede the statist development was three developments in 'civil society', namely:

1 The eighteenth century German development of 'stadtistics' as part of the work of the academy in which systematic descriptions of different states were generated as snapshots as the basis for comparison among them.
2 The late seventeenth and eighteenth century UK emergence of a tradition of 'political arithmetic' which led to the creation of life tables, an essential foundation of the insurance industry.
3 The early nineteenth century 'progressive' practice of statistical investigation in developing industrial cities by elements of the intellectual elite, and especially the newly emerging medical profession, often organized in 'statistical societies'.

Shaw and Miles point out an important difference between German 'stadtistics' and British political arithmetic. The former generated essentially a set of static descriptions at a single time point. The latter was very much concerned with 'past and present changes, with dynamic processes and causal regularities' (1979: 31). The significance of the use of the word 'causal' is considerable.

German 'stadtistics' was descriptive but the political arithmeticians, and even more the progressive urban statisticians, were interested in using measurements as a clue to the causes of things – of death and of disease in the first instance. This epidemiological objective was a major factor in the move towards mathematical methods as described by Desrosières.

The Victorian statistical movement, closely associated with the promotion of 'Healthy Towns', and typified by the Manchester and London Statistical Societies (now unified as the Royal Statistical Society), was particularly important. Cullen (1975) provides a full account of this. We should return to Williams's (1979) remarks in the epigraph to Chapter 1 and note his absolutely correct assertion that without systematic counting 'the society that was emerging out of the industrial revolution was literally unknowable'. Only through counting could change be grasped in general terms. Shaw and Miles draw an important parallel between these early nineteenth century flowerings of modernity and the social indicators movement of the 1960s (1979: 37) and we will return to this theme.

The United Kingdom history of the development of statistical investigation and statistical accounts of social conditions and social change provides a good example for the purposes of this book.[2] The decennial census begun in 1801 has been carried out every tenth year apart from 1941 during the Second World War. Civil registration of 'vital' statistics began in 1837. The recording of causes of death (although deeply contentious – see Bowker and Star, 1999; Prior, 1989) and the return of incidences of 'notifiable disease' played a crucial role in the development of public health systems. However, moves beyond this have taken place at particularly interesting times and have usually been driven by some form of social crisis. For example, in 1908 the Board of Trade produced a benchmarking report on wages, prices and rents in the principal industrial towns of the United Kingdom at a time of considerable industrial unrest and in the context of the Liberal Reforms of 1906 to 1912 which were an important element in the development of the UK welfare state. The social insurance system introduced at this time and massively extended in the aftermath of the First World War necessitated the collection of unemployment statistics and to some extent led to the creation of a concept of 'unemployment' and hence of a social category[3] and a set of appropriate statistics collected as a by-product of administrative intervention. The systematic organization of production during the Second World War, in which the future Prime Minister Harold Wilson – a statistician by trade – played an important role, was the basis of the production of a series of economic statistics describing both production and consumption, the latter represented by the Family Expenditure Survey. The creation of a National Health Service generated what were at first a rather unsystematic set of data relating to health service use.

The Health Service illustrates two related pressures on the generation of statistical information. The NHS was created by the nationalization of an existing system of hospitals and until the 1970s no significant administrative attention was paid to the match of secondary care (hospital) resources to health need. Agitation at that time, deriving originally it is claimed from systematic collection of data in order to develop a North East Regional Strategy, led to the work of the 'Resources Allocation Working Party' (RAWP) which generated a composite indicator of 'health need'. This was used as a key device in allocating resources for service development.

Davies (1968) had written about the concept of 'territorial justice', by which he meant the spatial allocation of public resources on some basis which reflected needs for services. Various devices attempt to achieve this, particularly in relation to the allocation of central funds to local authorities. Statistical information is essential for these purposes. However, modern administration has required more of statistics than differentiation of needs. Reasonably enough, there have been efforts to generate some measures of the outputs of public sector organizations. What in the private sector can be defined by the bottom line of the accounts,[4] that is the success or otherwise of the enterprise measured by rate of return on capital employed, has to be defined in some other way in 'not for profit' public organizations – hence the development of a series of performance indicators.

There is an interesting political argument about the status of statistics collected by the state. We can leave on one side the arguments about the ontological status of such measures. For us, as realists, they are social constructs but constructs derived from social reality. The issue here is about range and access. In the 1960s and 1970s Claus Moser (for much of this period Director of the Central Statistical Office), with the active support of Harold Wilson, argued for and developed a system in support of statistics as information for the 'public citizen'. There was a large expansion in the publication of statistical information and *Social Trends* was initiated as a general summary description of the character of social changes and as a way of documenting the involvement of government in those changes. This was very much in accord with liberal political perspectives – essentially a kind of extensive whiggism on fabian lines – which informed public intellectuals of Moser's generation in both the United States and the UK and was part of the background to the social indicators movement.

When the Tories came to power in the UK, Rayner was appointed to review the governmental statistical services. A full account of developments is given in Levitas (1996) but, in summary, the view taken was that only those statistics which government required for its own purposes should be collected and that there should be no 'citizenship' orientated subsidy to the publication of statistical information. Anything government did not require would be provided by the market if it was needed. Levitas considered that these developments reflected Thatcher's view that there was no such thing as society (1996: 10). Certainly the line of the Rayner review was very much in accord with that strange mixture of authoritarianism – the state should know and the public doesn't need to know – and economic liberalism – leave it to the market – which characterized the dominant force in British politics in those years.

However, there has been another view which seems to have prevailed and which is very interesting. This is one which regards the public not as Moser did as an assembly of active citizens concerned with the collective good, but rather as a set of individual consumers concerned with receiving good information in order to inform individual choices. This is well represented by the publication of performance data for specific schools in England and Wales. This is intended to inform parental choice within a frame of under-standing in which such choice will reward good schools and lead to the elimination of bad ones since each child is in effect a quota award of cash given so that schools are resourced through a formula based on recruited numbers. This is actually a rather libertarian view of information in a market framework.

It is notable that in 'public market' orientated information systems of this kind there is a real retreat from any consideration of cause. The argument, which has force in relation to individual social practices, is that parents seek-ing to maximize the achievement of their own children are not concerned with whether a school does well because is has a good intake[5] but rather want their child to go to schools which do well anyway – which generates exactly positive feedback effects.

In summary, the UK statistical system is a by-product of the need for the state to have statistical information about its changing environment, about its own activities, and about the relationship between those activities and that environment. However, 'the state' is embedded within a political process which, whatever the crises in the form, remains democratic. There are – because such forms always co-exist – two general accounts of the proper relationship between the public in a democracy and statistical infor-mation. One is that the public is literally the demos – the collection of citi-zens which needs to know in order to act in a political way. The other, which is essentially a depoliticizing version, argues that there is no collective public but instead a set of individual consumers who have a right to good product information. The latter currently prevails.

It is important to recognize that underpinning these two different concep-tions of the relationship between public and statistics are two quite different conceptions of the role of government in society. From the 'informed public' conception the view of the state is as of something different from market orientated institutions with a distinctive role to play. There is a separate and crucial public sector. This kind of approach informed all variants of a notion of capitalism as properly existing in a social market form[6] – that is, as a separate and distinctive political sphere existing apart from the market and acting on market relations in a non-market way. The German 'Order Liberals' who devised this conception considered that the very survival of market relations depended on such a separate and interventionist state. In contrast, the consumer model sees the public sphere as simply a rather specialized provider within a general market system. The products of this provider cannot be understood simply through information on prices and consumer evaluation of quality so other information has to be provided but this information is still geared towards individual market led choices.

The historical development of official statistics shows that these measures are intended to document the nature of changes in society. We can use a cybernetic analogy and think of them as in the first instance an information flow from the environment of the state to the state as a system. In the second half of the twentieth century that conception was extended through the development of economic statistics as a crucial element in macro-economic management to include 'learning feedback'. The state did not passively receive information about its environment. Rather it acted on that information and evaluated the consequence of those actions in order to inform future actions.

This kind of systemic account is useful as part of the story but there is more to it. Democratic states in complex social orders have to relate both to the general body of the citizenry and to special interest groups, including groups whose authority is derived from specific claims about knowledge. The actual development of statistics was in large part driven by the emergent 'scientifically learned' professions, especially but not exclusively the medical profession, in the nineteenth century. Statisticians, using probability theory as the foundation of a specialized branch of applied mathematics, extended those claims and acquired special status as a profession combining scientific and administrative expertise.

Statisticians are not, necessarily, desiccated calculating machines. They are human beings with experiences and motives. Moser, a refugee from nazism with a liberal and rational world-view, believed in the importance of an informed democratic public with a collective vision.[7] Some of his successors, in a political climate in which 'the Keynesian mode of regulation'[8] has been replaced by a 'hollowed out' state, still endorse public information but for the purposes of individual consumer choice. This division is a reflection of the crucial division in contemporary Western political ideology.

There is another element to be considered; that is the status of 'statistical science' in delivering knowledge about not only the social world, but also the crucial interactions between the social and natural worlds, about the ecological implications of industrial society and mass energy consumption. We may have, at least for the moment, managed to transcend the ecological implications of infectious disease in our 'unnatural' urban world, but our impact on atmospheric chemistry may be of even greater significance through the next century. Let us turn from the history of 'official statistics' to a general consideration of their nature.

Official and semi-official statistics

This is an appropriate point to say something about the nature of published and otherwise available statistical information. This takes different forms, and this section will provide a typology of those forms, and can be obtained from a variety of sources. It is pointless in a general text of this kind to attempt to provide a detailed guide to those sources. Instead I will point you towards the guides to those sources. It is essential to remember that the nature of sources changes and that such guides must necessarily be dynamic and respond to those changes. That means the guides to use are those on the Web.

Before embarking on classification of types of statistics and 'meta-guiding' as to sources, it is necessary to say something about all statistical sources in general. This takes us forward to themes which will be developed in Chapter 4, but a preliminary discussion is appropriate here. All statistics, whatever the actual detailed mode of their collection, are in the most general sense the product of social surveys. That is to say they are produced by systematic measurement across a specified range of cases. They generate what Marsh (1982) after Lazarsfeld called the case-variable matrix, in which for all our cases we have either a measurement or a record that no measurement has been obtained. In essence we create a spreadsheet, literally in the case of all computer based data analysis tools.

In contemporary versions of such tables the values are recorded as numerical integers. Interestingly, at the very beginning of modern data collection values were often recorded as textual entries. For example, the Royal Commission on the Poor Law in Ireland in 1837 obtained textual descriptions of every townland in Ireland under a set of headings sent to its informants. Now we turn these textual elements into types which become numerical codes.

It does not matter how statistical information is actually collected, whether through specific enquiry in either a census or sample form, or as the by-product of routine administrative processes. At the foundation of all social statistics is a case data matrix of this form.

This kind of spreadsheet is composed of 'micro-data' – data relating to specific individual cases. Such micro-data is not usually available in a published form but can be obtained in an anonymized version – that is, in a form in which the cases cannot be identified – in special instances. The most important examples of such available micro-data are the special samples of individual contemporary census records of individuals and of households obtainable from some national census authorities including the UK (see Dale et al., 2000). Such data sets are the basis of secondary analyses, of which more in Chapter 6. Note that the performance data about individual institutions, for example school performance data, are micro-data considered as description of the institutions although many components of those data sets are the result of aggregations of micro-data about individual cases. For a school its gender type, that is, male only, female only, or mixed, is a micro-data element for the school itself. The percentage of its relevant pupils obtaining five or more A to C grades at GCSE – the examination taken in England and Wales at age sixteen, is a micro-data element for the school but is the product of the aggregation of measurements for a set of individual pupils.

Published statistical information is generally the product of aggregation of individual cases. Much of this information, typified by the products of the UK decennial census, is presented in the form of aggregate indices at different spatial levels. An index is typically a percentage of all cases having a given nominal or ordinal value. The example cited above of percentage of relevant pupils obtaining five or more A–C GCSE passes is a typical example. Spatial examples include unemployment rates, percentage of households occupying dwellings of a given tenure, percentage of households headed by a female single parent of dependent children and so on. All such statistics require both a denominator and a numerator – they are essentially fractions. We need to know how many relevant cases there are and how many of those relevant cases have a specific value on an attribute. In many census based and other publications we are given all three of the numerator – the number of cases, e.g. total number of households in a metropolitan district; the denominator – the total number of households headed by female single parents of dependent children; and the index produced by rendering the second figure as a percentage of the first. In census style data we typically have these sorts of indices for a hierarchy of spaces. In the 1991 Census for England and Wales we had data for enumeration districts – the area covered by a single census enumerator and typically in an urban area containing less than two hundred households, local electoral wards, local government districts, counties, regions and nations (counting Wales as a nation as well as a region).

The Census is a special decennial data collection exercise. However, very similar data can be generated from administrative processes. The data contained on the 'National Online Manpower [sic] Information Service' (NOMIS) includes data about unemployment and the characteristics of the unemployed which is generated from the administrative practices of the UK Employment Service, the direct successor of Beveridge's Labour Exchanges of 1908, and its smallest spatial area is that of 'Local Office' – the modern equivalent of the Employment Exchange.

Although the use of spatial units as the basis of aggregate information is the most general way of constructing aggregates it is not the only way in which such aggregation can be carried out. Spatial data is important because it is the information base of much local administration and of central resource allocation to specific localities, but there are other demarcators which can separate cases apart from spatial location. An important example is gender. We can use micro-data for individual cases to construct aggregate measures for different genders in our society. This might be gender based aggregation of individual performances at A level, the academic examination taken at eighteen by English, Welsh and Northern Irish students at the end of secondary education, which will demonstrate that girls have improved their performance relative to boys and now do better. It might be the aggregation of information about incomes by gender from tax records and other sources which continue to show that men earn more than women at any given age and level of qualification and degree of engagement with work (that is, in terms of hours worked). There is an enormous amount of information of this kind, published not only for nation-states but also by international organizations such as the European Union and United Nations. Note that much of this information is not snapshot but takes the form of trend descriptions. We are interested not only in how things are but in how they are changing. This brings us on to the topic of social indicators.

Social indicators

The social indicators movement of the 1960s and 1970s is of considerable significance for quantitative social scientists, both in terms of its products – many of the series and, even more, composite indices, used by all levels of government and by international agencies are the creation of this movement – and because the debate about social indicators helps us to clarify our general concern with the nature both of measurement and of what is being measured. The social indicators movement had a great deal in common with the statistical societies of the nineteenth century. It was the product of professional concerns, although now largely of professionals employed in administrative positions and as university teachers rather than the doctors and concerned capitalists of the statistical societies, which reflected apparent social instability and change. In the United States, where the movement began, it reflected a tension about the functionality of the state's data collection exercises. As Cohen put it:

> Unfortunately, most government statistics are by-products of the needs of accounting and administrative routine, and thus tell us more about the operation of government than the condition of society. (1968; quoted Booth, 1988: 111)

The bloated administrative structure of the 1960s welfare/warfare state was quite well informed about the condition of its internal organs but lacked information on what was going on in its social environment. This was in marked contrast to the economic environment where a series of indicators were organized into representational models of the economic sphere. The urban riots of inner city Black America suggested that there was an urgent need to monitor and, if possible, explain, the character of social unrest.

The development of social indicator systems was a classic 'liberal modernist' response. Those who attempted to develop this programme, typified by US Vice President Mondale in the Johnson administration, had a genuine commitment to social reform and a typical liberal/scientistic belief in the value of rational and objective measurement as a means towards this. However, they were not prepared to challenge the bases of economic power or recognize the ideological components in the foundation of knowledge.

It would be absurd to say they had no impact, particularly in relation to the citizenship status of black Americans, but there was no conception of economic transformation.

It is interesting to recognize that there is now an 'ecological indicators' movement, although the end states sought by those proposing such indicators almost always include social as well as primarily natural objectives. Plainly one factor in the attempt to develop systematic social measurement *and* modelling was a jealousy of economics which as discourse had become a central part of governance. However, there is more to the issue that mere professional rivalry. Social critics in the 1960s and 1970s pointed out as ecological critics do today, that if all measures of progress are constructed around economic production and consumption then other things which matter for both individual and collective 'quality of life' become much less important as policy goals.

There are a variety of definitions and typologies of social indicators. One very commonly quoted is:

> the operational definition or part of the operational definition of any one of the concepts central to the generation of an information system descriptive of the social system. (Carlisle, 1972: 25)

The issue is what is meant by the term 'descriptive'. If this is understood in the traditional sense of descriptive statistics, then we have had social indicators since 1801 at least, and so we have. However, if description is understood as a process of representation, of modelling, then something different is going on.

Proponents of social indicators often argued for modelling, drawing explicit analogies with the value of economic modelling based on combining measured economic indicators with mathematical formalism. Land's 'integrated 21 equation model of how marriage, family, and population conditions, as indexed by macro-social indicators, affect each other and are affected by other social, demographic, and economic forces' (Land and Felson, 1976: 328) is exactly such a model.

Land and Felson's use of the word 'forces' and Carlisle's concern with the construction of operational definitions, both indicate the way in which variables were regarded as real, despite the inherently systemic conception which informed the construction of social indicator systems. The 'variables' were seen as external to the systems they described and causal to it. Hence, a central problem was that of measurement and the inter-relationship of autonomous variables with causal models:

> This then is the problem: social indicators, virtually by definition, specify causal linkages or connections between observable aspects of social phenomena which indicate, and other unobservable aspects or concepts, which are indicated. They can only be accomplished by postulating *implicitly* or *explicitly* some causal model or theory of social behaviour which serves to relate formally the variables

under consideration. All social indicator research represents, therefore, some social theory or model, however simplistic ... Only the explicit specification of the nature of the causal linkages within a model allows hypothesis-testing and thus the opportunity to establish that some indicator indeed indicates that which it claims to indicate. (Carley, 1981: 67–8)

If instead we think of indicators as traces of complex and evolving social systems, the approach suggested in Chapter 2, we see things in a different way. It is not that careful thought about and justification of measurement become any less important, but we avoid the trap of reifying some platonic real at the level of autonomous variable. In fact this is pretty well exactly what people have done with general social indicator systems. With 'general social indicators' they have used them to provide a descriptive account of the trajectory of social systems through time.

There is a large variety of typologies of social indicators but these can really be considered in terms of three classificatory principles. The first is that of objective and can be used to divide indicators into those *descriptive* of social systems and those concerned with the *evaluation* of particular social projects, usually through employing an accounting distinction among inputs, through-puts and outputs. The second is that of form. This has been systematized thus by the Conference of European Statisticians:

- Raw statistical series as basic counts or simple percentages.
- Identified key series of single variables of the kind presented in *Social Trends*. Total population is a simple example.
- Comprehensive systems of statistics – we can regard the set of measures about schools published annually as an institutional orientated example.
- Composite indices generated by the mathematical combination of sets of indicators. The United Nations Development Program (UNDP) index of social development is an example.
- Synthetic products of multivariate analyses – although we might regard these as a special case of composite indices. Factors generated by Factor Analyses typify here.
- Series fitted into explicit formal social models – there are no real long term examples of these.

The final principle, which is at best heuristic, is founded on the distinction between descriptive indicators and normative indicators. Given the whole sociopolitical milieu of social indicators there is always at least a normative tinge to them.

A good example of a social indicator is provided by the UNDP index of development:

> The concept of human development focuses on the ends rather than the means of 'development' and progress. The real objective of development should be to create an enabling environment for people to enjoy long, healthy and creative lives. Though this may appear to be a simple truth, it is often forgotten in the immediate concern with the accumulation of commodities and wealth. Human

development denotes both the process of widening people's choices and the level of their achieved well-being. The most critical ones are to lead a long and healthy life, to be educated, and to enjoy a decent standard of living. Additional choices include political freedom, guaranteed human rights and self respect. The concept distinguishes between two sides of human development. One is the formation of human capabilities, such as improved health or knowledge. The other is the use that people make of their acquired capabilities, for work or leisure. (UNDP at: http://www.undp.org/hd50/anatools.htm)

The concept of human development has been translated into an index which can be used to describe all nation-states – the Human Development Index (HDI). It is worth quoting UNDP's account of this in full:

The first *Human Development Report* (1990) introduced a new way of measuring development – by combining indicators of life expectancy, educational attainment and income into a composite human development index, the HDI. The breakthrough for the HDI was to find a common measuring rod for the socio-economic distance travelled. The HDI sets a minimum and a maximum for each dimension and then shows where each country stands in relation to these scales – expressed as a value between 0 and 1. Since the minimum adult literacy rate is 0% and the maximum is 100%, the literacy component of knowledge for a country where the literacy rate is 75% would be 0.75. Similarly, the minimum for life expectancy is 25 years and the maximum 85 years, so the longevity component for a country where life expectancy is 55 years would be 0.5. For income the minimum is $100 (PPP) and the maximum is $40,000 (PPP). Income above the average world income is adjusted using a progressively higher discount rate. The scores for the three dimensions are then averaged in an overall index. (UNDP)

The Human Development Index is a typical, if sophisticated, compound single measure which can be used in both the traditions of 'statistics', that is, it can be used to make comparisons among states, and to explore trends since it is computed each year. However, it is not a statistical system of social indicators. Attempts at whole system modelling have largely been abandoned or replaced by the rather different process of constructing simulations which we will consider in Chapter 7. None the less, we can consider the repertoire of social indicators as descriptive of the traces of social systems as a whole. Of course this means that there is no real distinction between those things which are formally called 'social indicators' and the kind of systematic information which has been collected since the beginning of the nineteenth century in emerging advanced industrial societies.

It is worth considering for a moment the methodological implications of treating social indicators as traces of complex systems rather than as free variables. If we think in this way then a compound social indicator like the HDI is an attempt to generate a summary measure which describes the current state of the system. Indeed, the HDI was not intended as a causal variable, although analogues to it have been used in causal modelling in epidemiology. We shall see in Chapter 6 that the use of single composite indicators as descriptors of current system condition can now be replaced with rather more sophisticated allocations of cases to types on the basis of numerical taxonomies. We can categorize rather than rank. Although this involves a 'lower' level of measurement, it actually produces a better description of something like human development precisely because changes in levels of development are not incremental but rather involve transformation of kind. For example 'health transition' in which the pattern of death in a society changes from one in which many infants, children and people throughout the course of adult life die from infectious diseases, into one in which such deaths become uncommon and the great majority die in old age from other causes, is not an incremental one. It is absolutely a transformation of form, a phase shift.

Tracing individuals

Martinotti, in an interesting essay on 'Transients and Public Life' (1999), remarks that:

> Valuable as it might be, direct observation tells only a partial story about urban society. After all, society is literally invisible and can only be inferred from the traces it leaves. ... The bulk of our knowledge of the social or invisible aspects of the city comes from the large body of systematic data collection that we call *statistics*. (1999: 77; original emphasis)

This conception of the nature of statistics is very much in accord with the view expressed in this text about them as traces of complex social systems. However, Martinotti goes on to make a most interesting point about

> *process-produced data* such as the various population registers. These are the traces that the human particle leaves during its passage through the bureaucratic maze. ... these traces, which are part of the organizational knowledge of our times, are extremely useful and reliable. (1999: 178)

Martinotti doesn't think much of censuses, either in terms of their accuracy, or because, as he notes, they only count people asleep in bed – not the most important aspect of their lives. However, individual household census records, available in the UK after one hundred years, have been used extensively by social researchers, and even more by people researching their family history, to document exactly the movement of individual human particles through space and the social system over time. Whatever the actual sources, these kinds of longitudinal registers of what happens to people, which include the special sample registers generated by longitudinal social surveys, show us how the dynamics of individual lives intersect with the wider social dynamic.

The historical use of such data has been regarded as relatively unproblematic given that the long dead are accorded few rights of privacy when confronted with the demands of science[9] but there are clearly issues of confidentiality in relation to contemporary lives. There are social surveys based on participation through informed consent and guarantees of anonymity, like the British Household Panel Survey. Whatever the, very real, ethical issues which surround cross-referencing, the historical use of such traces shows us that public records can record how the complex systems of individual lives change in relation to the social changes documented by social indicators.

Secondary data analysis

This is an appropriate point to introduce the idea of secondary data analysis. Basically, secondary data analysis is using data which has already been collected. In technical terms it usually means the use of micro-data or data at a low level of aggregation, which data has not been published in printed form. In a sense any interpretative use of even a highly aggregated measure is a secondary use, although of course the data has been aggregated for exactly the purpose of interpretation whether by state official, informed citizen, or careful consumer. However, in general secondary data analysis means taking the 'raw materials' of interpretation, the original data files, and working with them for some specific research purpose (see Dale et al., 1988; Hakim, 1982). The electronic storage of data records means that in principle data can easily be obtained and utilized – literally down the wire. Some data sets, notably the small areas statistics sets created from decennial censuses in the UK and the United States, are in effect sets especially made for secondary analysis. This is also the case with 'omnibus' surveys like the British Household Panel Survey. We will return to this topic, but it is obviously closely related to the general fields of social statistics.

Sources

The Web – I could conclude here. It is not, just, that there is an enormous amount of statistical data available on the Web. The statistical offices of most advanced industrial countries have excellent web pages and guides to available statistics and the way to understand these is to use them. Things can be more difficult in other places. I have often encountered difficulties in trying to obtain municipal and city level data in Poland, other than that published in the excellent Polish National Yearbook of Statistics. This data seemed to pass seamlessly from being a state secret not to be divulged to foreigners to being a commercial product only available if paid for. The latter state would not be so bad if I had been able to establish whom to pay and how much! And this in Poland, which is a country making a much smoother transition from soviet to capitalist systems than most others and in which in general public officials are helpful and courteous.[10]

International organizations, especially the United Nations, UNDP, UNESCO and the World Health Organization, publish extensive global data. The European Union is much more proactive with statistical investigations of its own whereas the global bodies generally rely on data provided by national authorities. There is a good deal of data, both aggregated and raw, at every level of governance. A good example is provided by lettings data about UK council tenants. Typically this will be published in aggregate form, even dis-aggregated say to the level of particular housing estate (project in US language). It may be possible to obtain anonymized individual household records, usually only if working co-operatively with the authority on some research project.

Blackman (1995) has written in a very interesting way about the use of this kind of data as 'intelligence' in local governance. For example, he used lettings data to describe the situation of particular council estates in Newcastle. He observed from trend data that a sudden increase in the rate of tenants with more than five years of residence leaving estates was an indicator, indeed a kind of warning klaxon, about developing serious social and management problems in that particular area. Blackman has interpreted this kind of statistic in complexity terms as a way of tracing the trajectories of places based on information about the trajectories of individuals and suggest that this kind of approach, the steering of the system, has considerable potential in public sector management (see Byrne, 1998 for a discussion of this). There are, of course, published statistical guides but they are nothing like as useful as Web guides with a search facility. That is what to use.

Conclusion

This chapter has argued for an 'emergent and historical real' understanding of the nature of statistics. In other words, it has rejected the extreme relativism which regards statistical measures as mere reifications, whilst at the same time arguing that *both* the data generated by the activities of states and other organizations *and* the set of mathematical techniques which are employed to manage and interpret that data, are socially located. As is so often the case when we argue for the social construction of anything, the best way to grasp the character of that social construction is by examining the historical processes of its development. Considerable reference has been made to the work of Desrosières, and in general the arguments advanced in this chapter accord with his understanding of the history and social location of social measurement. However, there is one important difference. Desrosières often seems to be saying that statistical measures are reifications which become real as they are used in political and administrative processes which transform social orders. That is not what is being said here. Rather, statistical measures are understood as social constructions which, generally, relate to and derive from aspects of changing reality. They are in origin reactive although they do indeed become part of the proactive process of governance as they shape what states and other bodies do in terms of social action. This may seem a rather functionalist position – which is actually a reasonable description of the argument Williams advanced in the epigraph to Chapter 1. At the time when statistical measurement was needed, out it popped. But of course 'it' didn't 'pop out'. Rather human agents drew on existing repertoires of knowledge to construct measurement and representational systems which met the needs that they perceived in their changing world. Humans can do that!

Note that this chapter has not only argued that our measures are social constructs, but has also suggested that the methods of statistical reasoning themselves are socially generated. Indeed, the methods may be rather more contentious than the measures. We will return to this issue in Chapter 5. First we have to consider the actual nature of the survey process which is the means by which measures about the social world are actually constructed in practice.

Notes

1 The contemporary fuss in the United States over 'creationist' efforts to de-privilege the teaching of evolutionary theory illustrate this very well. Belief must be subordinated to knowledge says 'Science'.

2 For accounts of the United States and France, see Desrosières, 1998.

3 Beveridge's intellectual contribution in writing *Unemployment: A Problem of Industry* was complemented by his administrative role as first Director of Labour Exchanges.

4 Note that different conceptions exist here. The bottom line is by no means necessarily short term profits on capital employed or even short term movements in share prices. Recent history in relation to the valuation of dot.com shares demonstrates that. However, financial information *appears* to give an objective measure in normal circumstances.

5 This is not by any means simply a matter of schools with good intakes not adding much value. That is what happens at the third level in Oxbridge where little value is added. Schools work in a literally complex way in which interaction both among children and of the character of the intake of the children with the character of school makes for a different form of institution. People know this. They know schools are complex systems and that there are interactions among intake characteristics, pupil culture and school orientation.

6 It is important here not to be misled by the theft of the phrase 'Social Market' by a UK right wing, free market think-tank. The products of that institution have nothing to do with the original order liberal conception of a social market economy, and it should be done for trademark infringement (see Byrne, 1999).

7 I regard myself as substantially to the left of Moser in politics but I have to say that I think he is absolutely correct in asserting this position and I support it without reservation.

8 This refers to regulation theory's specification of the character of the state's relationship with economy and society during the post-war period in the West when a consensus on the objective of full employment and, in Northern Europe at least, on the maintenance of an extensive welfare state, informed politics in general. This era is described as 'Fordist' and

regulation theory asserts that we are now in a 'Postfordist' era in which these arrangements, which were essentially universalist, have been replaced by a new flexible variant of capital-ist production associated with a 'hollowed out' welfare state and a turn to individualist con-sumerism as the hegemonic account of personal behaviour. See Byrne, 1999 for a developed discussion.

9 It is common, for example, for cemeteries to be excavated for archaeological and anthro-pological data. I thought little of this until I saw it done in the Isle of Whithorn in Southern Scotland, one of the oldest Christian settlements in Britain. At that point I understood absolutely the reasons why some ethnic groups wish to recover the bones of their ancestors.

10 I didn't meet discourtesy at all, just a kind of bafflement about what to do and how to do it typical of transition periods.

4

Measuring the Complex World:
The Character of Social Surveys

In Chapter 3 the idea of the case-variable matrix was introduced in a preliminary fashion. We can return to that idea as one of the components in the process of defining the nature of a social survey. Marsh defines a social survey as:

> an investigation where:
> (a) systematic measurements are made over a series of cases yielding a rectangle of data;
> (b) the variables in the matrix are analysed to see if they show patterns;
> (c) the subject is social. (1982: 6)

In (b) Marsh used, as was conventional at that time, the word 'analyse': we might say exploring patterns, yes, but analysing no, because analysis always carries a reductionist implication. In (c) the word social is really tautologous for social surveys but we should remember the nature of the boundary which Khalil and Boulding (1996) suggest should be drawn in the sciences – not between the natural and the social but between the artificial and the real and recognize that any observation of already existing covariation, that is, of variation not created in a controlled experiment and where things vary together rather than being held constant by the experimenter, is a survey, whether it deals with the social, the natural or, as in many important contexts, with both together.

Another, and very important definition, was given by Bateson:

> I conceive of a social survey as a social system consisting of three participants (client, researcher and informant ...) engaged in a common task: the production of knowledge. To understand the data construction process and its problems one must understand the respective roles and functions of these three participants and their mode of interaction. A survey, then, is an applied exercise in small-group psychology. It is also an applied exercise in cognitive psychology in that the knowledge production task can only be successfully achieved if full account is taken of the different knowledge processes of the client and informant. Finally, linguistics is also a central discipline for surveys. A survey trades in *meanings* [original emphasis], and meanings are embodied in language: a survey consists of a transfer of meaning between the three participants through the medium of knowledge. (1984: 8)

Marsh defined a survey in terms of what it produces. Bateson defined it in terms of the processes involved in that production process. These two definitions are perfectly compatible. Indeed Bateson explicitly endorsed the notion that the product of the survey, in the form of data to use his terminology, is a case-variable matrix with data items entered in the cells of that matrix. However, the distinction between product and process is worth preserving and will be important in our discussions here.

We need to recognize what a survey is not. It is certainly not simulation because it addresses the world as it is rather than creating an artificial rule-derived world *ab initio*. The survey is not the platonic forehand to use Hayles's terminology. Indeed, nobody ever says surveys are simulations. Likewise the survey is not an experiment – it is not a controlled artificial abstraction from the world as it is, the ancient platonic backhand. Rather its empirical engagement with reality makes it unequivocally part of the Aristotelian tradition and I have suggested that we should call it the Aristotelian smash (see Chapter 1).

It is important to realize that surveys are not experiments. They are fundamentally different and in my view much superior. This has to be said firmly because, whilst few people say surveys are experiments, there are many who treat them as if they were second rate ersatz approximations to experiments. This is a common assertion among statisticians and, under the guise of 'evidence based' social science, has now penetrated disciplines as an argument (see Oakley, 2000). Of course, there is nothing wrong with evidence based social science. Indeed the whole purpose of this text is to argue for a properly understood process of quantitative interpretation as one of the key components of such a science. What is wrong is the notion that the experiment, in the form of the randomized controlled trial, represents a gold standard to which all forms of quantification in the social sciences should seek to approximate. On the contrary, once we recognize the survey for what it is, the systematic measurement of the covarying real if we still use a language of variables, or more properly, in a language of traces, the documenting of the trajectories of real complex systems, then we see it as a much better process altogether than mere abstracted experimentation. Surveys allow us to picture what is really going on – to represent the complex systems of reality, even if such representation is at least in the first instance essentially retro-dictive. In other words, surveys can show what has happened but there are important questions to be asked as to whether they can generate knowledge which tells us anything about what might happen in the future.

The randomized controlled trial is a pretty ersatz form of experiment itself. It relies on random allocation, rather than direct physical manipulation, in order to hold non-relevant variation constant, and is wholly useless in the very likely event that interaction forms part of the causal process under investigation. Interaction means that the form of relationships in any given conjunction of variate values will not hold in another conjunction of variate values. Experimental evidence is used, properly, to generalize beyond specific experimental contexts on the basis of sustained linear laws derived from explicit theories. Much of 'evidence based' randomized controlled trialling is 'merely empirical', that is, it takes the form of reporting of relationships without an appeal to explicit theory as a foundation for generalizing beyond specific context. Moreover, given that experiments are abstractions from the world, they cannot be the basis of exploration of it. Experimental investigation is perfectly valid in contexts where there is no non-linearity, interaction, emergence. However, it should only be employed when there is good reason to consider that non-linearity, interaction, emergence, do not matter and there are sound arguments explicitly made to that effect. Outside treatment situations in a limited set of educational and health contexts, it is difficult to identify social contexts which can be described in those terms, and this is without mentioning any problems deriving from the autonomous actions of the human subjects of experimental social research – the dreaded Hawthorne effect.[1]

In this chapter we will cover three aspects of survey research. First, drawing on and arguing with Bateson, we will consider the processual nature of surveys. Second, drawing on and arguing with Marsh, we will consider issues of causal reasoning based on the product of surveys. Finally, we will consider the issue of representativeness both in the usual sense which relates to the extent to which samples correspond to the populations from which they are drawn, and in more general terms to do with our capacity to extrapolate from any given quantitative account to contexts other than that for which it was established. I make no apology for shaping much of this chapter around glosses on Bateson's and Marsh's arguments. I think these are important and surprisingly neglected and although I have substantial disagreements with their positions, I would never have been able to formulate my own arguments without engagement with theirs.

Knowledge production – the survey as process

Bateson's (1984) general account of the social survey as social process is based on a typology of social actors involved with each type holding a distinctive form of knowledge about the social world. The actor and knowledge types are:

1   *Informants* – synonymous here with respondents. People in general who hold *information* about the social world which is organized in the natural language of everyday life.
2   *Researchers* who carry out the survey process and generate information about the social world in the form of *data* which is organized as numerical entries in the cells of the case-variable matrix.
3   *Clients* who generate *expertise* in the form of summaries and models from the data.

The distinction between client and researcher is explicitly derived from Bateson's experience as a worker in the Social Surveys division of the then UK Office of Population Censuses and Surveys, which effectively acted as contractor for the execution of surveys which generated data for special purposes for government departments or for general secondary analysis. In academic investigations the roles of researcher and client are usually combined, although the research role can be contracted out to a specialist organization or firm.

Bateson's concept of expertise includes more than the organized derivative products of the survey measurement process. Expertise exists before the survey process and is privileged in the interpretation immediately of the products of the survey process, and ultimately in the generation of accounts of the social world. He puts it like this:

> Both the client and the informant 'know' the social world but the knowledge that the client has, and seeks to increase by means of the survey, is a specialist, technical, or scientific knowledge of the social world as a whole, whereas the informant's knowledge is of an everyday, intuitive, commonsense kind and covers only a very small part of this social world. Specialist knowledge, acquired systematically over time, is always more general, more abstract and more comprehensive than the particular, concrete knowledge acquired incidentally and eclectically in the course of everyday living. (1984: 23)

The notion that 'ordinary' people's knowledge of the social world is some eclectic jackdaw-like collection can be challenged. People have knowledge as a set of tools which enables them to function socially. We might argue as to whether this knowledge is always accessible to immediate conscious reflection – the weak programme of Bourdieu's conception of habitus[2] which leads Bourdieu to dismiss the qualitative interview as a basis of valid social knowledge although he admits statistical data which are to a very considerable extent the product of interview processes. However, people know because knowledge has worked for them in their lives in the past and may work for them in the future. Certainly Bateson's privileging of expertise, very much a product of the time his book was written, jars against Freire's arguments for participatory research in which informants must necessarily be engaged in the process of interpretation which underpins the refining of 'expertise' as the basis for social action:

> Participatory research is an approach to social change – a process used by and for people who are exploited and oppressed. The approach challenges the way knowledge is produced with conventional social science methods and disseminated by dominant educational institutions. Through alternate methods, it puts the production of knowledge back into the hands of the people where it can infuse their struggles for social equality, and for the elimination of dependency and its symptoms: poverty, illiteracy, malnutrition etc. (Heaney, 1995: 11)

Bateson distinguished survey elements based on indirect observation, those involving informants who are questioned about their own non-expert observation of the social world, from those founded on direct observation by the researcher. Thus a researcher might directly observe someone's gender but indirectly observe the industry in which they were employed by asking them to state it. Bateson included all survey items obtained from records as direct observation because they too were the product of expert observation. This seems fair enough in the example he gives of a payslip shown to an interviewer yielding a direct observation of wages (although it would not yield a direct observation of total income including income in kind and off the books). It is much more debatable when we are dealing with surveys of records – for example the construction of case-variable matrices describing inmates from the historical records of poor law institutions with a view to exploring variation in local systems of poor relief in relation to specific social, cultural and economic contexts, the essence of locality studies. Here we must consider all the issues that arise in secondary data analysis as introduced in Chapter 3 and we will return to them in Chapter 5.

My reading of Bateson suggests a further distinction that might be useful to us when we consider the nature of information, although I would follow Bateson's discussion of facts and opinions of which more in a moment, and see this as a matter of a continuum rather than a matter of two absolute categories. We might distinguish between information given by an informant which is the product of that informant's observation – how many people work in the informant's place of work, what type of school they attended as a child, the general health of their mother during their childhood – from information which is the product of introspection and involves the informant reflecting on and articulating a relational and meaningful account. This does relate to Bateson's own continuum of fact–opinion (1984: 29–30), where a fact holds constant among different observers and for the same observer at different times, but an opinion doesn't. However, Bateson distinguishes in terms of differential observation of an object that seems external to the subjects who report – what do different people observe or the same person observe at different times? It does seem useful to think of introspection as a process of articulating and organizing meaning which is more than just a subjective variation in impression of an object.

Measuring health illustrates this rather well. An expert observer might measure the degree of mobility of a case by asking them to touch their toes and seeing if they can – a common enough element in musculo-skeletal health scales in social medicine. That is direct observation. Indirect observation of relevant facts would include asking the subject whether they can tie their own shoe-laces without asking them to perform the task. A relevant opinion would be asking them how convenient they found steps up to bus platforms, where there would be variation among people with the same 'fact' scores on mobility scales. An introspection would be asking them to define their whole health state taking into account the World Health Organization's definition which incorporates physical, mental and social well-being. The example of describing mother's general health during childhood would move down the fact value continuum from 'pure' fact since all the temporal and social components of relativism and reference groups would influence the answer.

Asking about own health seems to me to require more introspection from the informant, although even asking about the health of a parent does involve elements of meaning which move it away from 'pure' observation.

Bateson's book represents the most important, indeed in many respects still the only, effort to understand what is going on when data is constructed in the actual interview process, although many critics of official statistics have recognized the social construction involved in the process of operationalization. He extended his approach by addressing issues of the validation of data which began to move beyond the kind of assertion of a platonically ideal truth which traditionally informs discussions of validity as an issue. Essentially, he argues that validity can only derive from process – in other words, validity resides in the character of the survey process as a whole rather than in the act of operationalization taken alone. I find this wholly convincing. Bateson, a social psychologist by trade, then attempted to move towards a scientific understanding of the processes of knowledge transformation and construction which constitute a social survey, by drawing on accounts of perception and cognition. He seems to me to have made an interesting start, although further development of this approach must also, as Bateson recognized, incorporate insights from socio-linguistics. That said, I do wonder whether we can 'derive' an abstract process of good survey practice, important though a social psychological, socio-linguistic and sociological account of the actual process undeniably is. In Chapter 9 I will suggest that validation may well depend very much on methodological triangulation rather than on a scientifically founded survey practice, although the development of such practice is an interesting objective.

It is important to relate Bateson's account of the components of knowledge back to our previous discussions of measurement and modelling. Essentially, data is constructed by measuring information through a process of classification – a central theme of Chapters 2 and 3. Expertise derives from the constructing of models, although we might note that pre-existing expert accounts of the world may very well shape the character of the models that are produced. Catherine Marsh's discussion of causal reasoning in relation to surveys can take us further with that topic.

Models from surveys – beyond the flowgraph?

In her important book, Marsh (1982) departed from academic convention and reflected on her own responses to engagement with survey research and with the literature about it. I very much agree with this approach, and in accordance with it wish to record the excitement and enjoyment I derived from reading *The Survey Method* on its publication. The subtitle is 'the contribution of surveys to sociological explanation' and it is that theme which I wish to pursue. In so doing I am going to propose a radical rejection of Marsh's approach but it is worth reiterating that such an approach would not be possible without the conceptual clarification of the subject which she achieved.

Here I am going to address the issue of establishing cause from the products of surveys. Marsh predicated her discussion of this issue on a comparison between the experimenter and the survey researcher. The experimenter working on an abstracted and limited subset of reality 'knows' the potential cause because that is what she (following Marsh's usage) made vary whilst other things were held constant. In other words, the cause is a single variable and the experimenter could distinguish cause from effect both by reflecting on the logic of the specific experiment and because the time ordering of the experiment meant that cause came before effect. Time ordering is important and we will return to it below. The logic of experimentation as described here is inherently positivist and asserts that there is a single cause for each effect. Now, Marsh did not believe in single causes. On the contrary she was explicitly realist, endorsed multi-causal accounts and appreciated the significance of interaction. At the same time she was working with Lazarsfeld's notion of variables and saw them as the causal factors. The basis of her approach to generating causal accounts from survey data was the construction of causal models in which the causal and the dependent elements were variables and in which causal processes were represented iconically in the form of flowgraphs. These flowgraphs embodied specific theories. Indeed, drawn without the attachment of numerical values to connecting arrows they are best considered as diagrammatic representations of theories of cause. Marsh argued for models:

> It is the model that stands between the researcher and unbridled empiricism in attempts to draw causal inferences for it forces the researcher into explicit theory-making activity. No body of data suggests a unique model of its own structure to the researcher and no one model can ever be shown to be the one and only way to make a good fit to the data. (1982: 72)

Marsh's discussion was primarily abstract but her account gelled absolutely with that of Hellevik, who developed a series of practical tools in his *Introduction to Causal Analysis* (1984) which had the subtitle 'exploring survey data by crosstabulation'.[3] In essence these approaches all form part of the general linear model which is best know in terms of regression derived techniques for describing relationships among variables measured at the ratio scale level.

Figure 4.1 is an iconic representation using a Venn diagram form of the relationship among four variables. If we consider Variables One, Two and Four to be causal and Variable Three to be caused, then the general linear equation which describes this relationship is:

$$b^1\text{variable1} + b^2\text{variable2} + b^4\text{variable4} + \text{residual} = \text{variable3}$$

where b^1 etc. are coefficients describing the form of the relationships between independent and dependent variables. In the Venn diagram the circles

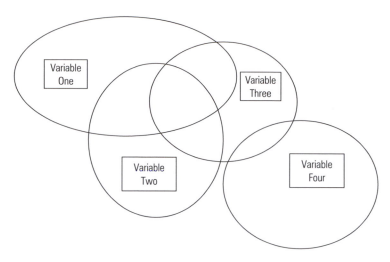

Figure 4.1   *Ven diagram representation of multiple causation*

represent the amount of variation in each variable and intersections between any two circles represent the amount of variation in common between the two variables whose variation is represented by those circles. However, the equation above describes a very simple causal process in which all the variables operate independently of each other. Figure 4.2 illustrates this as a flowgraph.

Suppose instead we thought the causal processes ran as indicated in Figure 4.3, with Variables One and Four wholly independent of each other but with Variable Two being in part caused by Variable One. Here Variable One both has a direct effect on Variable Three but also has a role operating through Variable Two. An example will illustrate. Suppose Variable One is the income level of an individual, Variable Two is a measure of that individual's housing conditions, Variable Four is the marital status of the individual and Variable Three, the independent variable, is the health status of the indivi-dual. Income level will affect housing conditions but may well be indepen-dent of marital status.[4] Income level will have a direct effect but also an effect operating through housing conditions. The additive and multiplicative rules apply. In other words, the total effect of Variables One, Two and Four on Three is the sum of the individual effects and the effect of Variable One on Variable Three operating through Variable Two is the product of the effect of Variable One on Variable Two times the effect of Variable Two on Variable Three. The direct effect of Variable One on Variable Three is the remainder when this product is taken away from the simple effect of One on Three. I employed models of this kind to explore exactly the relationship between housing conditions and health in Byrne et al. (1985), working directly with the approaches suggested by Marsh and Hellevik.

All this is fine so long as there is no interaction, so long as, for example, the relationships among income level, housing conditions and health are not

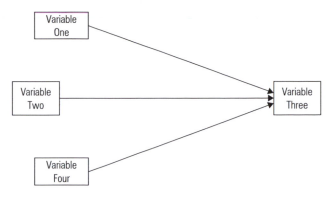

Figure 4.2   *Direct multiple causation*

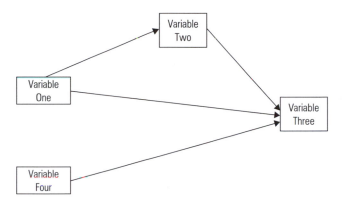

Figure 4.3   *Indirect multiple causation*

different for people of different marital status. Sure, even if there is such interaction we can get round the problem by fitting interaction terms into the equations and seeing them as an additional causal element, but this both becomes extremely clumsy with large numbers of variables and interaction terms and seems to be a very poor representation of the actual character of the real systems we are investigating. As we shall see in Chapter 6, we can use procedures of the kind suggested by Marsh and Hellevik but more as tools for detecting interaction than for the construction of causal models.

Let us think about the example of the relationship among health, income level, housing conditions and marital status and do so by considering a case. Here we will take account of the reality that income levels are not independent of marital status for many people. Let us take the case of a female single parent living only with her children on benefit in a 'difficult to let' social housing estate. If we have any sense we won't have measured income level as a ratio scale variable but will instead have some ordinal account of it. Housing conditions may be quite good in terms of amenity level but are likely to be bad if we use measures which rank the neighbourhood against other neighbourhoods in the locality and incorporate the self-assessment of the person concerned – our case.

Now let us consider forward movement in the life trajectory of this woman. She establishes a relationship with a partner in full time employment with a median level income and they decide to live together. The woman's children are at primary school so it becomes economically sensible for her to take a part-time job. The earned household income is now well above benefit dependency levels and moreover the payments made in support of the children by their father now accrue to household income rather than being confiscated almost in their entirety and set against benefit payments. The couple buy an ordinary middle income house in an ordinary owner occu-pied estate. Internal amenity levels are unlikely to change but the whole social context and social meaning of the housing situation will have been transformed. All the changes in this process are non-linear and interactive. We can best understand them by considering not the variables, but the case itself. The woman's life and the lives of her children have been changed in a qualitative way. I use this example because the process described in it is in fact rather common!

A simple approach to causality in understanding the dynamics of this change would say that change in marital status (or perhaps we had best con-sider what we are talking about as household form) was the causal factor but so many other things were going on at the same time and in interaction with that. We can quite properly consider household form as a control parameter for the system, something which if changed may change the whole charac-ter of the system by triggering changes in other things, but it is not by any means a simple, single and abstractable cause.

The approach which is a necessary predicate of focusing on cases does not by any means involve a reversion to the documenting of each individual and unique story – the ideographic turn. Rather, it involves classification, but not classification of snapshots – rather a repeated classification of frames in a variety of moving pictures.

To understand this let us return to our consideration of the significance of time. Marsh discusses this in relation to the problems of establishing cause on the basis of survey data, comparing the advantages of the researcher who always has time ordering as a way of distinguishing cause from effect in con-trast with the survey researcher who measures covariation which is often, literally, coincident, that is, things happen simultaneously. Let us think about this issue of time from the perspective of complex realism.

Plainly, if we think of systems as embedded in time, and moreover moving forward in the direction of an arrow of time, then we want to know about changes and know about them in a time ordered way. The ideal kind of survey for this is the longitudinal study which visits cases at intervals and records their character at each visit, but in even a single contact survey we can ask people about their pasts and get some time ordering.

The whole point of this is to explore change but not in the really rather trivial way of seeing change in relation to changes in the value of a single variable. What we want to see is the nature of changes in whole systems, which systems may be individuals, households, neighbourhoods, localities, regions, states, blocks, or the whole global system.[5] If we think of our cases as described in tracing terms by the values on *all* the variate descriptions of them we have measured and consider to be relevant, then we want some way of summing all that up – of specifying co-ordinate position. Moreover, following Emirbayer's dicta (see Chapter 1), that method must be relational. To use systems language we must be able to describe ensembles of systems and do so in a way that differentiates and categorizes. My argument is that we should here and now abandon causal modelling using variables and linear approaches. Instead, we should classify using traces and map changes through time both in the location of individual cases within classification sets and in the form of those classification sets. We should then explore the representation of personal and social changes offered by our time ordered classifications and look for what might be control parameters, which will seldom be one thing operating alone but rather a complex which might change the character of whole systems. This involves detailed comparison. Indeed it is rather like a dynamic and investigative version of the original comparative statdistics. Figure 4.4 shows what this might look like in iconographic terms. It demonstrates that most people stay in the same category,

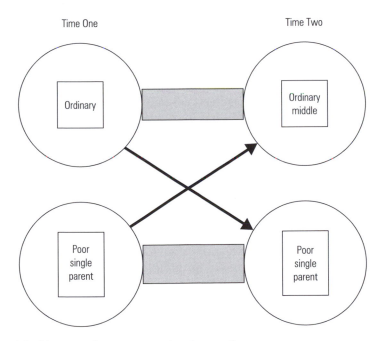

Figure 4.4   *Movement of cases among categories over time*

assuming categories stay the same themselves, for two time points, but some move. The interesting issue is then are there differences between those who move and those who stay. Detailed comparative investigation may reveal exactly combinations of control parameters.

In Chapter 6 we will examine how we can use existing computer based tools to enable us to carry out exactly this sort of modelling. Here, we now need to return to a consideration of the significance of the case and how we get our cases. That means we need to turn to sampling and issues of representativeness.

Representative before random – sampling in the real world

A central argument of this text is that it is cases which are real, and that variate measures are simply traces of those cases. Given this, it is appropriate to deal with issues of sampling, with the problems that derive from getting a part to stand for a whole, from a starting point which addresses cases rather than variates. It is conventional to consider these issues in relation to probability theory and the foundations of statistical inference. Statistical inference is important and we will discuss it at length in Chapter 5, but we need to begin by thinking about populations of cases rather than sampling distributions of disembodied variate measures.

Sampling is a special but extremely important example of the issue of generalization. It seems useful to distinguish among three terms here. I will use generalization to refer to statements made on the basis of evidence that is local but which are asserted to apply beyond the local context in which evidence for those statements has been assembled. Here the word 'local' is used specifically in the sense that it has in complexity theory, namely to refer to a specific context in time or space or both, which context might be large in both dimensions. Let us reserve the term inference for that specific form of generalization in which we say something about the components of a population on the basis of information about part of that population. Note the difference here between the words 'context' and 'population'. Finally, the word prediction refers to time ordered generalization in which statements about future states are made on the basis of evidence about past states.

The distinction between context and population is important. The term context describes the whole complex of multiple, nested, inter-penetrating and recursively related systems which matter to us in relation to explanation and history. It involves hierarchies (of data rather than causation) and aggregation as well as all specific and individual components. Population is a much simpler idea. Along with its synonym – universe, as used in statistics – it simply means all the cases at a given level in which we are interested. In statistical inference, in principle, we use the aggregate characteristics of the sample to give us an estimate of the aggregate characteristics of the population. We do not in principle consider emergent characteristics of context, although in practice sociologists if not social statisticians usually do this. The programme of exploratory categorization proposed here suggests that we should both calculate statistical estimations of aggregate population values – of population parameters – and explore in an effort to establish a description of emergent characteristics of the social level.

If we are going to do this we need samples which look like populations and can sustain statements about emergent context. How do we get them? Sometimes we don't need to. We have census information covering, in principle, all cases, although the actual quality of collected census information is variable over time and place and we should note that in many countries, including the United States, census estimates are corrected using sample derived measures. In general, well funded and organized sample surveys are more likely to contact all the members of a sample than are censuses to contact all the members of a population.

Randomness alone does not give us any protection against selecting a sample wildly unlike the population from which it is drawn. Probability theory allows us to make some statements about the population in terms of ranges – confidence intervals – and to test hypotheses of difference and correlation, but that is all. If we want a sample that looks like the population, we must stratify. That is to say we must use existing relevant information about our cases to sort them into categories and then we sample within the categories. This means that the sample has the same (or if it does not we know exactly the disproportionate differences) distribution of category membership as the population. We may over-sample in a given category in order to get large enough numbers of small categories to sustain probabilistic statistical significance, but we can weight back to reproduce population characteristics. For example, in Teesside where people in the 1991 census described by the respondent of the household in which they live as something other than 'white', constitute about 6 per cent of the population so that proportionate sampling would yield just thirty cases in a sample of five hundred, we may take sixty cases to cross an important numerical threshold in relation to probability and sampling distributions, but we must weight each case in this category by 0.5 when attempting to reproduce overall population characteristics.

We should distinguish stratified sampling which is random within categories from commercial quota sampling in which the characteristics of a population are reproduced not on the basis of the categorization of all available cases (the working universe as opposed to theoretical universe of all possible cases) by relevant criteria, but instead category blocks are simply filled by searching out people who fit them. Such an approach does not permit the use of probability theory in the construction of parameter estimates. None the less, stratified sampling and quota sampling do have an important objective in common. They are directed towards producing a part of the real whole which looks like the real whole in significant ways. This is the explicit rationale but implicitly these approaches directed towards representativeness also indicate an interest in emergent characteristics of social context.

The problem with stratified sampling is that we often don't have the information on which to stratify. We must always try to random sample from lists of the whole (or at least available – hence working universe) population, but even where we have such lists available, they are often nothing more than lists of case identifiers – in the case of individuals in a residence based sample, typically in the form of name and address. We cannot classify without information as the basis for classification. Any classification at the level of primary sampling unit, the level which provides the case rows in the case-variable matrix, which can be achieved should be achieved. However, we often have to turn to the hierarchical properties of data sets, and especially spatially ordered data sets, in order to achieve stratified samples.

Of course spatial classification is a stratifying process in itself. In a European Union study it is conventional for part of the sample to be drawn in each member state which ensures representativeness in relation to distribution of national populations within the wider union. In multi-level stratified sampling we make use of information available at a level of 'containing system' to make our sample of ultimate cases more representative. For example, suppose we wanted to conduct a survey of attitudes of sixteen-year-olds in the UK to mathematical education in state funded schools. We would certainly want to get a regional representation but we might also use the extensive data available about schools to sort schools into relevant types and then sample schools within the categories generated and then sample pupils within the schools. The actual mechanism of stratification at the level of school would involve the construction of a four-way contingency table with five classification principles so that a school would be for example:

religious
mixed sexes
non-selective
middle ranked achievement
middle ranked social deprivation

and would be in the stratification category of schools in that cell of the contingency table.

Properly constructed stratified random samples are more statistically efficient in probabilistic terms than simple random samples and pose no problems for statistical inference. However, statistical inference, although often reified beyond its limited but important value in relating the properties of a sample to the contextual and local universe from which it is drawn, is only a component in the far more important and scientifically significant issue of generalization. The ontological premises of this text are, I hope, unequivocal. The real world of the social/natural is composed of evolutionary and interacting complex systems. The epistemological consequence of this is that our knowledge is inherently local. We cannot appeal to universal laws applicable always and everywhere – the great nomothetic get out – as the basis for generalization. So how can we generalize? In particular how can we say anything about emergent levels, and in particular the emergent level of the social, on the basis of information about components of the social? This question will arise again, particularly in our discussion of modelling and simulation in Chapter 8. Here we need to consider it in relation to the nature of cases in the survey process.

One of the charges against which Marsh wished to defend survey research was that it was inherently atomistic. She quotes Mills making exactly this charge:

> Their fundamental source of information is a sample of individuals. The questions asked in these studies are put in terms of the psychological reactions of individuals. Accordingly, the assumption is required that the historical structures of society, in so far as it can be studied in this way, can be understood by means of such data about individuals. (Mills, 1959: 79; quoted by Marsh, 1982: 60)

Let us get rid straight away of the red herring about the psychologistic character of survey questions. Most survey derived information is 'fact' in Bateson's terms and I would argue that even responses founded on introspection can be social rather than psychological. Mills was responding to the psychologistic and reductionist character of survey analysis in his own socio-historical context.

The charge of atomism, of merely aggregating individual case properties, is much more serious, because aggregation does not permit examination of emergence. Marsh herself responded to this challenge by referring to the possibilities of hierarchical data analysis – essentially to the construction of data sets which reflect the nested character of social reality – and to the possibilities of relational sampling in which information about connections among cases is collected as well as the properties of cases. She was rather optimistic about the imminent availability of computing tools for managing these forms of data (1982: 61) given that almost all existing tools require the conventional case data matrix. In fact, as we shall see in Chapter 7, multilevel modelling approaches which do address the problems posed by hierarchical data remain atomistic since their objective is to explain variate characteristics of cases at the individual level.

Plainly, the first thing any survey based investigation of the social world must do is ensure, if possible, that data is collected at every relevant level. An example where this has not been done illustrates the difficulties, although there are important ethical arguments for the present arrangements. In the anonymized samples which have been generated from the UK census there is very limited information as to the spatial location of the individuals and households in the respective individual and household samples. Initially the only spatial information given was the local authority district in which the case was located. The perfectly sound reason for this was to preserve anonymity of sampled cases. However, this would have meant that there was no possibility of relating immediate neighbourhood characteristics, the relational characteristics of urban socio-spatial systems, to cases in any causal way. In order to get around this problem an area level classification has been written to each case record with, for example, forty-nine different types of area identified in the City of Manchester so that spatial data may be used in multi-level modelling (Dale et al., 2000: 34).

This is extremely helpful, although as we shall see in Chapter 7 the assumption that the purpose of this is to facilitate multi-level modelling in a linear tradition leads to gross misinterpretations of causal processes. What we have then is information about an individual, some information about the household of that individual,[6] information about the neighbourhood type of the individual, and a location of the individual to local authority district (or a population area of 120,000 if the district is smaller than that).

What this means is that we can bring in data from another level – in this case data about the local authority districts, and any other meaningful geographical level, for example, region, of which it is a part. We can relate households to the socio-spatial system within which they are embedded. Actually the UK Census Samples of Anonymized Records (SARs) are really very limited devices for this as they are cross-sectional and give such limited household and neighbourhood information, but they are not wholly useless.

It is useful to consider what an ideal data set for our purposes would actually look like. How could we get the kind of data which would allow us to relate individual, household, neighbourhood, region etc. (or any other meaningful nested set) as the basis for description of the local and possible generalization to other comparable instances? Such a data set would have the following characteristics. It would:

1 include full relevant data for individuals;
2 include full relevant data for the household of which the individual was a member, including data about all other individuals in that household;
3 include full aggregate data at a level which could be used to construct 'neighbourhoods' as part of the local socio-spatial system;
4 include full locality data describing the level of the local economic and cultural system;
5 include full data for all other relevant geographies;
6 be longitudinal at all levels so that changes in individuals, households, neighbourhoods, localities etc. could be charted through time.

If this looks impossible it isn't, quite. The original Cleveland County Council Household Survey conducted on an annual basis from 1977 to 1993 did have a panel element for individuals and households and if this had been maintained, if in other words a local version of the British Household Panel Study which charts households and their derivatives through time had been achieved, then this study would have met all the criteria above. Regrettably the panel element was dropped but it was possible to chart aggregate changes in household characteristics and relate these to longitudinal changes in neighbourhoods (in Cleveland sub-locality zones, e.g. East Middlesbrough, Outer Stockton), the locality and the regional and national economies.

The key method for this is the integration of different data sets. Individual and household level data can be related to neighbourhood data derived from censuses, locality data derived from administrative returns (for example, the detailed unemployment data from NOMIS and data from the Labour Force Survey on industrial structure), regional data and so on. We can relate individuals, households and measures at least of the urban and regional social systems.

In my view this offers the possibility of a social account which can then be generalized precisely by careful comparison with other locales that can be argued to be similar in terms of descriptive data and other forms of account. For example, in Byrne (1997) I compared the socio-spatial systems of Teesside and Leicester in terms of their differences. However, there were also very considerable similarities – one of the most interesting being the incidence of non-marital births in the poorer parts of both urban systems. The Cleveland Social Survey permitted the comparison of cohabiting and married households in that locality and showed that cohabiting households were characterized by lower educational levels and less stable labour market connections. Cleveland household level data sustains a causal account of 'parental relationship form', that is, married or cohabiting, in terms of labour market connection causes and longitudinal examination suggests that changes in 'parental relationship form' stem from changes in local labour market form. In other words, deindustrialization at the locality level engenders casualization which is causal to cohabiting rather than married parenthood: not a very surprising assertion, but a social one rather than an atomistic one. Given the similarities between deindustrialization in Teesside and Leicester, although there also important differences of timing and scale, it is useful to make a preliminary (subject to local examination) suggestion that the same processes operate there as in Teesside.

This kind of approach does enable us to resolve issues of nested reality as expressed in hierarchical data sets. Issues of relationships among cases are trickier and will be considered in Chapter 7.

Conclusion

This chapter has not taken the form of a set of instructions on how to conduct surveys. There are plenty of good cookbooks which handle that (e.g. De Vaus, 1991). Instead it has followed in the tradition of Marsh and Bateson and tried to say something about what surveys are. It does seem to me that an understanding of the nature of this form of social investigation is a precondition of any sensible interpretation of its products. In Chapter 5 we will take this further by considering a topic which is important both in defining the character of social surveys and in managing the interpretation of the products of social surveys – that of inferential reasoning using mathematical probability systems. The plural is deliberate.

Notes

1 So called after the findings of a study carried out in the Hawthorne plant of the General Electrical Company near Chicago in the 1920s. Experimenters varied illumination levels in workrooms and initially found increased illumination led to increased output. Then, in a stroke of genius, the experimenters reduced illumination to the previous level, and found that output rose still further – a really non-linear event! Of course the explanation was straightforward. The workers were responding not just to light levels, but to the social meaning of management surveillance, which surveillance was embedded in the research process.

2 In the strong, and usual, version of habitus the unconscious social practices and understanding which constitute habitus are never available to people's introspection. I would argue for a weak version in which practices can be taken for granted in contexts that are relatively stable but do become accessible to people in times of major social change when those contexts are transformed, when, as E.P. Thompson put it, Experience I – reality – walks in the door without knocking. The transformation of urban societies from industrial to postindustrial is the currently important example of such period of crisis; see Byrne, 2001.

3 Bulmer, the editor of the series in which Marsh's, Bateman's and Hellevik's books were published, explicitly identified them as a complementary set.

4 Although not in the contemporary UK. See Byrne, 1999 for a discussion of this.

5 There are other nestings which could have been proposed but as an urban sociologist I am suggesting the one I work with most often.

6 The household SAR file is not available at any geographic level below region which is a real problem because that file contains full household descriptions and descriptions of all individuals in the household and would be much more useful for proper nested system description.

5

Probability and Quantitative Reasoning

'The initial problem of the statistician is simply the description of the data presented; to tell us what the data themselves show. To this initial problem the function of sampling theory is in general entirely secondary. (G.U. Yule, 1942)

G. Udny Yule, the great British statistical educator of the first half of the twentieth century, made the above remark in a debate on the 'future of statistics' in which he reflected on developments and trends. He went even further, referring to 'a completely lopsided development – almost a malignant growth – of sampling theory' (1942). Yule was arguing, in much the same way as Tukey nearly thirty years later, for the value of statistical description and exploration, finding out what the data show. That this is the first task of social measurement, we should all agree. However, 'sampling theory', based on the application of probabilistic reasoning, has continued its 'malignant growth' to the point where the ideas of randomness which underpin it have become the foundation of what some authors (Oakley, 2000 for example) argue is the gold standard in quantitative social research – the randomized controlled trial.

In this chapter we are going to unpack ideas about probability and investigate the role of probability theory in quantitative social research. We will do so by differentiating the two different conceptions of probabilistic reasoning: the classical, frequentist, objectivist approach and the very different Bayesian science of clues which is inherently subjectivist. We will also consider the radical and innovative possibilities which arise from considering Popper's proposal of 'single case probabilities' in relation to complex systems. We will then explore the nature of probabilistic explanation, first by reference to 'statistical' experimentation and then by considering the role of probabilistic reasoning in relation to the design of survey samples and the exploration of the products of survey research.

Here we will begin our review with the important topic of the elaboration of contingency tables and developments of this practice in the form of loglinear and related modelling procedures. The account of modelling presented here will be radically different from the conventional identification of models as 'hypothesis' testing devices, although it will have a lot in common with the actual way in which modelling techniques are used by real social researchers. The whole point of the exercise is to get us beyond the tyranny of the hypothesis and the reductionist and mostly useless ontological implications of partial, abstract and unreal specificity in quantitative social science.

Objective probability versus the science of clues

Desrosières (1998: 7) argues that there is a fundamental tension between the idea of an objective and universal science and claims made for scientific knowledge as the basis of social action. This tension is a crucial, indeed for Desrosières, the crucial, source of transformation of science's own conceptualization and procedure. It is important here to distinguish between tension and contradiction, although in a dialectical mode of reasoning contradiction is an especially important form of tension with transformative potential.

The imagery is plainly structural. When there is tension in a structure in general there is a pressure for change and development. In the dialectical mode contradictions are tensions of such significance that they lead to a transformation of the whole structure itself. In science paradigm shifts might be considered to have this character. However, in more general usage contradiction implies opposite and cancelling out. That is not what we are dealing with here. Instead we have to understand science as changed by its relationship with the world of action and, with especial force in relation to statistical reasoning, understand the world of action as changed by science. The relationship is inherently and necessarily recursive. Desrosières elaborates thus in an extremely important passage:

> The complex connection between prescriptive and descriptive points of view is particularly marked in the history of probability calculus, with the recurrent opposition between *subjective* and *objective* probability; or, according to a different terminology, between *epistemic* and *frequentist* probability. ... In the epistemic perspective, probability is a degree of belief. The uncertainty the future holds, or the incompleteness of our knowledge of the universe, leads to wagers on the future and the universe, and probabilities provide a reasonable person with rules of behaviour when information is lacking. But in the frequentist view, diversity and risk are part of nature itself, and not simply the result of incomplete knowledge. They are external to mankind and part of the essence of things. It falls to science to describe the frequencies observed. (1998: 7)

Although the epistemic and frequentist position are linked by some fundamental premises in probability, and in particular the law of large numbers,[1] they are separated by the view of incomplete knowledge. The epistemic view is concerned with action and knowing is simply a basis for action. The frequentist is platonist and contemplative, knowledge of the world becomes a substitute for the contemplative's knowledge of god, and is valued for its own sake and according to its accuracy. It is a matter of engineers versus pure scientists in the same terms as Crutchfield (1992) distinguishes between engineering and scientific conceptions of modelling (see p. 20).

The epistemic view has become codified in Bayesian statistical methods which work on an iterative basis in which a specified 'a priori probability' is refined through testing to generate an 'a posteriori probability' which provides a better ground for specific action. Desrosières, following Ginzburg, considers that the Bayesian approach forms part of the science of clues as opposed to the Galilean sciences. The Galilean sciences are concerned with the establishment of general laws and engage with masses of information in order to infer such laws from that mass – from a description of general reality. The sciences of clues are concerned to establish local and specific chains of causation in order to explain particular events. We might consider that the sciences of clues, although they may well be quantitative, are essentially ideographic. They are concerned with the particular and are not part of the nomothetic programme directed at establishing general laws.

The contrast between the Bayesian science of clues and the usual form of statistical reasoning on a frequentist foundation, can be illustrated by considering the idea of null hypothesis. In formal statistical reasoning a hypothesis is a statement that can be tested by using a combination of measured data and a specified – in principle specified in advance – statistical method based on the laws of mathematical probability. However, we do not test hypotheses directly. Instead we test them indirectly by reference to 'null hypotheses' – in effect statements to the effect that what the hypothesis states reality to be like is not what it is like.

Let us assume that we have taken a random sample of students at a university. We have stratified the students by gender. When we examine the number of A level points[2] obtained by the males and females in our sample we find that males have an average of 18.5 points and females an average (in both cases arithmetic mean) of 20.1 points. It looks as if females have higher scores than males but our data comes from a sample. In the population as a whole there may be no difference or males may even be doing better than females. Technically we might not have distinctive populations of males and females but rather a single population and the observed variation is purely a product of sampling rather than a reflection of the real situation. Our null hypothesis is that there is no difference between males and females and we employ a statistical test to see how often in a theoretically infinite number of repeated exercises in which a sample of the size of our sample was drawn from a population, we would find a difference of the size observed when there was really no difference in the population. This gives us a measure of statistical significance – essentially the proportion of times in an infinite series of trials with samples of our given size that such an observation would come up if there really was no difference. Note that with large enough samples we may establish statistically significant differences when the actual differences are substantively trivial.

This kind of inferring to a population from a sample says nothing about cause. In this simple bivariate case we are doing no more than describe an apparent association between gender and A level performance – a correlation – and correlation is never cause. This kind of significance testing where the null hypothesis being tested is to do with inferring from samples to populations is always necessary and justified in such instances. We might gently remonstrate with Yule, who was no fan of sampling, and assert that the development of sampling theory is necessary precisely because we do need to infer from descriptions of parts to the character of wholes, from sample statistics to population parameters. And we might say – thus far and no further.

The Bayesian method is different precisely because it does not start from a null hypothesis. The null hypothesis is essentially an assertion of ignorance whereas the conditional probabilities attached in Bayesian methods are based on existing knowledge. The examples given in basic textbooks are always very simple – for example deciding the probability that a white ball is drawn from one of two different urns when we know that one urn contains half white and half black balls and the other contains two-thirds white and one-third black. Poker players familiar with stud variations of the game in which some of the cards are visible to all players and in which that knowledge can be added to knowledge of the composition of your own hand, use essentially a Bayesian method[3] to calculate the odds of a displayed card improving their hand and of the final hand being a winning hand. For example, in a game of one variant of stud poker with four players all of whom are still active, I might hold two kings with three aces plus two low cards in the five cards displayed. I can then calculate that the chance that another player holds another ace which will beat my hand – a full house of two kings and three aces – is six in forty-five. There are six cards in play about which I have no information. There are forty-five cards in total about which I have no information. There is one ace about which I have no information. Any one of the six cards in play has a one in forty-five chance of being that ace. The sum total of chances of that ace being in play is six/forty-fifths. High full houses are not very common and real calculations can be much more complex! Here I am using my knowledge of the composition of the card pack and knowledge about seven cards to calculate my odds. In this instance I would bet my shirt and my grandmother. This situation could be represented as a formula by entering values in Bayes's theorem, but the language description will do perfectly well for us.

Note that I might well lose both grandmother and shirt. However, assuming an infinite supply of both commodities and an infinite number of poker games in which this hand emerges, if I bet in this way every time, then thirty-nine/forty-fifths of the time I will win and my overall position will be optimal. Percentage play is important in poker but it is not the only aspect of the game, and particularly of any individual game.

The null hypothesis and Bayesian approaches both rely on the true and crucial basis of probabilistic reasoning. In a sense the null hypothesis is a special case of the Bayesian general case, the case in which we have no previous knowledge on which to construct our probability statement about what will happen in the future. Probabilistic reasoning is about what will happen in the long run, given an infinite series of events. It is no accident that its foundations are in gambling.

The problem is that wholly legitimate and useful reasoning of this kind has been extended beyond the event by associating probability with that bug-bear, the variable. If we look at traditional discussions of probability and cause, for example in Black (1999: 9), we find that the idea of probability is extended to cover reasoning about populations of cases as opposed to dis-crete events. In a population abstracted variates vary, tautologically. An asso-ciation that is observed in the population seldom holds for every case. We cannot assign causality in a universal way. So a jump is made from valid reasoning about long run occurrence of events to specific outcomes in rela-tion to an individual case. An analogy is drawn between my kind of poker playing strategy and the outcome of something for a specific case. It is valid to say that my kind of bet will come good in a given ratio in an infinite, or in practice with luck in a large number, of games. Note luck is required in any run less than infinite. It is valid to say that the chances of a vaccine causing damage if administered to a large population are such that 0.0005 per cent of those receiving it will be harmed – one in two thousand. There is no way in which that can be translated as saying that the individual immunized case has a one in two thousand chance of being harmed. That specific immuniza-tion is a unique, and statistically independent event. Probabilistic explana-tions hold at the level of populations but never for cases. This is not an argument against probabilistic explanation at the population level. If immu-nization against measles damages one child in two thousand but five children in a thousand – a ten times higher rate – are damaged by measles, then there is a good population case for immunization and an unanswerable case for massive support and compensation for the damaged children. Blalock put this with characteristic clarity:

> the mathematician finds it necessary to think in terms of a priori probabilities that cannot actually be obtained empirically and that are not dependent upon any particular sample data. … we shall use the term probability not to refer to single events … but to a large number of events, to what happens in the long run. (1979: 115–16)

This point is very poorly understood in many conventional texts. The char-acteristic of a population is presented as a probability in the individual case. It is not that and can't be that. This is bad enough. Experiments are often a deal worse, but before we turn to them, let us note the re-emergence of a novel late idea of Karl Popper's – that of the single case probability.

Single case probabilities – back to the specific

Williams (1999) and Ulanowicz (1996) have both drawn attention to themes raised by Popper in his late work. Both set their examination within a complexity frame of reference and note that Popper was concerned precisely with the fundamental problem of frequentist probability – how can we infer from probabilistic trends in a population to the outcome for a single case. In a way highly reminiscent of the conceptual basis of the qualitative approach, analytic induction, and very close to the procedures of Qualitative Comparative Analysis, both of which we will discuss in Chapter 9, Popper argued for a propensity interpretation of probability. Popper's own proposal for investigation here was repeated experiment but we might very readily interpret the Boolean sorting/crunching strategies of Qualitative Comparative Analysis as directed towards the establishment of single case probabilities. The pursuit of single case probabilities is in its infancy, but conceptually and perhaps quite soon practically, it is important.

Gold standard – or dross?

In many books on quantitative methods the 'controlled' experiment is presented as the ideal – the gold standard – in relation to which all other quantitative approaches are more or less adequate approximations. The move towards evidence based policy, first in medicine and then generally in public policy, almost invariably privileges experimental approaches. This is methodological rubbish but it is gold plated and highly scented rubbish. It is not that experiments are wholly useless, just mostly useless. There are limited and special circumstances in which we might derive some understanding of the social world, and the intersection of social and biological worlds, from experimental investigation but it is absolutely necessary that every claim to knowledge based on experiment justifies why this highly unusual and generally inappropriate method is being used. In other words, experimenters have to demonstrate the specific and unusual ontological context of no interaction and absolute superposition, of which more in a moment.

First let us consider the issue of control. In the ideal experiment in physics, control over variables is exercised by physical control. Power is supplied at a fixed voltage when we measure the relationship between resistance and current in an electrical circuit. In social and bio-medical contexts we can seldom if ever exercise this sort of physical control. We cannot hold things constant because we are dealing not with single instances of universals, the way any electrical circuit can stand for all electrical circuits, but highly differentiated cases. Any knowledge we generate is not knowledge about the individual case but knowledge about the population of cases.

The method of control utilized in such investigations is not physical control but rather randomization. Methods of randomization vary. Sometimes cases are simply randomly assigned to a treatment and non-treatment group. Sometimes cases are carefully matched on given characteristics and then each of the pair is randomly allocated – a more sophisticated controlling device but one seldom possible with individual cases and more usually employed with aggregates such as classes or entire schools of children. The process of random allocation is equated with physical control. We don't directly control the circumstances of the individual experimental case which we consider can stand for all cases. Instead, we randomly allocate lots of cases to treatment and control groups and infer knowledge about the causal relations for populations of lots of cases from our findings.

The typical experiment in the educational or bio-medical fields does have one thing going for it. It deals in at least one real variable – one thing external to the cases which operates or does not operate on them – the treatment. Treatments are real, not just traces of the character of individual systems. Treatments are external to systems and imposed upon them. If we take an example of procedure which in general I would regard as valid, then the application of a new method of teaching statistics and the comparison of it with an existing method where large numbers of students have been paired on scores on pre-existing mathematical ability and randomly allocated to existing and innovatory programmes, would represent external real variation in relation to the individual systems of the students. In practice we would probably apply the techniques to different pre-existing whole classes although in a very large university where basic (exploratory and descriptive) statistics were taught to all students regardless of programme and we had a SATs style score on entry, we might set up this experiment.

Of course we are dealing with reasoning human beings who impose their own meanings on the situation and act in accordance with them. The students in the groups really should not be aware that one set are being taught in an old fashioned way and the others in a new fangled and supposedly better (because why else would it be tried?) fashion. In bio-medical contexts a double tribute is paid to the implications of meaning for outcomes in the form of placebo administration and double blind trials. Placebos are harmless substances – for ethical reasons they must be harmless – given as if drugs to patients who then respond to the social context of treatment without its physical component. The insistence in pharmacological investigation that the placebo is harmless has implications. There is reason to suspect that patients who experience side effects, as with many anti-depressant medications, recognize that they are receiving a real drug because of them and this enhances the placebo effect as against other patients who for ethical reasons must know they are in a trial in which they may be given a placebo and have no side effects. The double blind system extends ignorance of form, that is, possibly effective versus placebo, from patient to actual administrator of the treatment. This is possible with pharmacological products but not in general with any other kind of treatment intervention.[4]

Note how hard randomized control actually is in any real social context. The techniques were developed in agriculture where randomization is much easier to achieve at the level of the individual plot of cultivated land. None the less, sometimes we can do it. And we can infer from it if the following holds:

1   There is no interaction between the intervention and some non-randomized characteristic or characteristics of the cases subject to the treatment. This is fine with a generally homogeneous population of university students. Students in schools, which vary much more than universities do, might actually be subject to very significant interaction between social background of the school's general population and cognitive development. Vaccines that work in the micro-flora environment of Northern Europe don't have much value in the context of the very different micro-flora of the tropics. Inference is necessarily limited to specific contexts with minimal base variation.

2   We can manage 'Hawthorne effects', that is, the significance of meaning for all actors in the intervention, in an appropriate way.

3   The outcome of the intervention is close enough to the termination of the intervention. There is more to this than just the practicality of getting results in a time scale which can influence quite rapid policy/treatment development, although that is not trivial. It is because significant gaps between treatment and outcome allow for the intervention of factors which are not controlled during the experimental period.

4   It is clearly understood that evidence derived from studies involving plural cases applies to the level of populations of cases and not to individual cases. There is no general and universal case.

5   The context of intervention is highly structured and thereby repeatable in other context.

6   The character of the intervention is discrete and specific, that is, one clear thing varies between treatment and control groups. The experimental method can test for the impact of one difference. There are statistical methods – two way analysis of variance for example – which have the advantage of allowing detection of interactions. However, if there is interaction then it is wholly invalid to generalize on the basis of experimental evidence. Not just difficult, as many texts suggest – invalid!

This specification permits experiments in important instances. It certainly provides a validation for experimental evaluation of many teaching and therapeutic innovations in the structured and replicable contexts of classroom or clinic. However, there is a rather tight boundary set around effective inference from experiments, even inference for populations which is by no means trivial and unimportant. There really must be neither the potential for significant variation in treatment nor any interaction effect. Experimental methods work best with single and specific interventions. They work with specific drug therapies and specific and highly programmed methods of cognitive development. If there is scope for variation in intervention, forget it. Likewise if there is significant interaction, if the relationship between treatment and the trajectory of the case is variable in relation to any variate factor in the environment of the cases which is not controllable by random allocation of cases, likewise forget it. Random allocation might deal with the variate character of cases as individual systems. It cannot deal with variates external to cases, variates in other systems, because the experimental design does not randomly allocate those systems. Bradley and Schaefer have remarked that:

> To test any primary hypothesis in a complex social situation with non-experimental data, we must swallow a large group of auxiliary hypotheses on related issues … If our study yields a falsification of the original theory … we will have a difficult time disentangling a failure of the main hypothesis for a failure of one of the peripheral hypotheses. Thus, we will have difficulty coming to a firm conclusion. The variation in Y from what was anticipated could indicate that our theory about X is untrue, but it could also indicate measurement problems of the observations or the initial conditions or poor controls, misspecification of the model (deleted variables or improper abstraction and modelling), errors in choosing proxies, or (when the analysis involves estimating coefficients in equations) misspecifications of the functional form. Whereas we might hope that knowledge generally proceeds by finding falsifications in earlier presumptions, the complexity of social realities implies that we will rarely get a clear falsification of any claim. (1998: 142–3)

My point is that the word 'non-experimental' is redundant in that passage. In most social experiments outside highly specific and regulated environments typified by the classroom and the application of a single technique which varies, all the problems identified by Bradley and Schaefer apply just as much to experiments as to the use of non-experimental techniques.

Let me go back to my example of statistics teaching to illustrate, remembering that this is something done in the kind of context in which experimental approaches are in fact valid. In UK universities there is plainly an initial achievement difference between students at old and new universities. The former require higher A level grades for admission. This does not indicate innate ability differences. The higher grades may be bought and paid for by a private education but they are achieved by whatever means. This means that classes of students in old universities may well have a higher average achievement in basic mathematics than classes of students in new universities. The characteristic of the class as a whole will certainly influence outcomes. In general, the higher the base achievement of a group in relation to cognitive development, the less difference procedures make to additional cognitive development. Different methods might not matter in old universities and be rather significant in new universities. This example by no means rules out experiment because we can sort our results by context. The problems arise when we cannot sort our results by context.

All this is a way of saying causal influences are always local, even if we are dealing with real monocausal influences with no significant internal system interaction effects. If we have internal system interaction effects then there is no logical basis for generalization from the specific experimental context to any other context whatsoever.

Understanding Head Start

What happens when we seek to move experimental methods outside the specific controlled context of classroom or drug treatment and evaluate large scale policy interventions? Oakley (2000) has recently reviewed the US experience of a series of such initiatives in the 1960s and 1970s, part of Rivlin's efforts at providing a basis for *Systematic Thinking for Social Action* (1971). Let us consider one of the most important of such initiatives – the early positive discrimination interventions in educational preparation under the 'Head Start' programme. Head Start is a good example for two reasons. First, it is very important and is widely asserted to have been successful in important ways. Second, a large scale re-evaluation of the programme is currently under way in the United States which is based around a central principle of randomized controlled trials. Let me make something absolutely clear: the purpose of my review of Head Start is not to question its intrinsic merits – in political terms I am wholly supportive of this kind of intervention. Rather, it is about the methodological understanding of efforts at interpreting the outcome of these sorts of programmes.

Head Start was established during the Johnson administration's 'Great Society' initiative of the 1960s. As such it was an important part of a genuine effort at improving the relative trajectories of the children of the poor, and particularly the black poor, through their subsequent adult lives. The intellectual context was one in which the notion of a 'culture of poverty' (see Valentine, 1970) held considerable sway. The 'culture of poverty' was understood to be an intergenerationally transmitted structure of cognition, belief, behaviour and aspiration which reflected a rational response to the oppression of previous eras, and in particular in the form of the female headed family with absent male, understood as a consequence of the US black experience of chattel slavery. However, in contemporary circumstances it was disabling and held back mobility into the new occupational positions which required historically high levels of educational achievement.

Pre-school programmes like Head Start were intended to be remedial and to positively discriminate. They would catch children early, introduce them to the aspirational and linguistic forms necessary for educational success, and 'compensate' for domestic disadvantage. Delivery of these programmes to the children of the poor but not the affluent, positive discrimination, was intended to bring all children as equals to the starting gate in the educational race of life.

If we consider the objectives of Head Start we have to see that these were plainly long term and to do with the condition in which participants would enter adult life. Changes in educational performance and cognitive skills, measurable through testing, were at best intermediate variables towards this long term goal.

Oakley (2000: 225–7) discusses the experience of the Perry Pre-School Project which preceded Head Start but followed exactly the model of treating cognitive skills as intermediate causes. This programme was directed at children with low measured IQs and randomly assigned them to either a treatment or control group. There were subsequent early differences in cognitive ability between the groups, with better development in the treatment group, but these differences disappeared during elementary school career. However, later differences in life trajectory were quite marked in some instances. In general, on a range of measures of life performance the treatment group at age nineteen were about 50 per cent better than the control group. For example, 31 per cent of the treatment group were in college or vocational training but only 21 per cent of the control group. The twenty-five young women in the treatment group had experienced seventeen pregnancies or births as compared with twenty-eight among the twenty-four young women in the control group. The direction of these differences was constant.

How do we interpret this? First, it would seem hard to sustain the model of intermediate cause by cognitive skills since differences in cognitive ability disappeared in elementary school. Something happened to the treatment children but it seems to have been social rather than in the realm of things measurable by psychologists. Second, if we move away from a conception of linear variables and think instead about category change, we have a rather different view of outcomes. Plainly the programmes did some good. More of the treatment children achieved something than those of the control group. But let us examine the actual patterns. Most of both groups failed. This was particularly marked among the young women in relation to the massive social disadvantages of early child-bearing. The measure of numbers of children/pregnancies is meaningless in itself. What matters is having one live born child (not aborted pregnancy – a common enough middle class teenage experience[5]) which changes the whole life trajectory of the person concerned. A mother is something different.

Measuring cognitive abilities or educational performance is not a process of measuring real things independent of human systems, of cases. These are artefacts of the measurement process which may or may not[6] correspond to traces of those real systems. In any event if differences in them disappear in elementary school, they cannot be causal to long term life events. What we have here is a compounding of the problem of inappropriate experimental design with a reification of 'variables' measured as continuous when the real issue is qualitative change of condition.

So now 'Head Start' is being re-evaluated and the Commission set up to re-evaluate it comprises thirteen psychologists, nine people with educational research backgrounds, two sociologists and three others. So, surprise, surprise, we find that they propose an experimental design. Having done so they remark:

> The Committee believes more consideration needs to be given to the option of using quasi-experimental or other embedded studies to supplement the information from the randomized impact study or studies. Some members believe quasi-experimental studies could yield useful information about Head Start, but others question the validity of these studies. All members agree that the amount of money spent on quasi-experiments should be small relative to the amount spent on a randomized study or studies. This option should be more fully developed and reviewed by the Department during development of the detailed research design.

The outcome measures proposed for both the experimental, specifically randomized controlled trial, and quasi-experimental interventions are relatively short term measures of cognitive development: precisely the things which were shown to have disappeared in the previous studies. The committee is asserting that it doesn't matter if these don't matter – what matters is that we have measurement tools for measuring them. One could not believe it if one made it up.

Let us escape from the byways of experimentation – a distinctly drossy rather than golden domain – and get back to reality by considering the employment of probability in the exploration of data derived from surveys of the world as it is.

Probabilistic reasoning in relation to non-experimental data

In Chapter 7 we will examine the use of loglinear and related modelling procedures in the exploration of survey generated data. These techniques use a form of probabilistic reasoning but it is not, in practice as opposed to theoretical assertion, the form of probabilistic reasoning which informs classical understanding of the testing of hypotheses. Gilbert puts it like this:

> This scheme of analysis differs in two main ways from the classical approach. First, statistical texts, especially ones pitched at an elementary level, generally consider the testing of hypotheses rather than models. The term 'model' has been used here partly because it is clearer than 'hypothesis', and partly because while a hypothesis usually concerns just one relationship, a model may and usually does involve a complex set of linked relationships. Secondly, the classical approach assumes that the analyst possesses, *a priori*, a carefully formulated hypothesis to be tested against the data. Following the confirmation or rejection of this hypothesis, the analyst must cease working with the original set of data. Improved hypotheses should be tested with new data. In contrast, the above scheme assumes that, while the analyst should have some prior theoretical notions about the form of suitable models, the investigation ceases only when an adequate model to describe one set of data has been found. The task is

essentially to explore in depth the structure of the data. This seems a more realistic view of research in practice than the classical one. (1993: 6)

This is not just an argument that our approaches should be exploratory, iterative and originate from a broad theoretical conceptualization of the situation, although all those things are true. It also involves a radical recasting of the use of probabilistic measures.

Essentially, these modelling procedures are based on a comparison between the actual observed data set as this presents the sample's pattern of relations among measured variate traces for cases, and that which is generated by a mathematical equation which describes the model being compared – note the avoidance of the word tested. The easiest way to examine this is to begin with Chi-squared and work forwards.

Chi-squared is the basic test for statistical significance for a simple bivariate contingency table. We compare the pattern of observed cell distributions with those that would hold if there was absolutely no relationship between the two variables used to construct the table, and if the difference[7] is big enough in relation to the sample size, then we reject the null hypothesis of no association between the variables. Loglinear and related techniques do this in reverse. They measure closeness rather than difference. As Gilbert puts it, we compare the real world as represented by our data set with the imaginary world represented by the values constructed by the model building process.

The method of testing goodness of fit of a loglinear model involves the calculation of G^2, a measure closely related to Chi-squared. However, as Gilbert points out:

> the consequence of this more exploratory approach to analysis is that the tests of significance lose their original meaning, and the probabilities they generate cannot be relied upon as indicators of the generalizability of the hypotheses being tested. … Nonetheless, tests of significance do have an invaluable role in loglinear analysis because they provide a most convenient means of quantifying the comparison of a model table with data. (1993: 72–3)

Bradley and Schaefer (1998: Ch. 7) present an important discussion of the implications of this kind of approach, the real approach of almost all quantitative social scientists to survey data. I disagree profoundly with the continued privilege that these authors attach to experimental approaches – in a world of complex and evolutionary systems that is wrong; there is an ontological misspecification – but they are dead right about what we are doing with probabilities.

> Classical statistics, using experimental data, yields the likelihood that we have correctly accepted or rejected a null hypothesis, but with non-experimental data the null hypothesis itself has a 'probability' or degree-of-belief attached to it. Probabilities here are degrees of warranted belief, not relative frequencies. Probabilities are indexes of the reasonableness-of-doubt that should be attached to conclusions – conclusions that, as in court cases, generally cannot be proved

or disproved but can be argued more or less persuasively. Probability is not a statement about physical events but an estimate of the level of believability, the relative weight of admissible evidence in the face of uncertainty and ignorance; it is an assessment of the likelihood of a particular conclusion, given a body of (imperfect) information. (1998: 148–9)

There are problems with the use of loglinear and related techniques which derive from their essentially linear form, although I will argue in Chapter 6 that we can get round this if we treat them as exploratory tools. However, these important and interesting techniques are not the bases of classical testing of hypotheses. In reality we almost never really test any hypotheses in social statistics other than those which are to do with handling the potential for simple sample variation. In loglinear modelling we frequently find several models which are consonant with our data set. Few commentators now argue for mere parsimoniousness – Occam's razor – that is to say taking the simplest statistically significant model. Instead other criteria, including qualitative information and theory, play a large part in model selection. There is little point in debating models that don't fit the data, although a lot in seeing why any models suggested by substantive theorization are way off beam. The arguments are about those that do, and significance levels are not the determinant factor.

Randomness, probability, significance and investigation

Frequentist statisticians treat randomness as an inherent quality of macroscopic nature. We can regard uncertainty as a fundamental aspect of quantum reality – Heisenberg's position – but we cannot scale up from quantum to macro levels. Instead we seem to be dealing not with inherent randomness but with uncertain knowledge. As Poincaré, the father of modern chaos theory, put it: 'A very small cause which escapes us, determines a considerable effect which we cannot ignore, and then we say that this effect is due to chance' (quoted in Ruelle, 1991: 48). Chaos is a deterministic programme. Chaos theory has no place for inherent randomness. Imprecision of measurement is the foundation of uncertainty in the chaos programme. If we could measure exactly, then we would know exactly. There is no randomness although there may be either or both of extreme sensitivity to initial conditions and complex evolutionary emergence.

In the social world we can, mostly, ignore the problems of extreme sensitivity to initial conditions. Complex systems are in fact rather robust, even if they are by no means homeostatic. We should not always ignore the possibility of sensitivity to initial conditions. Personal trajectories, life courses, can in fact display exactly that. However, complex emergence, which for loglinear modellers appears in the guise of difficult to interpret (here difficult serves as a synonym for impossible if the interpretation is analytical) higher order interactions. We really ought to dispense with all this mystic conception of the inherently random.

In practice probability is a tool in a science of clues – not a means to the nomothetic establishment of universal laws. Bradley and Schaefer (1998) don't use the expression 'science of clues' but they do make an explicit comparison between the work of the social researcher and the forensic procedures of a detective investigating a crime. Put this in the context of the Code Napoleon with a genuinely investigative as opposed to adversarial system, and the point becomes even stronger. Probabilistic reasoning neither proves nor disproves for us. It facilitates account. It helps us see what is worth bothering with and if relationships do hold in sample data. It manages the problem of relating sample to whole. It facilitates exploration of multi-level accounts of variate trace relationships. That is it.

This is a good point at which to clarify the significance of statistical significance. No level of statistical significance ever proves anything. Indeed, given the problem of Type II (Beta) errors, it can't really disprove anything either – the problem of the fallacy of affirming the consequent. However, it is a powerful tool in facilitating decisions if understood as that. All even half-way decent statistical textbooks explain that statistical significance is a function of sample size. Relationships that are not significant with small samples become so with large ones – we can place more reliance on our statements about the whole on the basis of information about a part when we have a bigger part to play with. This discussion is used, properly, as the basis for distinguishing between statistical and substantive significance. The former is about inference. The latter is about what matters in the world. This is why social scientists place so much emphasis not on significance but on measures of strength of association – correlation coefficients, phi, Cramer's V, and so on. Note the emphasis is on strength not form, on correlation not regression. In other words, there is far more interest in what matters than in how things might work – an implicit recognition of the importance of system relations rather than multivariable causation of dependent variables.

Conclusion

This chapter was intended to 'demystify' probability as a component of quantitative exploration and reasoning in the social sciences. It showed that there are at least two general approaches to probabilistic reasoning – the frequentist approach and the science of clues – which have profoundly different understandings of what we are doing when we think in probabilistic terms. It challenged the notion that probabilistically organized experimentation, the randomized controlled trial, represents any sort of ideal against which any other sort of evidence should be graded, and instead argued that the RCT is a useful but limited approach which can only be employed if the relationships being investigated are not characterized by the interaction and emergence which dominates the open systems of social and bioloigical reality. It referred to the potentially enormous significance of a shift in probabilistic reasoning from the population centred tradition to an understanding of probability as embodied in the causal propensities of the individual case. Finally, it examined how significance tests are used by social scientists, not in experiments, but in efforts to retrodictively model causal processes in the social world. In general it argued that probabilistic reasoning is important and useful but that it is well time we stopped worshipping the divine principle of the random.

So what is probability for in social science? Mostly it is about inferring from parts to wholes, from samples to universes. It has a useful role in helping us explore models as descriptions of how the world has worked in the context in which we have measured it. It has a role in very specific and limited circumstances for which a detailed ontological justification must always be provided in enabling us to carry out experiments where direct physical control is not possible. That is it – a useful tool but a lousy foundational principle. Oh! and if the mood takes you it helps you play cards as well, but only in the long run.

Notes

1 The practical implication of the law of large numbers is that provided a sample is itself of large enough size – in effect more than about forty cases in any relevant subcategory – then we can consider that the sampling distribution of all samples of that size drawn from the population will be normal for the estimates of the values of any given population value – parameter – regardless of the actual distribution of that parameter in the population. This allows us to construct sampling distributions and construct probabilistic estimations of parameters from sample statistics.

2 In England, Wales and Northern Ireland most students are admitted to university on the basis of their performance in the A (advanced) level examination. Students typically take three subjects which are graded A, B, C, D, E, U and Fail. An A counts for ten points, a B for eight and so on to an E, which counts for two points. Us and Fails get no points.

3 Perhaps I should say I do. Some players seem to rely on very different criteria or none at all.

4 Note placebo effects are wholly real and may be rather important. A GP doing a research course with me had been one of the clinical evaluators of Viagra as a treatment for impotence. The drug had very real and dramatic effects, over and above the actually rather dramatic effects of the placebo intervention, which included detailed health management and discussion with the GP as well as a placebo treatment. In any context with a social content we must regard the social content as part of the intervention. In this instance outcomes were essentially benign in all directions which is fine, but this would not always be so.

5 Adoption used to serve the same purpose for middle class and upper working class girls in the UK.

6 Actually I do think that skill performance tests and some cognitive measures, but not of course G (general intelligence), have some validity considered as traces.

7 Differences are squared to eliminate negative numbers.

6

Interpreting Measurements:
Exploring, Describing and Classifying

In this chapter we will start to get down to actually working with data – with sets of numbers – in order to get a grip on the world.[1] Remember that this text is committed to exploration. Our approach to data is not a matter of testing pre-established hypotheses but rather a process of continuing re-engagement, a quantitative hermeneutic. In contrast with Erikson and Nosanchuk, who provide an outstanding introduction to exploratory techniques (1992), we should not make any distinction between explanatory techniques which are applicable to 'good' data and exploratory techniques. Part of the argument of Chapter 5 was exactly that 'good' data generated in experimental and quasi-experimental procedures is of relevance only in specific and limited contexts. Exploration is the real and serious game.

In this chapter we will begin by considering basic techniques of data exploration and description, tools we can use to help us see patterns and relationships. In this category we will include graphical procedures that generate pictures – icons – for us. These are very useful tools but we have to be careful in their employment – not because they mislead in any specific instance but because in general they are variable centred. They tell us about variables first and cases in a secondary fashion. We have to invert this in thinking about what they show, which is easy enough provided we always remember to break the habits of variable centredness.

In the second half of the chapter we will deal with numerical taxonomy, with cluster analyses and the potential of neural net approaches. These techniques have the enormous advantage of being explicitly case centred. Variables are used as traces of cases rather than as things in themselves and what emerges from the procedures is sets of cases rather than models of variable relationships. To some extent in cluster analysis and explicitly in neural networking approaches, the whole idea of variables as causes is abandoned. This is not just a matter of technique. It is a fundamental meta-theoretical shift.

Throughout the chapter, reference will be made to tools available in SPSS, the most commonly employed statistical package in the social sciences. I remain convinced that basic statistical exploration and reasoning should be taught through the medium of MINITAB, which is explicitly designed as a relatively open teaching tool in contrast to the rather black box character of SPSS. However, SPSS is a superb data management tool and offers a user friendly and accessible set of procedures which enable us to execute all the procedures we are going to discuss here. Learn on MINITAB, practise on SPSS – that is the way to do it and the way I teach it to postgraduate students in my own institution.

Basic exploration and description

Let us begin with what you will see when you read an edited data file into SPSS. You will see a rectangular matrix of data arranged in a spreadsheet form with each row representing a single case and each column representing a single variate trace of that case. The spreadsheet is the flat file of the case/variate trace data matrix.

SPSS has an excellent data labelling system which enables you to assign names to the variate traces, value labels to specific values of ordinal and nominal variate traces, and to assign a missing data code. We will assume that all this has been done. Most universities offer basic courses in this data management and SPSS's own help facility will guide you through it. There are also some good introductory texts. We are concerned with the first pass after these jobs are done.

Note that phrase: the first pass. When we have considered how we might explore the variate traces we have to start with, those we constructed in our operationalization up to and through the execution of a survey instrument or had provided for us in a set of secondary data, we will consider how we might create new variate traces from combinations of those which exist at this first stage of exploration.

The spreadsheet representation of an SPSS data file for a large number of cases and a large number of variables is an imposing site. One by no means excessively large example I have worked with comprises some 120 variate traces for each of the more than three thousand 1991 Census enumeration districts in what is now the North Eastern Standard Region of England.[2] If this was printed out on A4 sheets in 10 point type, given that each case occupies twelve lines as we have to wrap the original row to fit it onto the paper, it would generate nearly 40 000 lines of type and about 500 sheets of paper if we allow eighty lines per sheet. Just looking at this, even if we confine our visual inspection to a single variate trace, will not help us much. Simple visual inspection might enable us to make some sort of sense of a data listing for two or three variate traces for twenty or thirty cases but for 120 for more than 3000 – I don't think so.

So what can we do? Well for single variate traces we can explore and we can summarize. Exploration is basically a process of rearranging the data so that we can order it in some way as a device for seeing if there are any meaningful patterns in it. Summarizing, through standard descriptive statistics, is a method of reducing the whole column of measurements for a single variate trace to a much smaller set of measurements which tell us about the overall character of that variate trace. Graphical displays are essentially part of the exploration mode of interpretation.

In SPSS we can access Tukey's standard exploratory tools through the Analyze menu. Tukey's original exploratory tool, developed in the 1970s for the manual exploration of data, was the stem and leaf layout in which a continuous or ratio scale measurement is split into components. In the case of percentages the first of these would be the number of tens in the numerical representation of the measurement, varying from 0 to 10. These are the stems as below. The actual value within the decile between 0 and 9 would be the leaf. For percentages the only possible leaf in the tenth decile would be 0. (See Figure 6.1.)

```
10 - 00000000000000000000000
 9 - 0111112223333344444455555555566666788899999
 8 - 001223334445555566667777899
 7 - 22333334578
 6 - 000111235557888899
 5 - 0111112222233444455566677788888889999
 4 - 00000122233444556789
 3 - 00111122233344455566666667777888999
 2 - 0011122233334444456667778889
 1 - 000000000111111112223333334444444444455555566677777888999
 0 - 000000000000000000000000111222333345555566777888889999
```

Figure 6.1   *A stem and leaf diagram*

I simply made this distribution up for illustrative purposes but let us imagine that for the cases recorded in it, the values actually measure something real. Let us assume that they are the scores on a test of basic mathematical competence achieved by students at the beginning of a basic statistics course. What can we see. The distribution is plainly not normal, not the characteristic reverse of the pattern of wear of the stone threshold of an ancient building – look next time you enter one. It is if anything multimodal with several peaks but the key feature, which should make the teacher's heart sink, is that there are a lot of students with very low or even zero scores. The advantage of stem and leaf over simple graphical representation as a bar graph for deciles is that stem and leaf preserves the original individual values but for the teacher this doesn't really matter very much. The difference between 43 and 47 has no significance for the planning of teaching.

Suppose we decided on the basis of this data that we had more or less four groups of students – high basic ability, i.e. scores of 70 or more; moderate ability, i.e. scores between 40 and 69; low ability, i.e. scores of 20 to 39; and virtually no ability, i.e. scores of less than 20 – we might want to see the proportions in each category and could do this rather well by constructing a pie chart. In making a pie chart we do two things which are rather important. First we turn a continuous measurement into an ordinal one by cutting up the continuous scale into four ordered categories – high, moderate, low and none. Note that we have some basis for doing this because visual inspection of the stem and leaf and bar graphs does suggest that there are four groups here. There is a sort of normal distribution between 70 and 100 and similar sorts of normal distributions between 40 and 69 and between 20 and 49, although the latter two overlap. Finally, there is a large group with an even pattern between 0 and 19. This cutting up is not a clean procedure. We have overlapping 'normal' distributions and the assignment of a case with a score of 19 to the no ability group and one with a score of 20 to the low ability group is not really likely to reflect a substantive difference in their respective mathematical abilities. However, as a working device, it might do.

The second thing is that we create a new variable from an existing one using the RECODE facility in SPSS. We create a variable of ordered maths score in addition to our original variable of maths score percentage. In other words we convert scores between 70 and 100 into the number 4, 40 and 69 into the number 3, and so on. These integers are ordered codes for the categories high, middle, low and none. We could express the distribution of cases on this new set of ordered categories as a pie chart.

For the task suggested, organizing teaching sets in a statistics course, this kind of exploration and representation of the variate trace is all we need. However, this is merely a useful administrative exercise. Suppose we were interested in thinking about why the mathematical competencies might differ among this group. We might have some other measures which described the cases – gender, whether (in the UK) privately or state educated, and grade obtained in mathematics at GCSE. For the moment let us concern ourselves solely with this group of students rather than treating them as a sample of all possible students. Can we explore the differences among this group in any easy fashion?

This is one of the purposes of descriptive statistics. We can calculate measures of centre and spread for our variate traces for the different categories. Typically these would be mean and median for centre and range, standard deviation and inter-quartile range for spread. Descriptive in SPSS will generate all of these. For exploratory purposes, the resistant (resistant to being overinfluenced by extreme values) median for centre and inter-quartile range for spread are the best to use. We can represent these, and also extreme cases, outliers and far outliers,[3] in a very useful graphical device, the boxplot, shown in Figure 6.2. The middle line in the box is the median value, the ends of the boxes are the upper and lower quartile values, the line shows one spread from the box, the small stars are outliers and the large stars are far outliers.

One of the great advantages of boxplots is that we can print them for several variate traces set to the same scale and compare. Another is that the identification of outliers and far outliers is a case centred element which allows us

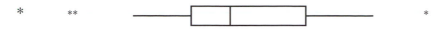

Figure 6.2 *A boxplot*

to look at the unusual. If we partition a data set – separate the cases for example by gender and then match boxplots – this gives us a good visual impression of differences by category although we must always be careful when organizing by variate trace.

There are other graphical techniques which enable us to explore the relationship between variate traces, most of which are various developments of the simple scattergram in which we plot one variate trace as the *x* axis against another as the *y* axis. These are useful if we focus on the plotted points which represent cases and pay attention to the way these occur together, rather than thinking primarily about what the plot tells us about the relationship between variate traces.

One disadvantage of most exploratory techniques is that they operate only with continuous data. Some of the graphic approaches allow us to visualize nominal and ordinal data. We can construct bargraphs or pie charts of nominal and ordinal values, which are iconic representations of frequency distributions. These are useful approaches. There is another approach which is even more useful and is case centred. This is correspondence analysis available in the analysis menu in SPSS. Simple correspondence analysis is described thus by Phillips:

> Correspondence analysis seeks to represent the interrelationships of categories of row and column variables [these terms refer to the organization of a contingency table] on a two dimensional map. It can be thought of as trying to plot a cloud of data points (the cloud having height, width, thickness) on a single plane to give a reasonable summary of the relationships and variation within them. (1995: 2)

Everitt (1993: 31–2) shows how bivariate correspondence analysis can be extended to handle three or more categorical variables. These approaches are particularly appropriate as a kind of preliminary pictorial search for clusters of cases. Let us now turn to the premier cru exploratory approaches – the classification techniques available as cluster analyses and through the use of neural nets.

Making sets of categories – taxonomy as social exploration

> All the real knowledge which we possess, depends on methods by which we distinguish the similar from the dissimilar. The greater number of natural distinctions this method comprehends, the clearer becomes our idea of things.

> The more numerous the objects which employ our attention, the more difficult it becomes to form such a method and the more necessary. (Linnaeus, *General Plantarum*; quoted by Everitt, 1993: 2)

In this section we are going to look at ways of sorting cases into categories. We are not going to consider how to sort them into pre-existing categories, the task of procedures like principal components analysis. Rather, we are going to be concerned with category sets which emerge from the exploration of our data. Bailey (1994) distinguishes between the terms 'typology' and 'taxonomy'. Typologies are conceptual – taxonomies are empirical. Although there is some value in this distinction in practice our typologizing is always guided by empirical information and our taxonomies are never 'purely' empirical but are always in part the product of the pre-existing understanding we bring to our exploration.

I think these numerical taxonomy techniques have been massively underused in social science, particularly in the UK, although the techniques are readily available in a range of computer packages including SPSS. There are a variety of reasons for this. One of the most important is that frequentist statisticians are deeply uneasy about clustering methods because in general they are not constructed around a central concern with inference from samples to universes. At one level this is a valid concern. There is no one set of categories which can be generated by clustering or neural net classification procedures. Differences in choices about which variate traces are to be used in classification,[4] about which clustering method (algorithm) is to be used, and in particular in the composition of the data set, can all generate somewhat different classifications. What look like meaningful classifications can be generated from random data. Plainly frequentist statisticians have a point when they worry about whether a different sample from the same population would produce a different classification and deplore the absence of anything resembling tests of significance in the most commonly used clustering procedures.

However, meaningful emergent classifications have one important quality which reflects the character of the far from equilibric complex systems from which they are generated – they are robust. Actually it seems to me that this property of robustness is a better source of validation than statistical inference because it more closely resembles the idea of repeatability which, supposedly, underpins the validation of experimental evidence. Basically, if there is a real underlying taxonomy to be found then different clustering methods will produce essentially similar classification account when applied to the same data set. Also, different data sets drawn from the same locality – here this word is used to indicate within the spatio-temporal boundaries of local but not universal knowledge – generate the same typology if there is a real taxonomy. Validity is established by process rather than by inference. Of course another important process in the establishing of validity is triangulation of the account derived from measured data with that derived from other processes of social investigation. Comparative investigation and triangulation are certainly good enough for me as bases for asserting the validity of our taxonomies.

Everitt puts this in a very direct pragmatic fashion:

> any classification is a division of the objects or individual into groups based on a set of rules – *it is neither true nor false* (unlike say a theory) and should be judged largely on the usefulness of the results. (1993: 4; original emphasis)

We might well consider that the usefulness of results is to a considerable extent a function of the degree of correspondence of our classification with real divisions in the world – a realist qualification of Everitt's pragmatism – but usefulness certainly matters.

It is worth reflecting on the intellectual history of numerical taxonomy. Although efforts were made to establish quantitative bases for taxonomy as far back as the 1930s, it was the ready availability of computing power for number crunching which made such techniques a practical proposition. Sneath and Sokal (1973) promoted the approach in biology with particular reference to biology's long concern with the differentiation of species. Clifford and Stephenson (1975) extended this approach to deal with the classification of ecological systems and this domain is of more relevance to social scientists given that both similarity and contiguity – both common characteristics and common location – matter in ecological systems. There have been numerous (if not numerous enough) examples of cluster analyses in the social sciences[5] and the procedure is widely employed across the whole range of scientific activity.

The central principle of numerical taxonomy is simple. All the methods, neural net as well as clustering, seek to establish classifications which minimize within group variation among cases in the categories and maximize between group variation, that is, variation among the categories as such. It is worth contrasting this approach with analysis of variance – a variable centred technique which deals with variation. In clustering the focus is on the cases. In analysis of variance the focus is on the variables with the actual category structure being determined by that of one or two of the variables themselves. Clustering techniques are case centred and case driven.

There are a variety of actual procedures which are used in clustering. Everitt (1993) and Bailey (1994) review them and there is a good discussion of the advantages, disadvantages and implications of different approaches in both texts. In general procedures are based on the construction of a matrix of cases and variables and the calculation of some sort of coefficient, either of similarity or more commonly dissimilarity, which is employed to allocate cases to categories. A commonly employed method is Ward's in hierarchic fusion clustering. This procedure starts with all individual cases considered as distinct and separate categories. The two which are most alike, with degree of similarity measured by minimizing the amount of information lost when there is a fusion, are joined. Information loss is represented in terms of an error sum of squares. At the next stage the two most similar clusters are again fused and so on until all cases are in a single cluster.

Clustering methods in statistical packages typically provide for the construction of a dendogram. This is a diagram illustrating the pattern of fusions and often with the pattern set against a scale. Figure 6.3 illustrates the approach.

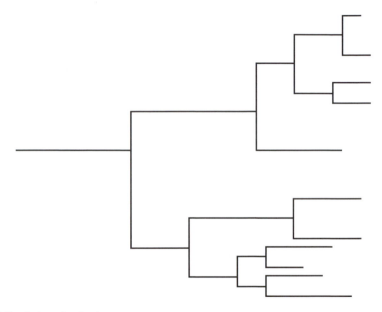

Figure 6.3   *A clustering dendogram*

When there are very large numbers of cases complete dendograms take up an awful lot of printout and it is advisable to use the following procedure to determine how much of the dendogram to examine. Hierarchical agglomeration methods typically generate a coefficient which indicates what is happening at each clustering stage. In Ward's method this is an error sum of squares (ESS) showing how much information is lost when clusters are combined to reduce the total number of clusters by one. This is listed in SPSS output from the method and simple visual inspection will reveal when the value of the ESS increases markedly at a clustering stage. Typically there are tiny increases for a long time and in the final clustering stages there are dramatic increases. This can be represented graphically, as in Figure 6.4.

Figure 6.4 suggests that when four clusters were fused to form three, two very different clusters were forced together. This suggests that we should carefully examine the character of the clusters at the four cluster level. In SPSS this can be done quite easily. The clustering procedures allow us to create a new variable which indicates the cluster membership at any given clustering stage of all cases. Here we would select the four cluster stage and write this variable to the data set. We can then partition the data set using this cluster membership variable as the partitioning principle. If our variate traces are measured

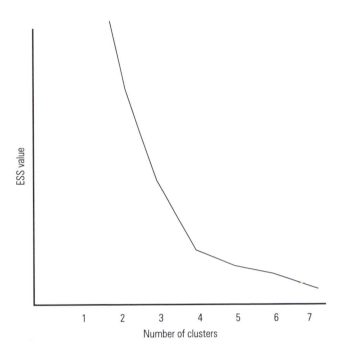

Figure 6.4   *Plotting the ESS*

at a continuous data level then we can compute means and standard deviations on all variables for each cluster using the MEANS procedure in SPSS and then we can describe our clusters in the form of a table.

Note that we can describe our clusters both in terms of the variate traces which were selected as clustering principles and in terms of all other variate traces for which we have measurements. This is rather important in relation to exploring possible 'control parameter sets' – starting to see if we can say something about the character of causal mechanisms – and we will return to it. Clustering techniques cope well with nominal or ordinal data. Sometimes ordinal data can be treated as if continuous. If treated as nominal then, as with simple nominal data, the procedure involves breaking up each of the categories of the variate trace into distinctive binary attributes. An illustration can demonstrate. Suppose we have classified households into five categories, namely:

Single persons
Couples, no dependent children
Single parents with dependent children
Couples with dependent children
Other

and called this variate trace 'Household Composition'. We can then create five new variate traces in which a case either does or does not belong to the category and is given a value of 1 if it does belong and a value of 0 if it does not. We will have the following variate traces:

Single person household	1 or 0
Couple only household	1 or 0
Single parent household	1 or 0
Couple with children	1 or 0
Other	1 or 0

The Recode facility in SPSS enables us to carry out such transformations with relative ease. Parametric variable centred procedures can be very sensitive to the transformation of ordinal or categorical data into binary attributes and consequent treatment of these attributes as continuous, but clustering procedures are much more robust and essentially we can carry out such transformations without concern and for most clustering procedures. We can use cluster labelling again as a way of exploring the character of cluster levels of interest. Here we can select cases by use of a cluster label value, that is, select only the cases in a particular cluster and generate a frequency distribution for that cluster. Repeating this for all clusters enables us to construct tables which again allow for comparison among clusters.

Cluster construction is important but the real art of cluster analyses lies in the interpretation of the results, and it is worth emphasizing that all the standard texts on the technique use that word 'interpretation' in discussing this phase of the procedure. Everitt remarks that:

> Interpreting the results from a cluster algorithm is often dominated by personal intuition and insight. If the investigator can make sense of the clusters produced, the cluster analysis is frequently deemed to have been a success. (1993: 142)

He then goes on to say: 'This may, however, be unsatisfactory ...' (p. 142) and discusses some procedures which have been suggested to establish whether the clusters observed are the consequence of any real structure in the data, which is supposed to correspond to reality, or are rather merely products of the application of the computing algorithm to that particular set of data. Two practical approaches here are the partitioning of the data set – split it in two randomly, cluster again and see if the same sets of clusters emerge – and deletion of variables. I actually would prefer to employ deletion of variables for another purpose – for exploring control parameters. There are also various graphical methods which can be employed. It is important to note that none of these procedures claims the (supposed!) magisterial authority of significance testing in frequentist statistical reasoning.

An alternative to clustering procedures in classification is the use of neural net approaches. Perhaps it is better to regard neural net approaches as a complement rather than a bald alternative. If we adopt a processual attitude to the establishment of valid taxonomies, then the generation of essentially similar classifications by different forms of numerical taxonomy is an important indicator that the structure we observe is real. In any event neural networks can classify as well as model. I want to postpone discussion of the essential character of neural networks to Chapter 8 because the most important characteristic of these techniques is that they themselves are connectionist and complex and can therefore be considered as representations of real complex systems. In other words we can 'model' with them, or more properly might be able to engage in prediction.

Neural nets can classify. Indeed their major current commercial use is exactly in classifying. Anyone purchasing books on-line is likely to be offered suggestions which are based on the data mining of the whole customer base of the bookseller. Suggestions are constructed by assigning each purchaser to a category based on previous purchase choices. This is a continually updated process – new purchases by self and others modify category structure and category membership. We have introduced an important term here – data mining. Let us consider what that term implies.

Basically data mining is a product of the existence of enormous electronic data bases. Data bases now can be extremely large – containing more than 10^{10} bytes of data. For example, every transaction by someone holding a supermarket preference card is recorded through the swiping of bar codes for that card and each purchase. Commercial organizations have developed tools in order to use this information to facilitate their marketing strategies, both in general terms and in relation to targeting specific individuals. It is important to note, as do those who comment on data mining for commercial users (see for example Two Crows, 1999: 1) that data mining identifies associations, not causes. We will return to the issue of the relationship between classification and cause in the last part of this chapter. Data mining is not any particular procedure. I can dig a hole with a teaspoon, tablespoon, trowel, mattock, spade, JCB, or stick of dynamite – very different tools but all capable of digging a hole. If I want to dig a hole in a soft-boiled egg I will use a teaspoon. If I want to dig a hole on an 0.6 acre rural building site in order to install a septic tank I will use (or hire) a JCB. Different tools for different contexts.

Although neural network systems can be used to classify, it is easier to describe them by considering their use in modelling so detailed discussion of them will come in Chapter 7. I want now to turn to issues of classification and cause.

Can classifying help us to sort out causal processes?

In the realist frame of reference we do not see causes as single factors whose presence inevitably generates an effect and whose absence means that the effect does not occur. Rather cause is a property of complex and contingent mechanisms in reality and such mechanisms, moreover, are not universal but only relatively permanent – inherently local. Traditionally, in quantitative reasoning causes have been understood as variables. In this text the very expression variable has been rejected and replaced by variate trace of complex and evolutionary system. It has been argued that the whole direction of quantitative reasoning should be shifted from the variate trace to the case, the complex embodied real system. Can we get anywhere with cause if we think in this way?

If cases rather than variate traces are the most important things, then it is by exploring and comparing cases that we might be able to say something about causes. I am going to make some controversial and I trust innovative suggestions about how we might go about this, using the classificatory procedures which have just been described.

Let me begin by considering the implications of 'deleting variables' in classification. In a complexity based understanding of far from equilibric systems, the term 'control parameters' is often employed. Let me quote myself – and note that I would want to replace the word variable in this passage if I wrote it now:

> When we examine real dynamical systems we often find that their trajectories are governed by particular variable aspects of them rather than by all aspects of them. Note that we are not necessarily dealing with single variables. Rather we may be dealing with several variables and with the interactions among them. However, we are very likely to be able to describe the actual development of a system's trajectory through state space in terms of the effects of a set smaller than that which is used in constructing the state space. The variable(s) in this set are control parameters. It is likely in systems with a complex determinant form that changes in the values of control parameters will produce non-linear changes in the system's trajectory which may involve either catastrophic or chaotic transformations. One implication of the existence of control parameters is that strange attractors may have dimensions less than that of the state space, and that this dimensionality may be fractal. (Byrne, 1998: 171)

I have argued that the actual form of the data matrix which is used in all forms of numerical taxonomy, both neural network techniques and cluster analyses, is actually a representation at a given time point of the state space for the ensemble of systems which is the set of cases in the data set. The entries in the variate trace columns of the data matrix are the co-ordinates of the given cases in this state space. We must be properly reluctant to consider that aspects of individual cases are causal to the form of the state space. In other words we have to be very wary of looking at something measuring the characteristics of an individual system and considering that that something can cause the character of the ensemble.

Class provides an excellent illustration of this point. Rose and O'Reilly's (1997) discussion of socio-economic class (SEC) suggests that we use a single measured attribute to define the class of any given individual. However, the class structure is not something that can be determined by aggregating the nominalist measures of individual classes and presenting these as an account of it. Class is a process and so far as we can measure it, it is certainly multidimensional. Classifying, using lots of measures of variate traces, can provide us with a momentary representation of class structure. Nothing we do in terms of the manipulation of nominal variate traces will change what this is, but relational variate traces are a different matter. I have argued (Byrne, 1999) that the existence of an attractor set describing the lives of individuals and households which we can call 'social exclusion' is a product of the degree of inequality in the social order as a whole. We derive relational variate traces of this kind from the measurement of individual cases but they are not properties of individual cases. However, we can do some interesting things by 'deleting variables'. I have classified two data sets derived from the 1991 Census and for the 1991 Cleveland Social Survey using appropriate indicators of 'social deprivation'. The census data variate traces are percentage indices for enumeration districts, for example, percentage of households containing one or more dependent children with no employed adult in that household. The Cleveland Social Survey variate traces are categorical measures for individual households – this household does or does not consist of at least one dependent child with none of the adults being in employment of any kind. What is interesting is that there is very little difference in the classification systems generated for both data sets, that is, clusters of Enumeration Districts and clusters of households, whether or not the tenure of the household is included. In the 'deprived/excluded' clusters of both households and enumeration districts, households resident in social housing predominate but it makes little difference to the cluster structure whether or not the variate trace housing tenure[6] is used in constructing it.

How do we interpret this? We might consider, correctly, that the cluster structure is rather stable and hence real – following Everitt's (1993) suggestion that selection of variate traces is one method of testing for this. We might conclude that housing tenure is not 'causal' but what does that term mean? What is being caused? Is it the location in the classification structure of any individual case – to use the complexity terminology, the ensemble attractor for that case? Or, is it the whole character of the classification structure itself – the actual set of ensemble attractors in the state space? My argument is that it is both and moreover that housing tenure is simultaneously part of the complex causal mechanism for both individual location and social structure and, recursively, a caused element in relation to individual characteristics and social structure.

Let us, to use a favourite expression of my 6th Form physics teacher,[7] 'think this through'. The actual socio-spatial form of any particular place is, at any given time,[8] a function of the character of the housing tenure system and in particular in postindustrial European cities, of the spatial arrangement and segregation of neighbourhoods by tenure. The socio-spatial form of a locality is one of the important determinants, in a system of complex and contingent causes, of the social structure of that locality. At the same time the policy regime of particular places may be promoting the residualization of social housing as a consequence of deindustrialization and 'exclusive' planning. At the individual level the residual character of social housing means that people who suffer contingencies which residualize them – the female single parent impoverished by divorce for example – are likely to end up resident in social housing. At the same time discriminatory practices against residents of social housing and/or the consequences of simple transport difficulties in getting to available employment, mean that residence in social housing can be part of the complex and contingent set of causes which perpetuate social exclusion for any given individual. Actually the way tenure 'works' in our clustering is wholly compatible with precisely the recursive and multi-level account which has just been presented. This is very far removed from linear causal modelling for individual cases but does have something serious to say to our understanding of social and political change.

Change happens through time. Can classification procedures help us in understanding social and political change? What is absolutely incontrovertible is that the classification procedures can be employed to describe change. Consider cohort data sets represented by the British Household Panel Study. In this study a panel of original households and households derived from that original set are reinterviewed at quite short intervals and a range of variate traces of those households are recorded. There have been studies that record unidimensional movements of those households, particularly in relation to position in the distribution of household income but, not yet published in any event, studies that deal in classifications at time points and record changes.

It is very important to recognize that there are two possible sorts of changes involved when we construct time ordered classifications from a cohort data set. The first relates to changes in the character of the classification system itself. In a study of Northern Tyneside (Byrne, 1989) I found that there was a radical change in the socio-spatial system of that locality as demonstrated by classification of Enumeration Districts in it for the two available time points 1971 and 1981. Note that there were no problems of sampling estimation here. I had data for the whole population of relevant enumeration districts and have since re-checked the data by partitioning and use of several clustering methods and found the classifications to be highly stable for each time point but different in important respects between the two time points. To summarize, the stepped inequalities of the industrial era had been replaced by a much more polarized inequality characteristic of the postindustrial era and these inequalities were expressed in terms of employment engagement, asset ownership and household form. Over the same period inequalities in internal housing standards – amenity levels and density of occupation – had virtually disappeared. In other words, time ordered classifications give us an account of historical change in social structures.

The other level of change is in the classificatory location of individual entities in the data set. Interestingly, in the changing socio-spatial pattern of Enumeration Districts in Northern Tyneside some did change relative location. Some inner areas moved from relatively deprived by category in 1971 to not deprived by category in 1981 and had firmly consolidated this status by 1991 when I examined the data set for the census of that year. This was of course a consequence of 'gentrification', in some instances in existing housing stock and in others by the replacement of social housing with expensive owner occupied housing. The indication from exploration of unidimensional measures of household situation, for example of position in the scale of income distribution, suggests that changes for households occur in the same way. I have discussed the implications of this for our understanding of 'social exclusion' in Byrne (1999). The point is that we can chart movement – for sure. The question is can we understand the sources of movement – can we delve into causal mechanisms.

I am going to argue that we can and do so by considering another sort of data set which charts changes, a very common sort of data set – that generated by the recording of cases through an administrative system. Wendy Dyer at the University of Durham has been examining a data set, in the form of a relational data base,[9] constructed by her which describes the movement of clients through a 'custody diversion' process[10] in the North East of England. The specific nature of the process is not important here because we can generalize the account to any administrative/interventionist system which processes cases through a series of 'treatments'. Basically, the raw material is the data file, electronically recorded as part of a relational data base. The processing of cases through time can be examined in terms of a series of classifications of the cases at stages in their career within the system. It is important to note that the temporal dimension is not calendar time although calendar duration has to be recorded as a variate trace. Rather it is stage in the process. Systems of this kind do 'process' cases and what is interesting and important for us is what difference the processing makes to the outcome for the case. We can certainly describe this using stage ordered classificatory procedures. We can distinguish categories of entry, that is, distinctions among original cases; categories of processing, differences in what is done to individual cases; and categories of outcome, what happens to the cases at the end of the process. We can map movement through the state space of the intervention process. The suggestion is that by re-examining internal characteristics of cases and processes in interaction we can determine what kind of complex causal processes produce good rather than bad outcomes. Note here that there is no suggestion that there is a single 'good treatment'. There may well be a variety of ways of arriving at a good as opposed to bad outcome, even for cases with inherently similar original characteristics, but we need to distinguish good processes from bad. Moreover, we can relate original differentiation in cases to differentiation in outcomes as mediated through differentiation in processes. What works for some (what being plural) won't work for others and we can explore to see what this is.

What is being attempted here can be understood with the help of Katherine Hayles's (critical) comment (1999: 233) on simulation procedures to the effect that information technologies seem to enable us to look directly into the inner workings of reality. We will return to this issue in Chapter 8. Let us perhaps agree that we can peer into the elements of the particular world, the world of a processing system, although that peering is exactly into the world in its complexity, rather than any elemental version of it. In effect we are using the data management capacities of IT to look at lots of things at once – exactly distributed processing whatever the actual form of the computer operation. We are using IT methods to compare what is and to try to distinguish what has happened to systems which have had very different trajectories over time.

This seems to be explicitly anti-reductionist but at the same time to facilitate carefully qualified and delimited generalization. It cannot be said strongly or often enough that generalization must always be generalization within limits. Our knowledge is always local – nevertheless it is knowledge.

There is one final point to make about classifying before we turn to modelling and Hacking has made it for us:

> in the case of natural kinds, classifying in itself does not make any difference to the things classified. Thinking of things as a kind, and giving a name to that class of things, does not of itself make any difference to the things so distinguished. ... entities – people and their acts [are] of a kind [that] can change in response to being grouped, that the group thereby changes. In this way human kinds have feedback, a looping effect unknown in the inhuman world. (1992: 189–90)

Here we are setting a subsidiary boundary within the 'natural' as defined by Khalil (1996). The point has already been noted in relation to Desrosières's discussion of the general character of statistics. Our processes of social measurement play a part in remaking the social world which they describe. Hacking is making the same point in a more specific way. When we group things – his example being the particular actions which are now defined as 'child abuse' – our groupings become part of the repertoire of social actors and influence the character of their actions. We shall return to these issues of 'reflexivity/recursivity' in general terms in Chapter 9.

Conclusion

This chapter has had two related objectives. It was intended to argue for classification as a central principle in the exploration of the dynamic character of the social world and of the trajectories of individual and other systems within that world. This means that it developed the arguments about classification presented in Chapter 2 by reviewing how ideas about classification have shaped recent scientific practice. It was also intended as a guide to the use of readily available procedures in the actual conduct of classificatory social research. As is so often the case in science, new practices develop before the revolutionary potential of those practices is recognized for what it is. That is certainly the case with numerical taxonomy. The final injunction here must be – go to it! Social scientists have enormous data resources and the thing to do now is to use them to explore and to compare, with the theme of comparison being one to which we will return in Chapter 9 when we look at the convergence of qualitative and quantitative procedures.

Notes

1 'Get a grip' is a very useful phrase. It relates both to understanding and to the actions of changing.

2 Given the ease of obtaining large secondary data sets and the convenience of providing them to students, we should work with such sets, which are the kind of thing students will identify in real research processes. Even data labelling is now being automated through scanning procedures and the use of packages like FORMIC.

3 In Tukey's terminology a step is 1.5 times the inter-quartile range. An outlier is a case more than one step above or below the appropriate quartile value – away from the boundaries of the midbox. Far outliers are two or more steps away from the boundaries of the midbox.

4 This is a crucial point at which pre-existing theory informs the outcome of the empirical exercise. The choice of criteria as the basis of a classification has fundamental implications for the character of the classification and is intrinsically theoretical and a priori. Garson puts it like this when he identifies 'a growing consensus in the research community ... that whatever methodological procedure is used, the critical factor is judicious selection of the menu of independent variables' (1998: 10).

5 My own first use of the technique was in classifying English and Welsh Local Education Authorities in the 1970s; see Byrne et al., 1975.

6 More precisely for the household level data set, the set of binary attributes derived from the original categorical variable.

7 Probably the ablest teacher I have ever been taught by so I am more than happy to use his mode of expression.

8 Time matters because the implications of tenure in a postindustrial locality are very different from those in that same locality when it was industrial.

9 Relational data bases can be distinguished from the 'flat file' as represented, for example, by a case entry in the SPSS spreadsheet. In the flat file all data about and relevant to the case is stored in one location as one row of a data file. In a relational data base file elements are stored in different locations – for example there may be different components for each passage of a case through the system – but can be brought together by use of a common identifier for the case. Relational data bases have the enormous added advantage of permitting storage of data about other hierarchical levels to which a case may belong, for example data about households, and the capacity to bring this back to the level of individuals within that household. In a flat file format all data for all levels has to be written to the lowest level if it is to be used at that level. In other words, all information about housing conditions in a household would have to be written to the data entry for every member of the household. In a relational data base only one household level record is required.

10 Custody diversion projects have been established in the UK in an attempt to cope with the difficulties that arise from the shift from institutional to community care for mentally ill people when mentally ill people enter the criminal justice system in consequence of committing criminal offences. It is generally agreed that ordinary custodial sentences are inappropriate. Custody diversion takes people identified as 'mentally ill' (with the original identification of course being a crucial processual stage) and employs a variety of strategies to handle their future trajectories with the objective being no re-offending.

7

Linear Modelling: Clues as to Causes

This chapter is a ground clearing exercise. It is intended to get 'the General Linear Model' out of our way so that we can proceed to better things. By now it should be clear that this text's commitment to 'complex realism' means that it argues against linearity, analysis and the reification of 'variables'. The General Linear Model is founded on a frame of linear equations, works with 'variables' and is essentially a programme of understanding causes through the analysis of data. In an ideal world we wouldn't start from here in outlining a programme of quantitative interpretation of cause.[1] However, this world is not ideal. Linear Modelling exists and comprises an important set of techniques in quantitative social science, some of which techniques are quite useful. Others, it has to be said very firmly, are not and are founded on the most fundamental of ontological errors about the status of 'variables'. We need to sort the useful from the dross.

Moreover, and more importantly at this point in the development of quantitative social science, we have to deal with the experiences which we have as social scientists. Almost all of us have been brought up on the General Linear Model (GLIM) as the account which enables us to understand causal processes, even if more modest statisticians are often careful to point out that there is no logical foundation for inferring from a model to a causal system. Recently, particularly in the UK, some rather excessive claims have been made for the potential for linear modelling techniques as 'the foundation' of a new and better quantitative programme.[2] The UK Economic and Social Research Council (ESRC) has attempted to prescribe the achievement of a high level of competence in linear modelling as the most important component of generic research training for all the PhD students funded by it, although this has provoked considerable opposition in the academic social science community. This is very much the time to put linear modelling in its place, which is that of a limited part of the exploratory repertoire of the quantitative social scientist and nothing more. It may well have a more important role in relation to the interpretation of the products of experiments in domains where experiments are useful, but when we deal with the products of surveys, with accounts of the world as becoming – that is, as a set of nested complex evolutionary systems, as inherently dynamic – then mundane exploration is as far as it goes.

Statistical models

The General Linear Model is by far the most important example of a 'statistical model' and all the procedures we are going to discuss in this chapter are basically variants of it. It is therefore useful to begin by attempting to define statistical models. Bradley and Schaefer in a book that represents an important sceptical move in understanding 'the mathematization of the human sciences', define the general idea of modelling in a way we have already encountered, that is, as a simplified representation of the way the world works:

> Modeling is the process of *formalizing* our framework for understanding the world around us by *abstracting* from a reality that is otherwise too complex for us to understand. In fact modeling is the central intellectual method that characterizes most empirical and mathematical approaches to the social sciences. (1998: 23)

If we refer back to Hayles's discussion of the platonic backhand and forehand we might see modelling as crucial to both and in both founded around simplification of complex reality. Remember Cilliers's precise and severe warning against any effort to describe complex systems in anything other than complex terms. Modelling as 'simplification' offends exactly against that canon of complex reasoning. Bradley and Schaefer's observation that 'Humans always impose structure through abstraction and modeling may be merely a way of forming this structure solidly' (1998: 37), should be amended to read: '*Some* humans *have* always imposed ...'; it is time to do things differently or rather to reinforce the alternative tradition of exploration of the whole as the basis of articulation of understanding.

Krzanowksi provides us with a very clear account of the nature of specifically statistical modelling:

> Analysis ... assumes *inter alia* that the available data forms only a subset of all the data that *might* have been collected, and then attempts to use the information in the available data to make more general statements about either the larger set or about the mechanism that is producing the data. ... In order to make such statements, we need first to abstract the essence of the data-producing mechanism into a form that is amenable to mathematical and statistical treatment. Such a formulation will typically involve mathematical equations that express relationships between measured 'variables' and assumptions about the random processes that govern the outcome of individual measurements. That is the statistical *model* of the system. Fitting the model to a given set of data will then provide a framework for extrapolating the results to a wider context or for predicting future outcomes, and can often also lead to an explanation of the system. (1998: ix)

Everitt and Dunn were far more cautious, and logically correct, when they stated that: 'In this text ... a model is considered to be a way of simplifying and portraying the structure in a set of data, and does not necessarily imply any causal mechanisms' (1983: 5). However, the search for cause is the general motivation and almost invariably those who use statistical models generalize beyond the data set to which the models are applied. Gilbert's definition conveys the motive for modelling very clearly indeed:

> A model is a theory or a set of hypotheses which attempts to explain the connections and inter-relationships between social phenomena. Models are made up of *concepts* and *relationships* between concepts. (1993: 2)

That brings in all the complications of operationalization but it does sum up what people are about when they engage in modelling.

There is one other component to the statistical model (and to the stochastic model which in this sense of stochastic is a statistical model which develops in a temporal and/or spatial fashion). That is an essential element of randomness. Generally speaking, the models are considered to have two components, namely a systematic component which corresponds to the researcher's conception of causal processes, and a random component which reflects the degree of variation in expressed effects. There are two ways of treating this variation. One is to follow Poincaré and to consider it as the outcome of causal processes which we have either not defined or not been able to measure to a sufficient degree of accuracy. The other is to think of randomness as an inherent property of nature. Statisticians vary between these positions, often in the same text. The first is a story of determination but incomplete knowledge. The second is one of randomness as real in itself.

We can see how this works if we consider the usual algebraic form of the linear equation. In a relatively simple example of the general linear model, that of the multiple regression of a single dependent variable on a set of more than one 'causal'[3] 'variables', we can express the model thus:

$$y = b^1x^1 + b^2x^2 + b^3x^3 \ldots\ldots + b^nx^n + \text{error term}$$

Error term is often described as residual. It is that part of the variation in the 'dependent variable' for a given case which is left unexplained by the model. The fit of the model overall is evaluated by comparing the sum of the variation 'explained' across all cases for the 'dependent variable' with the sum of the variation left unexplained. In the above equation we can see many of the things which characterize linear models. In particular we can see that it has been traditional to express models in the form of equations in which the systematic component is considered to be the equivalent of a mechanistic and deterministic expression of a relation in Newtonian mechanics. Following this tradition, great emphasis is placed in theoretical terms on the value of the coefficients, the *b*s in the equation, which describe the form of the relationship between 'causal' 'variables' and the caused element. There is an addition to the Newtonian form in that the 'random' element is also given serious attention through the use of probability distributions as discussed in Chapter 5 but the basic account of cause remains mechanical. At least it does in principle. Other than in econometrics, which bizarre activity is beyond the scope of this volume, and to a lesser and even useful extent in demography and epidemiology, social scientists actually pay very little attention to the form of causal relationships. They are far more interested in the strength of those relationships – in correlation coefficients rather than beta coefficients.

Other than when they are essential for illustration, this text forswears equations wherever possible. In my opinion sets of equations are all too often a screen behind which the essentially trivial products of linear reasoning can safely be hidden. In discussing the use of the General Linear Model in causal reasoning we can often turn to an alternative, the iconic representation of a Venn diagram as in Figure 7.1. In Venn diagrams the relationships between two sets are indicated by the degree of intersection of the circles representing the sets. Here the sets represent the variation in the individual 'variables'. The dark hatched area in the y set represents the amount of variation in y 'explained' by the set of 'independent' 'variables' – R^2 in conventional notation. The remaining area represents unexplained variation.

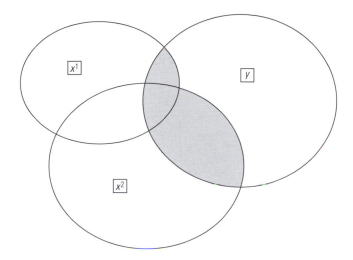

Figure 7.1   *Multiple regression as the General Linear Model*

Usually in causal accounts derived from the General Linear Model cause is assessed in some way that involves a measurement of the amount of variation 'explained' by the model. These models are often called 'structural models' because they describe the structural relationships among the 'variables'.

There is another variant of the use of models in which the objective seems to be not so much explanation as prediction – the general focus of Markov chain derived models and much of the repertoire of time series techniques. Here we have an interesting move. Statistical models are handled in a non-analytical way. There is no effort to decompose/analyse in order to establish causes. Rather the objective is to achieve a good retrodictive fit with the intention of using this to predict the future without any necessary causal understanding of generative processes. In other words, in important respects the models are black boxes. We will come back to this theme in the next chapter when we consider neural net approaches. In the remainder of this chapter we will go through the common and important examples of the use of the general linear model in the exploration of survey generated (but not experimental) data.

Flowgraphs: partial correlation and path analysis

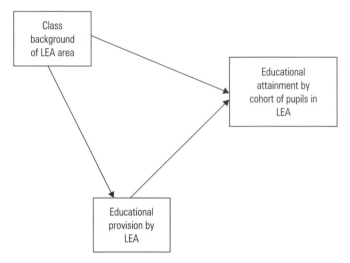

Figure 7.2   *A flowgraph*

Figure 7.2 describes a model of the relationship among three things – the class composition of the population of a Local Education Authority (LEA),[4] the educational provision made for children in that LEA area, and some measure of the educational attainment of the cohort of children who receive that provision. It suggests through the use of directional arrows that both class background and resources influence attainment and that class background has an impact on resource availability. This was basically the model that Byrne et al. tested in their 1970s studies. The measures of class background, provision and attainment can be compound indices – the product of taking several 'variables' in each relevant set together rather than a single measure. It is important to note that this is single level examination so no issues of ecological correlation arise. The cases are the LEAs and all the measures are at the LEA level with class background and attainment measures being aggregate measures for the LEA as a whole. We can represent relations among the 'variables' as in the modified version of Figure 7.1, which is Figure 7.3.

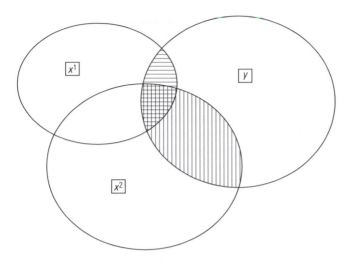

Figure 7.3 *Partial correlations*

In Figure 7.3 the horizontally hatched area represents the squared partial correlation coefficient between x^1 and y, that is, the amount of variation in y explained by x^1 which is not in common between x^1, x^2 and y. The vertically hatched area represents the equivalent for x^2 and y. The cross-hatched area is the common variation for all three 'variables'.

The problem with regression derived models is that the approach is inherently variable centred and does not describe the reality of the trajectories of complex systems. Let us turn from this old friend of mine to a set of procedures which I have always considered to be wrongheaded and dangerous – those which interpret measured 'variables' as indicators of 'real' latent 'variables' – reification squared and, in the case of structural equation modelling, cubed.

Working with 'latent' variables – making things out of things that don't exist anyhow

In the platonic world-view held to by many statisticians and quantitative researchers there exist somewhere 'true variables', real forms, of which our measurements are imperfect representations like the shadows beyond the fire in Plato's myth of the cave. The problem we have, in this frame of understanding, is that we cannot know the real by measuring but only imperfect indications, indices, of it. Everitt and Dunn put it like this:

> In many areas of psychology, sociology and the like it is often not possible to measure directly the concepts that are of major interest. Two obvious examples are intelligence and social class. In such cases the researcher will often collect

information on variables likely to be indicators of the concepts in question and then try to discover whether the relationships between these observed variables are consistent with their being measures of a singly underlying latent variable, or whether some more complex structure has to be postulated. (1983: 191)

Following E.P. Thompson, we have already been horrified by the notion of the complex relation of social class being expressed as a single variable. There is a massive and abundant literature on the problems that have derived from the reification of the notion of General Intelligence (G) as a single factor. It is interesting to note that the techniques from which these kinds of procedures derive have a most suspect history as part of the efforts to promote a eugenics programme through rational scientific reasoning in Britain in the inter-war years.[5]

Basically, as with the examples of multiple regression and partial regression/ correlation outlined above, the raw material of these kinds of investigations is a matrix describing the relationships among a set of ratio scale measured variables.[6] For the simpler and older set of procedures generically described as 'factor analysis' the basic underlying model is that indicated by Figure 7.4.

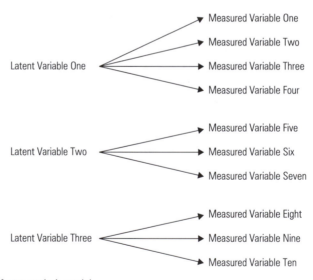

Figure 7.4   A factor analysis model

There are a range of factor analysis procedures available in all standard statistical packages. Essentially the factors – Latent Variables One to Three in Figure 7.4 – are generated by mathematical manipulation of the data matrix and are specified in a form which describes the correlations of the latent 'variables' with the actual measurements. Typically the factors are then labelled in a way which reflects the pattern of those correlations. The factors are made from the data matrix, which itself is based on the measurement of the variate traces of real complex systems. Factor models are sometimes called measurement models because the focus is on elucidating through indirect measurement the true nature of the 'latent variables'.

Factor analysis – bad: structural equation models – worse! In structural equation models we have a causal proposition in which there are considered to be two sets of index measurements in the data set. The first set are indices of underlying latent 'explanatory variables'. The second set are indices of underlying latent 'response variables'. Linking these is a series of linear 'structural' equations. Essentially structural equation models combine measurement models as with factor analyses and structural models as with multiple regression. Figure 7.5 shows the nature of such models.

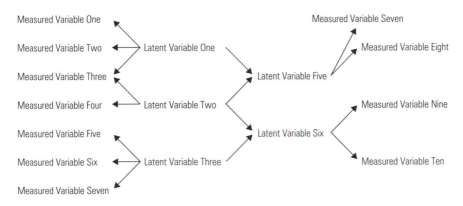

Figure 7.5   *A structural equation model*

In structural equation modelling we find an interesting departure from the principles of formal hypothetico-deductive reasoning. Basically the postulated models – note the plural – are tested against the data set to find the simplest (most parsimonious in the jargon) that fits the data set without being 'under-identified', that is, has more than one solution to the simultaneous equations, or 'over-identified', that is, has more equations than are needed to provide a unique set of solutions for all parameters. The approach is iterative with a start set of values for the parameters – the various coefficients which describe the structural model. The procedure works out the model that fits best.

It might be thought that it would be impossible to specify detailed hypotheses in advance in structural equation modelling. After all, the procedure elucidates 'reality' by establishing the latent causal and caused 'variables' whilst setting up the form of the relationships among them. However, in practice it seems that researchers assign particular measures to an underlying latent causal or caused 'variable'. Thus Bynner (1994) illustrates the approach by reference to a study by Bachman et al. (1978) of the relationship between social group formation and delinquency in adolescent males. The competing hypotheses were in essence that young men become delinquent in groups to establish status versus that delinquent young men seek out fellow delinquents to form social groups. There is a third 'null' hypothesis that neither relationship holds. In this study the researchers assigned certain measured variables to be the basis of the latent variables for delinquency and assigned all other variate elements to single measured variables – not a lot of latency going on.

Essentially in this study the underlying conception of what mattered derives not from a truly empirical investigation of potential latent 'variables' but from the theoretical presuppositions of the researchers. They did test their theory against the data and found it to be weakly sustained in a particular time ordered model. There is an empirical element. There is nothing wrong with the prioritizing of theory in setting up models but it sits oddly with the kind of abstracted empiricism which is applied to the rules for testing models. The example offered by Bynner makes reasonable sense, subject to the strictures about using 'variables' in models which are developed further in the conclusion to this chapter. However, it is interesting that there was so much theoretical specification and that is what made the thing work, after a fashion. Let us turn to multi-level modelling which represents a genuine attempt to cope with a real problem in exploring and interpreting data.

Multi-level models

> Most social science data are structured hierarchically. Examples are the clustering of students within schools, individuals within households with neighbourhoods, and repeated measurements within individual subjects. … Researchers dealing with large and complex structures, such as longitudinal panel surveys or studies of educational performance, require modelling techniques which respect the hierarchical and cross-classified structures in their data. (ALCD, 1997a)

In the discussion of Figure 7.2, I was careful to point out that the 'dependent variable' was not educational attainment for any individual child but rather the aggregate educational attainment of cohorts of children passing through educational systems. It is perfectly valid to relate data across a single level. The problem of cross-level inference arises when we infer from relationships at one level to relationships at another. Robinson's classic paper (1950) showed that the relationship between being native born in the United States and being illiterate was small and positive if measured for individuals and large and negative if measured for aggregates defined at the state level. We can say that for states literacy was higher the greater the proportion of the population native born. We cannot say that individuals were more likely to be literate if native born. If we are looking to explore relationships at lower levels within a hierarchy we must take account of this.

Note that this classical illustration of the 'ecological fallacy' relates to the higher level comparison of two variables which are constructed from the aggregation of lower level data. This is not at all the same thing as comparing variables which are properly measured at different levels. Often the higher levels are not merely aggregates. They are rather containing systems within a nested structure with properties that are relevant for the lower levels. This is particularly evident in education, where in England and Wales, the LEA, school and school class all have an impact on the individual pupil. But we cannot measure those impacts in any way at the individual level, only for the higher level containing unit. Multi-level modelling is a method of trying to deal with this real structure of data. As Goldstein puts it:

> the multi-level modelling approach views the population structure as of potential interest in itself, so that a sample designed to reflect that structure is not merely a matter of saving costs as in traditional survey design but can be used to collect and analyse data about the higher level units in the population. (1995: 5)

Much of the literature on multi-level modelling is concerned with educational performance and it is worth discussing the context of the technique. Typically, in educational multi-level models the 'dependent variable' is some measure of performance, usually in terms of achieved standard in a public examination. Often the measures are those used in the new consumer information sets of performance statistics. Goldstein and his colleagues (Goldstein and Spiegelhalter, 1996; Plewis, 1994) have paid particular attention to patterns of differences among schools and have argued that these can be demonstrated to be insignificant *if* school populations are treated as samples and variation year on year is considered. Draper (1996: 417), in the discussion of Goldstein and Spiegelhalter's paper, made a trenchant criticism of this assumption and argued, for me convincingly, that there was no random element at the institutional level at all because we had information about all of them. Goldstein and Spiegelhalter's argument is actually a very clear illustration of statisticians' belief in randomness for its own sake. There was data about all the components of the population but that data was treated as sample data from a hypothetical infinite population.

There is another contextual element to deal with here. The 'dependent variables' in educational research are typically attainment measures. When we think about the actual life trajectories of the systems represented by individual children we must surely recognize that any given component of cognitive development or knowledge acquisition or even credential achievement, only works in complex interaction with all the other components of the individual child as a system. However, in pedagogical research it is perfectly appropriate to be interested in improving performance in relation to any single set of measures. Understood in this way the kind of retrodictive, and essentially asocial, multi-level modelling engaged in by Goldstein and his co-workers can be understood as an effort to use survey generated data as the basis of quasi-experimental evaluation. In other words, the search is for the causes of the specific measured dependent variables in a way which gets past the problems associated with cross-level inference.

Plewis's discussion of multi-level modelling is clear and interesting. He describes models in which both mean attainment levels vary among schools and associations between 'causal variables' are stronger in some schools than in others. This latter development means that the models address issues of interaction both within and across levels of data. It is worth emphasizing that when Plewis turns to graphical representation of his findings what he does is specify three types of school – in other words, a statistical model generates a classification. For me it is the classification that is interesting because it points to policy interventions which might change the school's classified status towards one which generates better pedagogical results.

Although I find the treatment of population data as if it were sample data at the very least contentious, it is interesting that multi-level modelling which makes, as it were, an ontological effort, does seem to be quite useful as an exploratory technique. Its explanatory power may be limited, but then as always with the General Linear Model in whatever form, there is an inherent attempt to impose linearity on a non-linear world coupled with the problem of the reification of 'variables'. Before we turn to the one set of procedures which I think can be made to work in a way that is cognate with a complex realist dynamic social world, let us, briefly, consider models which don't analyse but do attempt to predict.

Statistical black boxes – Markov chains as an example

This discussion will be extremely brief! In general Markov chain models describe sequences in which what comes next depends only on the immediately preceding state. A typical use is in speech recognition. A word 'hidden' in noise can be recognized by reference to what has just been said. There are several discussions of the application of Markov methods in social science, particularly in relation to longitudinal data (see Langehiene and van de Pol, 1994). The most interesting thing about this family of approaches is what it is for. Markov models seem to offer little analytical guidance. Rather, finding a Markov variant that can be retrodictively fitted to a data set is the basis for prediction – as in the current use in attempting to separate sequences of genetic bases which are components of message carrying genes from the 'static' in the genetic code. Given this, Markov methods seem to be a special set of 'off the shelf' black boxes. They are not wholly black box in that there is a mathematical description of the workings of the mechanism – the specification of the model – but there is no real process of reasoning about why one particular model fits as opposed to another. In other words, there is no real discussion of isomorphism between theory and model. If it fits, use it to predict. Fair enough for practical clearing of noise – we might say, and go on to say – but not for any sort of understanding of how the social world works.

Loglinear techniques – exploring for interaction

> Statisticians, like theologians, are generally concerned with the here and now
> only to the extent it reflects the unknown and unknowable – that is the profes-
> sionals focus on problems of estimation (sampling error) while we amateurs
> sweat over what these particular data are trying to say. This division of labour is
> sensible. They know how to whip out theorems and we know what we are
> trying to find out. (Davis, 1984: xv)

In this section we are going to examine procedures which social scientists
actually use quite a lot in trying to find out things of some significance for
both understanding and the development of policy. With the exception of
the educational uses of multi-level modelling, that is not really very much
the case for the procedures we have discussed previously in this chapter.
However, loglinear and related techniques are used, extensively, and we
should know how and think about whether they have anything to offer to
those of use working in a complex realist frame of reference.

Basically the techniques we are going to consider are about 'how to get more
out of contingency tables'. Contingency tables are the typical products of
survey research. We relate categorical 'variables' to each other and construct
cells occupied by cases sharing the same value on two or more 'variables'.
The cell members belong to a category which is polythetic in Aristotelian
terms. Everybody who has ever used MINITAB or SPSS should know how
to construct a multidimensional table. Now we are going to see how we can
make more out of such tables.

The traditional mode for handling elaborated tables reflects the form in
which statistical packages deliver them to us. Figure 7.6 shows how we
might draw the three-dimensional table relating three categorical 'variables'
on a two-dimensional surface.

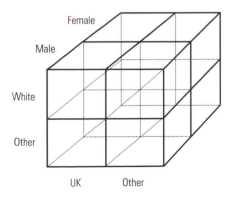

Figure 7.6   *A two way table relating gender, ethnicity and citizenship*

The usual way of elaborating tables of this form is to slice them up into two-dimensional tables. In the case of the above table we can slice three ways. We can examine the relationship between ethnicity and citizenship separately for each gender, we can examine the relationship between gender and citizenship separately for each ethnicity, and we can examine the relationship between gender and ethnicity separately for each citizenship. Typically, we construct these tables and then use Chi-squared to see if relationships are significant in our 'slice' and a categorical measure of association such as Cramer's V to measure the strength of any significant relationship.

If we really want to analyse, a procedure that requires us to 'believe' in the reality of 'variables', then Hellevik (1984) provides a very clearly explained and easy to implement set of procedures for so doing. When I believed in 'variables' this was my bible because it is so lucid, but if 'variables' have the same status as Santa Claus, then we have to do something different.

Fortunately there is something different we can do in the form of the loglinear analysis and its relatives. These techniques are variable based and involve the exploration of contingency tables constructed from cells which are polythetic categories, but they have one enormous advantage – they find interaction if it is going on.

The general approach can be illustrated by considering loglinear methods. What we have when we start is a multidimensional contingency table which 'describes' our data set. We can use statistical packages to reconstruct this contingency table from the marginal values in it which the package will calculate for us from the raw case 'variable' data matrix.

If we specify all possible relationships that might exist, then the package will simply regenerate the original data set. In the case of the table illustrated in Figure 7.6 the possible relationships are:

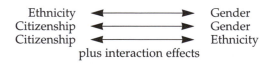

In other words everything might 'cause' everything else and the value of any given third variable would affect the form of the relationship between the other two variables.

In effect, what loglinear methods allow us to do is to specify simpler models, which as social scientists we should always specify on some pre-existing knowledge basis rather than just fishing through the data in an empiricist fashion to find the simplest, and see how well these reproduce the contingency table. The procedure calculates a significance level, usually G^2 which is analogous to Chi-squared, and which here is used not to test a specific hypothesis but rather as an exploratory tool which enables us to assess the degree of fit of a given theoretically founded model (see Gilbert, 1993: 72–3).

In the example (wholly hypothetical) illustrated by Figure 7.6 we might find that the following model had a significance level of 0.42:[7]

Ethnicity  Citizenship

with nothing else being necessary. In other words we could reproduce the table to a high degree by considering only the relationship between Ethnicity and Citizenship. Note that like Chi-squared, G^2 doesn't summarize the strength of the model. It merely indicates that the model generates a statistically significant reconstruction of the table. The equivalent of measures of association in a simple bivariate table is the coefficient of multiple determination which measures the proportion of the total variation in cell frequencies 'explained' by the model. This is not particularly useful as its value tends to be high for any model which has a reasonable degree of fit, in contrast say with Cramer's V which can tell us that a highly significant relationship observed on the basis of a large sample can have little substantive significance. It is more conventional to use 'odds ratios' which summarize the implications for the value of one 'variable' which flow from changing the category measure on another 'variable'. This begins to look rather causal in terms of its implications since odds ratios are used, for example, to make a comparison between marriage survival rates respectively for couples who have and have not cohabited prior to marriage.

Let us consider a real example which illustrates the impact of interaction. In Byrne et al. (1985) we found that when we expressed the relationships among housing conditions, health status and age group for a sample of council tenants in Gateshead, we had to fit an interaction term between age and housing conditions to reproduce the model. For all age groups under the age of 65 there was a positive relationship between housing conditions and health status – the better the housing the better the health. For those over 65 the better the housing the worse the health and obviously vice versa.

This surprising finding is easily explained. In other words we could relate it to a real social process.[8] Gateshead council housing in the middle 1980s included a substantial component of 'sheltered housing' for older people. All of this housing was 'good' by all the indicators we had to measure the quality of housing. A key method by which people gained access to this housing was by medical certification of pre-existing ill health. In other words poor health, absolutely properly, got you good housing if you were old. This process operated for other age groups but without a dedicated category of good housing associated with it and therefore did not affect the general form of the relationship between housing and health for those age groups. In other words although there was a process of medical certification it did not have substantive effects.

The use of loglinear procedures can go beyond fitting overall models using G^2 as a measure of correspondence. These procedures have been quite extensively used in the study of social mobility and here particular attention has been paid to residuals in a standardized or adjusted standardized form. Basically the use of these measures when plotted out either in a three-dimensional histogram for tables with three original dimensions or in summarizing plots for higher dimensional tables, facilitates an exploration of which parts of the actual situation as represented by the contingency table do not fit the overall model.

A more analytical approach depends on the implications of structural values. Real structural values are cells in a contingency table which have their values fixed in advance in some way. For example, if we crosstabulate household type against numbers of dependent children we know that all single person households will have not children present. This is a pre-existing structural value but tables can be constrained in a way that treats selected cells as structural and thus allows for a 'control' analysis of other effects. In mobility studies we might treat the cells representing men who remain in the same social class as their father as structural and thereby examine the effects of father's social class only on those who do move class position (see Gilbert, 1993: 88). This process is 'partitioning' and it creates 'topological' models.

Analysis is taken further in logistic regression in which one 'variable' is explicitly identified as 'dependent' and the objective is to explain variation in it by reference to the other 'variables'. This is essentially equivalent to multiple regression but with categorical rather than continuous 'variables'. The distinction is between the objective of reproducing the overall situation as described by the data – the formal objective of loglinear models – and 'explaining' the values of a single 'variable' in the system.

Logistic regression is an explicitly linear technique which treats 'variables' as if they were real and possessed causal powers. In contrast basic loglinear techniques can be understood as attempts to describe the character of whole systems through accounts of the character of the variate traces of those systems and of interactions among the variate traces. We can illustrate the difference by considering how we might use loglinear procedures in handling longitudinal data.

Let us consider a data set of our ideal form for exploring complex trajectories and emergence through time, say that of a Cleveland cohort of households which have formed a panel over the period in which that locality has been transformed from industrial to postindustrial. We have here hierarchical data at three levels because we have data about each of the following:

- The individual members of the households, for example, gender, age band, economic activity.
- The characteristics of the household as a whole, including both 'whole household' characteristics such as housing tenure and those formed from an examination of individual level characteristics such as a measure of 'employment engagement' of household members.

- The character of the locality in which the households live measured in terms of the structure of employment base, degree of socio-spatial polarization and so on.

In Chapter 6 we have discussed how we can use data measured at the middle of these three levels in order to construct, through the use of numerical taxonomy procedures, category sets at different time points. We can then chart the movement of households among these category sets over time. Essentially we are constructing descriptions of ensemble attractors in a social state space and charting both the change in the character of the attractors over time and movement of individual household systems among the attractor sets.

Clusters – our method of specifying attractor sets – can be understood as something like prototypical classifications systems. There is no requirement that all members of a cluster should be alike on all the variate traces which have been used to construct the clusters. In contrast, a cell in a multidimensional contingency table is a polythetic class because all cases in that cell are identical in terms of all the measured variate traces which have been used in constructing that cell. If we think of cells as classes, even if somewhat inflexible polythetic classes, then we can handle our interpretation of them in a different way.

For example, if we have time ordered data then we can construct multivariate tables at different time points. In terms of complexity theory this is a process of taking Poincaré slices at time points. We can chart movement of cases among cells over those time points and consider what has changed for those cases over that time. In essence we can try to delve into the complexity of the case and see if we can identify control parameters. Note, and this is very important, we may find that changes are to be understood as caused by complexes of aspects *and* of the interactions within those complexes. The key difference is that we fossick in cases rather than focus on variables. It is as much a matter of reinterpreting what we are doing as of doing something differently.

The use of control parameters here cannot be simply considered as equivalent to 'variable'. There may be true external variates, variates that may well operate at a different level from that of the case as with the change from an industrial to a postindustrial system. Here the change is a holistic property of another significant system at another level. The other true variates may be external impositions in relation to specific cases, although this is not commonly found outside clinical or pedagogical sessions as we saw in Chapter 2. Far more commonly we will find that what makes things change is some complex subset of the overall complex system.

Classification techniques and loglinear exploration of contingency tables are always complements. That is to say we should always adopt both approaches with our data. We can go further in that we can combine the approaches through using cluster membership itself as a categorical variable for input into a loglinear model or even, with great caution, into a logistic model. Crosstabulation is in principle one of the easiest ways to actually relate cluster membership at one time point to cluster membership at another, at least in broad descriptive terms. We can simply crosstabulate cluster membership at time one against membership of what may be a different set of clusters at time two in order to get a global picture of stability and movement. This would seem a far better way of exploring mobility data than the search for single variable explanations of change in position. In a logistic model we might construct several clusterings at time one and map the relationship of these among each other and with an outcome measure at a subsequent time point.

The key difference is that instead of imagining 'variables' in the ether which are acting externally on the cases, instead we see how the complex locations of the cases within different systems interact with each other to produce an outcome for the case. In a mobility example we might locate a case in clusters derived separately from measures of familial context and educational experience and have a subsequent measure of occupational location. This would enable us to chart how for cases relations work together to generate different futures.

Conclusion

A lot of effort has been devoted to causal model building in the social sciences. A number of grandiose claims have been made for the potential of these approaches, although all who have seriously considered the issue are cautious about the logical assignment of causal power on the basis of model fitting. There is a lot of camouflage in the exercise. One cannot blame professional statisticians for taking issues of sampling distribution seriously but the constant reporting of regression coefficients and their analogues has no justification.

Outside economics, demography and epidemiology there is no programme of detailed model specification in the social sciences. By this I mean that there has been no effort to construct a general mathematical model which describes in a direct fashion the character of social life. As noted in Chapter 2, the social indicators movement of the 1960s had the objective of a social model, analogous to the economic model which could then be used to predict the consequences of macro-social interventions. This objective has long been abandoned. Given the absence of a general interpreted social model, or even of much in the small scale interpretations of particular social contexts in a form that can be represented by any kind of dynamic model, it seems appropriate to conclude that much of the mathematical reportage in quantitative articles which deals with form of relationship rather than strength of relationship serves the purpose of a smokescreen in concealing the banality of the import of the application of the model. There isn't much to say but it can't half be said fancy.

I don't think all linear modelling is useless, but for it to be really useful to us we have to think of it as one of a set of tools which might enable us to get some insight into the workings of complex systems. That requires a reforging of the technique to modify it from its apparent analytical purpose. We will now turn to two related approaches – simulation and neural net modelling – which are by no means intrinsically analytic.

Notes

1 And we haven't because time ordered comparative classification has already been proposed as a way of exploring causal processes in terms of control parameters. See Chapter 6.

2 Revealingly, in a key text in this project (Dale and Davies, 1994) the models are described as a set of 'methods'. The setting of method as prior to model has the effect of rendering less apparent the provisional and metaphorical character of any quantitative exploration.

3 Cautious statisticians refer to 'antecedent' 'variables'.

4 LEAs administer schools in the UK. They are units of local government which are multi-purpose and are described as LEAs in their educational capacity.

5 This is fully detailed in MacKenzie (1979). It is only right to note that the eugenics programme advocated by Pearson was not racist in character but rather reflected a commitment to an intellectual (as opposed to aristocratic, plutocratic or racial) elite.

6 Ordinal variables are often treated as ratio and nominal variables are incorporated by transforming them into binary attributes and treating the resulting values of one and zero as continuous. However, in principle, for sample based data these procedures impose considerable demands in terms of assumptions about measurement level and the actual true distribution of 'variables' in the populations sampled. They are 'parametric' procedures.

7 When we calculate G^2 in loglinear procedures we want as high a value for probability as possible in contrast to Chi-squared where very small probability values indicate significance. For G^2 we are assessing the degree of fit of the model. With Chi-squared we are rejecting a null hypothesis of no relationship.

8 Conventionally the word mechanism would be used instead of process but in my view the conventional use of this word is to be avoided. It still has Newtonian implications.

8

Coping with Non-linearity and Emergence:
Simulation and Neural Nets

Given the complex, non-linear, emergent character of most of the things that interest us in the social world, is there any way in which we can attempt to model that social world? If we are dealing with non-linearity and emergence then we cannot turn to any formal modelling procedure based on a system of simultaneous equations because we will not be able to establish an analytical solution to the equations. Differential calculus will fail us in the non-linear case. The general linear model is so popular because linear models can be resolved analytically but that is a pointless exercise if the processes being investigated are non-linearity and in consequence a linear description bears no relationship to reality.

This is actually not a new problem in science, and particularly in the application of science. Turbulence is of great importance to the designers of ships and aircraft but in general there has been no analytical solution, no mathematically specified formal description, which enables aircraft designers and naval architects to assess the effects of turbulence on the planes and ships they design. Instead they have turned to simulation – historically to the literal building of scale models of planes and ships which were tested against air-streams and wave patterns in wind tunnels and tanks. These models were analogues and were set in analogous environments to see how they would perform.

An engineering structure can be built to scale and then the effects can be scaled up but until the development of cheap and powerful digital computers there was no equivalent way in which we could construct such simulations of social processes. Now we can, not as physical analogues but in virtual form. Our virtual models are simulations and simulations can include the potential for emergent behaviour. We can create complexity in a virtual sense.

Simulations are one important approach to the modelling of social processes and the search for the character of mutable social structures, but there are some real methodological problems in employing them. Another approach works in quite a different way. If simulations seek to model reality, then neural nets seek to model the cognitive capacities of the mammalian brain in engaging with reality.[1] Neural nets are connectionist, distributed, processors. They do not work in the linear way of traditional computing nor are they driven by a predetermined algorithm in the form of a program which defines what they do with data. Instead they are inductive – they learn from the structure of existing relationships – existing knowledge – and use the 'comprehension' acquired to classify and to predict. They do have algorithmic bases but those algorithms specify the mode of learning, not the mode of action. The great advantage of neural nets is that in principle they can handle non-linearities and develop predictions for non-linearity systems. Again there are methodological problems with neural nets. As with simulation, we have to ask can any technologically founded model 'represent' complex emergent reality. Cilliers (1998) at one point offers us the possibility that it might – that we can 'do with technology what we cannot do with science' and then (forthcoming) seems to retreat by asserting that nothing can be a model of a complex system but the system itself. Here it will be argued that we can *explore* using neural net methods and that simulation might have exploratory potential. Certainly both approaches have a far firmer foundation than linear modelling. They are at the very least moves in the right direction. In this chapter we will deal with them in turn.

Simulation – interpreting through virtual worlds

It is worth asking 'what is simulation?' and Troitzsch (1998: 27) gives us an interesting answer. We can come at simulation, he suggests, to solve the problems which we encounter when we cannot resolve non-linear equations systems and then we might regard simulation as a shift from analytical to numerical methods – from elegant formal mathematical representation to the solution of problems by crude iteration. However, following Ostrom (1988), Troitzsch suggests that simulation can also start from natural language descriptions translated into programming terms. In other words, we can come to the computer language accounts of simulation either from formal mathematical modelling or from language. We might therefore regard simulation as a new, third, system in which we manipulate symbols as a way of representing the world, which complements the existing systems of mathematics and language. There is much to commend this conception.

In any event, simulation involves modelling and, as with all modelling, involves a simplification of the character of reality, which is an important source of problems if we are working in a complexity frame of reference. There are numerous accounts of the general process of simulation but all follow much the same pattern. Troitzsch (1998) specifies six steps thus:

1   Identification of some part of reality as a discrete[2] real system composed of different real elements. This system is generally called 'the target'.

2   Specification of causal links between the elements – this has much in common with the kind of specification which underpins the representation of a linear causal model as a flowgraph but here we can anticipate and cope with interactions.

3   Identification of the properties of the components of the model. In the most advanced forms of simulation – agent based simulation – these components are in a sense themselves systems with specific capacities to act.

4   Specification of the 'laws' governing the system – that is, description of the form of relationships among elements in the system. Note these 'laws' are inherently local to the system.

5   Combination of the laws into a fully constituted model describing the system as a whole.

6   Running the model as a simulation.

We might add:

7   Validation of the model by some appropriate process.

The formal element in the simulation is the program that drives it forward through successive iterations. In general, in simulation this involves the translation of a textual account expressed in natural language into a formal set of instructions about the operation of the system and the properties and behaviour of its components. Gilbert and Troitzsch (1999: 6) regard the necessary specification which underpins this process as one of the major general advantages of simulation as a process.

The question 'what is simulation for?' is worth considering. There are two possible answers. Simulation can be considered as a tool of scientific understanding, in which case the purpose is to produce models which assist us in scientific explanation. Alternatively, simulation might be considered as a tool for prediction, not in the sense of using predictions to validate a scientific theory, but rather in a pragmatic 'engineering' fashion so that all that matters is that the predictions are accurate without us having to know why they are accurate. Gilbert and Troitzsch (1999: 17) consider that in fact all simulations have to be adequate both as aids to explanation and as devices for prediction. Whilst we might agree that any explanatory system will have the potential for generating predictions, it is by no means as obvious that a system which is adequate at predicting will in fact work in the same way as the world about which it is making predictions. It may not actually be a model of it. This is much more of an issue in relation to neural net approaches but we might consider that a simulation approach will be able to predict how a real system will behave in a way that is useful without actually being much like that real system at all.

There are a range of simulation procedures available. Here we are going to consider two in order to review the general character of the approach. We will begin with micro-simulation, a procedure in which there is no emergence and no attempt to contend with non-linearity, and then consider multi-agent models in which there is certainly first order emergence and in which Gilbert and Troitzsch consider we might also be able to deal with second order emergence.

First order emergence describes emergence that derives solely from interactions among individual components operating in a given environment. Second order emergence deals in the first instance with the reflexive cognitive capacity of human beings to comprehend and act in relation to forms which are the emergent product of human interaction. We might also, although this is a contentious point, consider that second order emergence implies that we must consider that institutional forms – emergent products – may themselves have the capacity for agency. And we might consider that the environment – in the form of the combination of natural and built – is not necessarily a passive canvas on which interaction takes place, but itself has a reflexive relationship with human action. This is particularly the case if we consider culture as in part emergent from and external to individual action – cultures as ways of life.

Micro-simulation – projecting on the basis of aggregation

In micro-simulation a large sample drawn from a population is considered to be a model of that population. This is the essential element in considering samples as representative – as parts which can stand for the whole. However, the sample is not treated as a model of the aggregate population as such. In other words, micro-simulation does not deal with aggregate estimates of population parameters. Rather, it is a case centred approach in that the sample is seen as a representative selection of the individual cases which comprise the general population.

This distinction is crucial because micro-simulation does not work by transforming characteristics of the whole sample considered as a model of the whole population. Rather, the method operates at the level of individual case. Micro-simulations are commonly used as tools for predicting demographic changes and for assessing the impacts of public policies. A recent example is provided by the Fabian Society's proposals (2000) for increases in the taxation of higher incomes. The report of an inquiry commissioned by the Fabians has suggested that incomes over £100,000 per annum should attract a marginal rate of tax of 50 per cent. We cannot assess the impact of such a change by transforming aggregate population parameters. Instead we have to look at the incomes and tax payments of each individual tax payer and assess the change in tax take for that individual which the new regime would imply. We can then assess the total revenue implications by aggregating up the individual figures.

Calculations of this kind are regularly performed in fiscal and demographic studies. This approach is one of 'static' micro-simulation. In effect everything about the individual cases remains the same apart from the external change – which in the language employed here we might consider to be an external, and hence real, variable. Dynamic micro-simulation accommodates rather more closely to complexity thinking. In the dynamic version micro-simulation allows for changes in a range of the properties of the individual cases. This is typically done in demographic projects where the individual cases are allowed to age and reproduce in accord with life tables which use existing data to describe the likely trajectories of those cases.

Micro-simulations require not only large numbers of cases in the sample but also, in the dynamic form, considerable retrodictive information about the past trajectories of cases. Panel studies, typified by the British Household Panel Study (BHPS), would seem to provide exactly the data base necessary for good dynamic micro-simulation. They are based on large samples and there is, once a few runs of the panel have been achieved, good information about the previous trajectories of cases which can be supplemented by relevant external information such as the life expectancy data contained in life tables. Let me illustrate the possibilities by a hypothetical example.

Suppose we wanted to model the impact of changes in unemployment on family form. With BHPS data we could see what the impact of unemployment had been on family form in the past. In other words we could assess the likelihood – a probability estimate – that unemployment of the male in a two person mixed gender household for a given duration would lead to household break up. We could then use the BHPS data as the basis of a micro-simulation in which we drove the data forward with normal demographic changes and with, say, a doubling in male unemployment of that duration. This begins to look very like the social models which could perform in the same way as economic models – the holy grail of the social indicators movement. However, there is one very great difference. Economic models are based on sets of simultaneous equations describing the behaviour of the economic system as a whole. Our household trajectory model would be based on aggregating the behaviour of individual cases. This approach seems to have distinct possibilities although there are problems because of the non-availability of user friendly software for running dynamic micro-simulation models. We can put that one on the shopping list we are going to present to the IT industry.

Dynamic micro-simulation allows for interaction among variate characteristics of the individual cases at the intra-case level. In other words, we can estimate the probability of a particular trajectory for a single case given the interactive effects of two or more changes in variate characteristics of that case – for example of the overall effect of unemployment, having a first child, and an increase in housing costs, on the stability of the relationship of a couple who were previously childless. We can then aggregate the overall effects to a description of the aggregate character of our new population in which unemployment rates have doubled over a three year period and otherwise households have followed the individual trajectories which we established for them from retrodictive examination of the panel data set. However, we cannot assess the effects of interaction among households, given the form of those households. For that we need a different approach – multi-agent modelling.

Dynamic micro-simulation would seem to have considerable value as a predictive technique in relation to forecasting the social consequences of economic changes. However, we should note that the technique is essentially linear. It can cope well with descriptions of the consequences of continuous, in the sense of continuous measurement, changes in crucial parameters – with changes of degree rather than with changes of kind. Moreover, it is essentially non-social in that it deals with aggregates of cases rather than with emergent social forms. However, the focus of the technique on cases rather than variables is important and useful.

Multi-agent models – interacting entities

Multi-agent models are based on interacting agents and what results from the interaction among those agents. Gilbert and Troitzsch define agents as: 'self-contained programs which can control their own activity based on their perceptions of the operating environment' (1999: 158). Such agents are autonomous, have social ability, react and are proactive. An alternative but related definition is offered by Doran et al. thus:

> An important conception of artificial intelligence studies is that of 'agent': a process, however simple, which collects information about its environment, makes decisions about its actions, and acts. This use of the term 'agent' differs somewhat from its use in other areas of science, where it is often used to denote anything endowed with causal powers. (1994: 200)

Drogoul and Ferber elaborate on the nature of the whole process:

> Multi-agent simulations are used primarily to represent situations in which there are many individuals each with complex and different behaviours and to analyze the global structures that emerge as a result of the individual's inter-actions. The purpose of such simulation is to take into account both quantitative and qualitative properties of the situation, as opposed to traditional simulations which only link properties to quantitative parameters. (1994: 130)

Drogoul and Ferber point out (1994: 31) that in a multi-agent simulation the model does not comprise a set of simultaneous equations but is instead based on entities. The entity set includes the active agents, passive objects, the general environment defined as the topological space in that agents operate around objects, and the communications that enable relationships among agents.

The attraction of multi-agent simulation is that it seems to address the issue identified by Doran and Palmer when they remark: 'It seems unrealistic to model human societies without paying attention to the particular character-istics of human cognition' (1995: 104). In however simple a fashion, agents are cognitive entities.

However, there remains the issue of emergence. Certainly multi-agent simu-lations display emergence. Things happen in the simulation which are derived from interaction among agents but which are not to be understood in terms just of the aggregation of the properties of individual agents. There is macro-structuring derived from micro-action. Gilbert (1995) discusses this in a particularly clear way but his turn to structuration as a way of resolving the conceptual difficulties of relating structure and action is revealing. Carter (forthcoming) in a commentary on Pleasant (1999) points out that the essence of structuration is that all human behaviour is rule governed and every interaction involves an 'instantiation' of the rules: 'Structuration is thus able to combine the hermeneutic emphasis on the meaningfulness of human behaviour with a recognition of the structured nature of social life: every instance of meaningful action is also an invocation of (transcendental) rules' (forthcoming).

This is exactly what is going on in a multi-agent simulation. Every interac-tion is a product of rules because the agents are only autonomous in terms of the implementation of their rules, but, as Gilbert (1995: 155) clearly recog-nizes in what is really a rather important criticism of the structuration approach to which he turns, any adequate model of human social action and its consequences must address meaning. The thing about human beings is that we can change our rules of action! We have a degree of real auto-nomy, individually and even more importantly in the form of collective social actors.

There is another and related problem with multi-agent simulation. An exten-sive recent (web) discussion on the 'simsoc' list addressed precisely a ques-tion raised first by Penn about 'what are the real entities?'. Sawyer pointed out that a crucial component of this question related to the character of macro-social phenomena. Are macro-social phenomena, Durkheim's realm of the social, real or are they just epiphenomena of agent interaction? Sawyer spelled the issue out in a particularly clear way, pointing out that current multi-agent models are inherently nominalist, in the same way as micro-economics and rational choice theory are nominalist. Only individuals exist. Macro-social consequences can derive from the actions of individuals but the macro-social never acts. If the macro-social was considered to have agency then it too would have to be modelled and assigned causal powers. As Sawyer noted, realists of all varieties do accept that macro-social entities exist and have causal powers. Hayles's remark is exactly pertinent here:

> In a significant sense, … AL [artificial life] researchers have not relinquished reductionism. In place of predictability, which is traditionally the test of whether a theory works, they emphasize emergence. Instead of starting with a complex phenomenal world and reasoning back through chains of inference to what the

fundamental elements must be, they start with the elements, complicating the elements through appropriately non-linearity processes so that the complex phenomenal world appears on its own.

What is the justification for calling the simulation and the phenomena that emerge from it a 'world'? It is precisely because they are generated from simple underlying rules and forms. AL reinscribes, then, the mainstream assumptions that simple rules and forms give rise to phenomenal complexity. The difference is that AL starts at the simple end where synthesis can move forward spontaneously, rather than at the complex end where analysis must work backwards. (1999: 231–2)

We might consider that not only the social but also the natural and in particular the intersections of the natural and social might have causal properties too. Certainly, at the very least, I am uncomfortable with any story about culture which reduces it to a series of rules inscribed into individuals. Here Archer's (1998) discussion of morphogenesis offers important insights. Cultural rules change in human interactions although they provide a framework for those interactions in the first place. So cultural change changes the ground of human interaction and human interaction changes the character of culture itself. If multi-agent models are going to be useful, then they have to address these issues.

We should now also consider the nature of 'the environment'. In multi-agent simulation this is really not much more than a topological description – the specification of a range of co-ordinates which locate the ground of agents' actions. However, any sensible materialist account recognizes the interaction among social actors, social action and environment as real material context. This applies both to the built and to the natural environment. The built environment illustrates the point clearly. Any account of social action in urban space has to take account of the causal potential of the complex of built and social which constitutes socially meaningful space. Cellular automata have been used to model segregation practices in a way that is essentially a simplification of multi-agent modelling. Real segregation depends on cultural matrix – no European (which includes British) city is remotely as segregated as the typical US city – and on the actual socio-spatial forms of residential space. We cannot model this without some way in which environmental context has causal liabilities.

The issue of simplification is even more important. Every account of simulation begins by specifying that models are simplifications of reality – for example multi-agent models involve the very gross simplification of assigning causal powers to agents and to agents alone. Simulation lets in non-linearity in relationships but it does not, as yet, sustain an adequate account of real social emergence. This is the problem Cilliers (forthcoming) confronted when worrying about our ability to model a complex system as anything other than itself. Given the emergent potentials of complexity, how can any simplification help us in understanding how a given real complex system works? The immediate answer is that it can't. However, there is a chink of light. A complex system is a complex system is a complex system. A simulated complex system might be considered to represent a valid metaphor for a real complex system. To do this it would have to be a complex system of the same order – certainly nominalist systems without social and environmental causal entities will not do. An adequately specified complex system would help us in reviewing how things might work.

The issue is not just a matter of scale. If we return to the analogy with the ship in the wave tank, the naval architect understands all the simple structural and mechanical components of the vessel, but has to turn to modelling in order to handle the interaction of the vessel with the non-linearity causal liabilities of its potential environment. Here scaling up will probably work. We do not have anything to manage that is simple when we try to model social systems. An example can illustrate. Suppose we are trying to model a school in relation to its performance as measured through a set of conventional indicators of success. The way any given school works involves complex internal interactions and interactions of the discrete system of the school within the cultural, socio-spatial and policy environments which surround it. Moreover, the character of that school is shaped by individual decisions by parents exercising 'parental choice' and by decisions made by other schools' governing bodies in terms of entry criteria.[3] We can try linear models of a loglinear or logistic form and they might tell us something, both in terms of identifying the linear components of causal mechanisms and as predictive devices. However, if we wanted to model what the school is like we have to turn to a much more complex and non-linear story riddled with interaction effects at every level.

If the purpose of our model is not 'complete explanation' but rather the model is understood as a heuristic tool which enables us to explore the implications of alternative strategies of action, then metaphorical adequacy will do. It will not do on its own. Heuristic simulation cannot be more than a part of a wider 'integrative method' in which the entire repertoire of quantitative and qualitative techniques might be brought to bear in our provisional and iterative engagement in understanding the social *at the same time as we make the social*. Easton put it like this in a spin-off from the simsoc debate referenced earlier:

> critical realism combines elements of natural realism and constructionism. It accepts the fallibility of any causal explanation. 'Through a glass darkly' is the key phrase. It also accepts that some explanations that appear to be commensurate with the empirical level may be far from reflecting the real that lies beneath. Only more data, greater creativity, and critical debate can help to indicate where better explanations lie. I think it is far more helpful to accept the temporary and partial nature of many or indeed most of our explanations, at least in the social world, rather than to seek the elusive holy grail of complete understanding. For me simulation is a way of thinking through the 'real' deep processes that give rise to a particular event. (Personal communication, 2000)

This seems to me to be exactly right. Simulation can be a tool but it is simply part of the toolbag. Moreover, I would contend that for simulation to be a useful tool we need models that allow causal status to social collectives and to environmental components. We have to have agent – social – environmental models. Otherwise we are left with elegant but unreal nominalism as typified by rational choice theory. All that said, simulation certainly gets beyond the mechanistic conception of the variable as force. There is at least potential here.

Neural nets are not models but inductive empiricists

Neural nets are, typically, digital versions of parallel connected processors – nodes. The connectionist form is similar to that of the mammalian brain and the net and its components learn in a fashion that follows Hebs's law and depends on the strength and frequency of inter-node communication. Typically neural net approaches are discussed in books on computer modelling (Liebrand et al., 1998) and rule based emergence (Holland 1998), but we might consider that this approach really has very little to do with modelling and should be regarded as a tool for enhancing our perception and cognition rather than as any kind of representation. This gets us round Cilliers's problem identified earlier. Cilliers was attracted (1998) by the connectionist character of neural nets which he saw, correctly, as corresponding in form to the connectionist character of real complex systems. However, he realized that whilst neural nets are complex systems, we really have no way of establishing if they correspond in any meaningful way to any real complex system (Cilliers, forthcoming). Gernet explains why this is so. For neural nets:

> connection to traditional human thinking is poor: even if all internal parameters can be measured and registered, there is no chance for an interpretation of these data; no rules, correlations, coupling coefficients or other elements of our traditional thinking can be identified; no explanation is given for the way in which a result has been derived. (1998: 91)

The essence of the neural net approach is that a network is trained either to classify or to generate predictions on the basis of an inductive engagement with a data set where the classification/prediction of results is already known. The network can be described as fiddling around until it gets it right and then it remembers how it got it right. Basically it is a matter of specifying the weighting of neural connections and it is interesting to note that random noise is often used to 'jiggle' the operations of a net so that it does not 'settle down' at local optima but tries to establish a best account for the system as a whole. Most neural nets are 'backpropagation', which means that communication only feeds forward without recursive feedback when the system's character changes. This is simpler than the connections in real complex systems, where we must consider the possibility of feedback – that is to say, all connections can be bi-directional.

Typically a neural net has three or more layers of nodes. There is an input layer which receives data and an output layer which renders results. Between these the hidden layers process by adjusting connection weights. Garson notes that:

> the hidden layers do more than conjure up a 'black box' imagery: the algorithms of neural analysis result in neural weights to which it is difficult to assign a causal explanation. (1998: 16)

Note that the algorithms that drive virtual neural nets are not instructions about what to do to data. Rather they are instructions about how to learn from data. Neural nets are fine for Crutchfield's (1992) engineers who want data management tools but not for the scientists who want explanatory models. This is a robust technology. Its connectionist form means that it copes readily with interactions and non-linearities, is not much affected by the nature of sampling distributions when dealing with sample data, and is not restricted to dealing with a single output at a time.

There is a variant of neural network approaches, Kohonen architecture, in which outputs are not specified in training. The network can be regarded as 'unsupervised' and the output is an emergent product of its perception and cognition. Kohonen approaches have been used in classification procedures although this approach requires that the number of classes be specified in advance. We can certainly combine statistical cluster analysis, which works on the basis of an iterative sorting algorithm in a top-down fashion, with Kohonen approaches, at the very least as a mode of processual validation. If the two approaches yield similar classifications, then we might think we have found something real.

What are neural networks? It seems to me that they are not models as such because it is impossible to demonstrate any representational correspondence between any given neural net and any given real system. However, they do enable us to process large amounts of quantitative information, in the same way as our brains process information, but much more rapidly. They are in a way idiot *savants* who can use numbers to describe and can do this with great speed. Considered in this way, they are first and foremost exploratory tools. They help us to see the patterns. They are aids to Aristotelian intuitive induction.

Prediction is more problematic. Neural networks certainly can generate predictions, which predictions can be based on retrodictive examination of non-linearity causal systems. However, there is a real leap of faith involved in prediction if there is non-linearity about. In other words, whilst we may have set up something that can produce what really happened in the past in terms of co-ordinate measures describing the traces of a real virtual system, because we can never know

either: that our neural net is in any way an explanatory description of the system so that even for incremental change it can predict what will happen next;
or: that the future trajectory of the system will resemble its past trajectory in an incremental way. We cannot rule out phase shifts.

The implication of this for me is not that we do not use neural networks as predictive tools, but that we realize that our predictions have to be grounded by multiple integrative approaches that will include qualitative reasoning and modelling.

So neural networks offer us a validating tool for our large scale stamp collecting – for classification – *and* a toolset for making predictions as part of integrative consideration of potential futures. If we abandon the holy grail of complete representation and instead set out on an integrative programme of engagement for understanding as a basis for action, then neural network techniques at the very least have potential for us.

Models as icons, which are also tools

Simulations and neural network products might be considered as models, provided we are prepared to spend some time thinking about what the word 'model' means in this context. In traditional linear science the search is for models that reproduce the essential and (by implication at least, although usually this is asserted explicitly) have simple features that explain – that is, provide an adequate account of causal structure – real systems. In an aesthetic sense, which has rather different connotations from the philosophical one in which we have used the word thus far, they are realist. So, for linear science, models should be simplified, analysable accounts which can be mapped on to real systems as causal descriptions. A corollary of this is that models can generate predictions. In a very simplistic sense a videotape from a surveillance camera is an analogy to this kind of model. It represents real events over time in a place.

Let us consider the difference between an icon and a videotape. Although the term 'iconic' has become virtually synonymous with pictorial representation, its original meaning in Orthodox Christianity (which is really quite close to the meaning of icon in the phrase 'computer icon') is rather different. A religious icon on the iconostasis of an Orthodox church does not represent Jesus or Mary or a Saint. Rather, it shares in their essential character. It symbolizes them because it shares that character. There is no requirement for it to reproduce aspects of that character in a pictorial form. All 'Miraculous Madonnas' are icons in this sense. Like the computer icon, the religious icon 'calls up' that for which it stands.

My argument is that we have to understand simulations and the products of neural nets as being simultaneously both tools and icons. They are tools because they can be used to explore. We can dig with them. They are icons because, to the degree that they incorporate emergent potential, they share the essential character of real emergent systems. Again let us turn to Hayles:

> Information technologies seem to realize a dream impossible in the natural world – the opportunity to look directly into the inner workings of reality at its most

elemental level. The directness of the gaze does not derive from the absence of mediation. On the contrary, our ability to look into programs like Tierra is mediated by everything from computer graphics to the processing program that translates machine code into a high level language such as C++. Rather, the gaze is privileged because the observer can peer directly into the elements of the world before the world cloaks itself with the appearance of complexity. (1999: 233)

Of course Hayles is, rightly, sceptical about the adequacy of such a gaze – asserting as this text has that any simulation can only be an account of the world if it replicates exactly the complex mechanisms of the world (1999: 234). If we take the position that simulations/neural network products are both tools and icons, then we can get past the impasse that this seems to pose. Only contemplatives need to bother about the intrinsically real nature of something outwith the scope of human action. Contemplatives can be cosmologists, holy hermits or, if they wish, both at once. Those of us who are agents never merely meditate – we make. Here I am digging into the implications of the word tool. Religious icons are aids to the contemplation of the nature of the divine. Our icons are not for contemplative understanding but rather are means by which we can make the social world itself – the theme of action research, which will form the substance of the conclusion to this book. In other words, our provisional engagement will always be active – we change what we observe on the basis of that observation. Models are not just macro-scopes, tools that enable us to make sense of the large and complex through the way in which they enable us to process quantitative information, although that is an important aspect of what they are. We do more than look. We make.

There is more to this than engineering pragmatism. Engineers want things to work and are prepared to be blasé about why they work. They will design past turbulence without a formal mathematical representation of turbulence. We have to recognize that we are intrinsically part of the social systems ourselves and that our models are conceptual toolkits for perception and cognition as a basis for ongoing action. We are not simple systems making accommodations with complexity – the engineering situation. We are complex systems engaging with complexity. More of this in the conclusion. Let us turn to practical issues of how to use simulations and neural network techniques.

Using the tools

Thus far when referring to procedures I have always been able to point to aspects of the SPSS package and say, in essence, do it with SPSS. We can do that for neural networking. SPSS produces 'Neural Connection' and Garson (1998: 112–35) provides an account of how to use this package. He also (1998: Ch. 7) offers an example of the package in use. The task set was the prediction of household income from ZIP code real estate data organized in several 'independent variables'. In effect this is a regression problem but the neural net approach enables non-linear relationships to be accommodated and is much more robust in relation to data form than regression approaches founded on the General Linear Model. Garson's is the best general introduction to neural networks for social scientists. There is also a lot of useful material in Liebrand et al. (1998).

SPSS does not, at the time of writing, have an add on simulation package so it is necessary to examine specialist tools. The best general introduction is Gilbert and Troitzsch (1999). This employs LISP based procedures. Terna (1998: http://www.soc.surrey.ac.uk/JASSS/1/2/4.html) provides a clear example of how to use the Swarm toolkit in social science contexts. The best single source for examples of simulation in social science is the on-line *Journal of Artificial Societies and Social Simulation* (vol. 1, no. 2, http://jasss.soc.surrey.ac.uk/JASSS.html). Most of the examples of simulation which are intelligible to social scientists in general come from the interface of archaeology and anthropology. It is interesting to note that these are almost always essentially efforts at retrodictive fitting. The authors postulate models and then see if they can regenerate an account that is compatible with the fragmented but time ordered evidence which characterizes this field of work. The results are often interesting and these examples do seem to be of work that is peering into the complex real causal 'mechanisms', almost invariably 'mechanisms' that involve the interface of social and ecological systems. These approaches are efforts to make sense of data – they are primarily exercises in induction. In contrast, although the unorthodox economists who use these approaches have often forsworn economics' obsession with equilibria and emphasis on deduction, much of economic style simulation still seems to be 'game theory' driven and too close to rational choice theory for comfort.

Conclusion

At present a realistic assessment of the potential of neural networking in general social science use is that it offers a useful method of validating cluster generated typologies and has some potential for predictive exploration. Given that there is a reasonably user friendly tool in place we can expect to see much more use in coming years. Simulation still has not yet got the kind of tool which enables somebody like me – reasonably computer literate, Windows experienced and happy with a graphical user interface – to get started on simulations based on my data. I still can't suck it and see. However, by the time this book is published appropriate tools will almost certainly be available. Go to it!

Notes

1 Here there is a clear resonance with Lakoff and Johnson's discussion of 'embodied mind' (1999).

2 Discrete not necessarily in any permanent sense but 'discrete enough' for at least a temporary heuristic boundary to be established.

3 For example, the common practice of privileging children resident outside the catchment area of a primary school but who have siblings in the school means that middle class parents can establish a long term claim on a desirable school to the detriment of the intakes of other schools to which their children might have gone.

9

Qualitative Modelling: Issues of Meaning and Cause

The first edition of Bryman's *Quantity and Quality in Social Research* (1988) makes interesting reading today. This book deservedly attracted appreciation as a practical, and at the same time theoretically well founded, discussion of methodological issues, which achieved its author's objective of enabling researchers to make sense of their own ways of working. However, in this important text, published just a dozen years ago, there was no discussion of computer based qualitative modelling.

Bryman's objective was to break down what he saw as a mistaken conception that research methods were recursively dependent on particular methodological positions – for example, the belief that positivism prescribed surveys and surveys should always be executed and interpreted in a way that met the requirements of the positivist canons. He asserted that good real research often depended on the combination of quantitative and qualitative approaches. This is true, but what we are now dealing with is not just the utility of combining quantitative and qualitative methods but rather a convergence of the approaches through the use of computer based modelling techniques.

There was more to Bryman's argument than just the proposal of an eclectic combination of approaches. His endorsement of notions of methodological triangulation supported a view that different perspectives could work together to establish the real character of the social world. Now we have to ask whether there is really very much difference between quantitative and qualitative procedures in terms of their underlying processes of description and explanation given that for both forms we are now using really remarkably similar tools in an effort to open up the nature of complex systems. This is the question we will address in this chapter.

There is one crucial issue which we need to raise now. That is the relationship between qualitative research procedures and the establishment of both meaning and cause. It is quite conventional to consider quantitative procedures as being concerned with establishing cause and qualitative procedures as being to do with the elaboration of meaning. Bryman put it like this:

> The most fundamental characteristic of qualitative research is its express commitment to viewing events, actions, norms, values, etc. from the perspective of the people being studied. ... The strategy of taking the subject's perspective

is often expressed in terms of seeing through the eyes of the people you are studying. Such an approach clearly involves a preparedness to empathise (though not necessarily to sympathize) with those being studied, but it also entails a capacity to penetrate the frames of meaning with which they operate. (1988: 61)

However, later in the same book (1988: 119) Bryman draws attention to Willis's assertion that qualitative procedures, and in particular participant observation, often are covertly positivist in that the researcher regards the researched as data objects and sources of data rather than valid interpreters of their own social world and social actions. Certainly it is difficult to comprehend Bourdieu's concept of habitus as in any way associated with a qualitative programme concerned with the elucidation of the meanings of acts for actors. Bourdieu actually validates participant observation and social measurement because they depend on the observer's conceptions, and disallows qualitative interviewing as a research process because actors do not have access to the origins of those actions which derive from and constitute habitus.

In other words, the meaning in qualitative research is often the meaning given by the researcher. For all her valiant efforts, Marsh (1982) really did not demonstrate that the respondents' meanings informed the interpretations which underpin Brown and Harris's account of *The Social Origins of Depression* (1978). Specification of state of mental health remained an expert task in the measurement processes of that research.

The more I read and think about this the less convinced I am that contemplative observation of social action has anything much to do with elucidation of meaning. Of course the hermeneutic programme derives from the examination of holy scriptures in order to elucidate their meaning, but this action is undertaken by created beings in order to interpret the revelations of their omnipotent creator.[1] This is not the same at all as the scientific observation of social action in an effort to understand. At the end of this chapter we will return to the idea of dialogical research in order to see how the exploration of cause through a concern with meanings might be part of a programme of critical research but for the moment we might think that what is really being sought is a story of cause which allows for the construction of the social world through human social actions.

In other words, social constructionism, the ontological position[2] which, as Cicourel using MacIver put it, asserts that

the social structure is for the most part created. … Unlike the physical nexus [the social type of causal nexus] does not exist apart from the motives of social beings [and requires a methodological strategy that fits the distinctiveness of social events.] (1964: 1; [] indicates Cicourel)

is concerned rather more with cause than with meaning. We can be social constructionists and engage in qualitative research and be interested primarily in generating a causal account of the nature of the social world. Plainly, if the social world is created by human actions, then it can be recreated anew and different. There are no universal laws to be established here, but we can establish local accounts good within the spatio-temporal boundaries of the systems which they describe. Complexity theory and social constructionism are wholly compatible. We can engage in Pawson and Tilley's Hermeneutics I (see my Introduction), qualitative investigation in order to elucidate cause, with cause understood as Pawson and Tilley understand it, that is as causal liability and potential deriving from the mechanisms of a realist ontology.

From analytic induction through grounded theory to computer modelling – qualitative exploration of cause

The term analytic induction is due to Znaniecki (1934) and derives from his distinction between the practices of scientists who worked with many cases, either on the basis of a statistical experiment or through surveys, and 'bench' scientists who worked instead with a single or small number of cases which were studied very intensively. Induction based on many cases was, in Znaniecki's terms, 'enumerative induction' and at best could yield probabilistic accounts of the nature of reality. In contrast, the intensive analysis (that word again) of the single case could yield a deterministic account of reality. Analytic induction is analogous not to the statistical experiment involving randomized control, but to the actually physically controlled experiment. This distinction is rather important because analytical induction sought to establish laws by the demonstration of what amounted to constant conjunction and in statistical experimentation that cannot be done. However, Znaniecki did not propose controlled experimentation as the mode of social analytical induction. Rather he suggested intensive qualitative study. Moreover, although analytic induction uses the idea of hypothesis, it is very different from the hypothetico-deductive method. In hypothetico-deductive reasoning a hypothesis is formulated and tested against data, usually not through direct testing but indirectly by testing a null hypothesis which denies the associations asserted in the working hypothesis. Testing is through measurement and statistical calculation. Analytic induction is much more iterative and works by a process of case based constant comparison in which hypotheses are continually reformulated in order to develop an adequate overall account of the social processes being considered.

It is quite conventional in texts discussing qualitative 'analysis' to move from Znaniecki's specification of analytic induction to a discussion of Glaser and Strauss's (1967) proposals for a qualitative strategy concerned with the establishment of grounded theory. Whatever the details of intellectual inheritance, this makes a good deal of sense. In the original form of their approach Glaser and Strauss argued that researchers should, quite early in their research engagement, begin to develop a categorical scheme which describes what is being found. The researchers should continue with this process until they have 'saturated' their categorical scheme, that is, generated an adequate scheme in relation to the purposes of their research. This should then be translated into a general specification of each category which will act as a guide both for the development of description and as a way of stimulating further conceptualization. An important part of this process is the delimiting of the explanatory range of the category set. The whole process is inherently inductive in that, in principle, theoretical schemes derive from empirical investigation. It is important to note that there are two sources for the construction of components of and relations among the category set. The first is the conceptual apparatus of the disciplines themselves. The second are the in vivo codes which derive from the language of those observed and/or questioned in any particular piece of qualitative research. The issue of coding is very important and we will return to it in a moment. First we should note that grounded theory, like analytic induction, is again an iterative process. There is no null hypothesis set up in advance, or even working hypothesis for reformulation as in analytic induction. Instead researchers engage in a constant dialogue with the data until an end state of 'adequate description' is achieved. Essentially the process involves developing concepts from the data and then searching through data to see if they hold up at all and, if they do, then what are the limits of their applicability.

Note that this is not a variable centred approach. As with analytic induction, the search is for the countervailing case and modification is made to take account of that case. Thus the sampling strategy proposed by Glaser and Strauss – theoretical sampling – is not one that organizes the selection of cases in order to sustain probabilistic based reasoning about variables. Rather the range of coverage of the investigation is extended in order to bring in new 'instances' which extend the comparative range on the basis of which theory may be reformulated. Sampling is completed when no extending new instances can be located. Note that the case is not necessarily an entity here – that is to say, the entity need not be a person, group, institution or other pre-existing system. It can be an example of action. There is no case-variable matrix in grounded theory, although in the use of grounded theory in practice, usually in a much watered down form, the language of variables is often employed.

The original term used by Glaser and Strauss was category, which implied that their programme was essentially one directed at the generation of typologies. As Fielding and Lee put it:

> the analyst embarked on the constant comparative method will soon begin to think of different types of category, and to explore categories in terms of their conditions and consequences, as well as their relation to other categories and their properties. This is essentially a process of conceptual clarification, through which the nature of a particular category and its properties are delineated. (1998: 30)

There is at least one more iterative stage of engagement with data through the formulation, linking and reduction of categories but the essential point to make here is that what results is not just a typology of components of social action but rather an explicitly delimited, which is to say local, formal theory connecting components of social action. In other words there is a notion of causal liability, and moreover one which is inherently contingent. This is very close to the perspective of critical realism.

Lee and Fielding's (1996) review of 'Approaches to Qualitative Data Analysis' is most suggestive here. They are setting up an account of practice as a preliminary to a discussion, and indeed advocacy, of computer based qualitative research. They identify three sorts of approach as suggested in Figure 9.1, namely the translation of qualitative into quantitative information through content analysis, various forms of qualitative classification which are intended to generate accounts of social causation, and what they term 'discursive approaches', which means postmodern idiosyncratic interpretation.

Type	Method	Objective
Content analysis	Code and count	Statistical description and modelling
Qualitative classification	Code and interpret	Construction of formal theory
Discursive approaches	Delineation of narratives	Cultural interpretation

Figure 9.1   *Forms of qualitative analysis*

The debate in *Sociological Research OnLine* between Lee and Fielding (1996) and Coffey et al. (1996) illustrates the distinction between qualitative classification and discursive analysis rather clearly. It began with Coffey et al.'s (1996) argument against qualitative data analysis packages which depend on coding, and for 'a fine grained hermeneutic analysis' (1996: para 7.4). Coffey et al. asserted that 'complex texts may be more faithful to the complexities and contours of social life' (1996: para 9.3) and turned to the possibility of the multi-layering of hypertext as a mode of representation. This approach resonates well with Geertz's proposal (1973) for 'Thick Description'. Note that the very use of the word 'faithful' would be regarded by pomo purists as a fatal concession to realism but we might see Coffey et al.'s arguments as being for representations that take the same form as social reality rather than as ones that can be considered to model it in a way that will enable either explanation or prediction.

Lee and Fielding (1996) argued that qualitative data packages based on coding were not necessarily tied to grounded theory approaches. They could be regarded as in the first instance procedures for the management of data, and moreover that the grounded theory approach itself was in the first instance a data management strategy. Taking an entirely appropriate empirical turn, Fielding and Lee (1998: 179), in a necessary continuation of this argument, show that many researchers working on a coding basis do not cite grounded theory as the frame of their approach, although almost all take a realist position on representation. The essential issue is the status of coding in qualitative work.

Coding qualitative materials

The best way to illustrate what is involved in coding in qualitative work is by an example. Byrne and Doyle (1997) conducted research based on the responses of focus groups to a series of images illustrating the transformation of 'the cultural landscape' after the end of coal mining in South Shields. The stimulus to the research was the extraordinarily rapid elimination of the physical structures of mining from the Durham coalfield after the closure of the remaining mines in 1992. In South Shields the impact was particularly impressive because the very large structures associated with Westoe Colliery were on a rise and could be seen from almost everywhere in the town. The starting point of the research was a conception that this remarkable elimination – there are literally more physical remnants of the Roman occupation of the town which ended in the fourth century AD than of mining which ended some ten years ago and was for nearly 200 years one of the town's principal employers – would have some meaning for people in the place. The project was part of wider exploration of the implications of the transition from an industrial to a postindustrial society.

In one sense this was a rather more complicated project than most qualitative research because it had not only textual documents – the transcriptions of focus group discussions in response to the images – but also the images themselves. Moreover, the images included some simple graphical representation of the scale of mining employment in South Shields over two hundred years, in addition to photographs and early nineteenth century etched views. However, the actual coding process was carried out only on the text with the images coded when mentioned in the text.

Coding was initially carried out using NUDIST4, although the project has subsequently been transferred to NVIVO to facilitate modelling. The coding began with the researchers reading over the transcripts and discussing general impressions of them. The actual sequencing of images had imposed a kind of historical narrative on the discussions and that flow was important in terms of structuring the nature of the account. One obvious classification strategy was to divide components into those which referred to the past, the present and the future, and the nature of discussion allowed a further subdivision of the past into a past of which the respondents had personal knowledge and a past before their own life experiences. The researchers had decided on first reviewing the transcripts to make each speech act by a participant the unit that would be coded, so a speech act might refer to the participant's childhood and be coded as 'remembered past'.

It is important to note that speech acts could be coded in multiple ways. Another issue which 'emerged' from the transcripts was a discussion of the dangers and unhealthiness of mining, so a coding category was set up which identified speech acts dealing with this. In grounded theory terminology this was an in vivo coding. A component could thus be coded as 'personal recollection of past' and 'dangerous/unhealthy'. Here we had two different coding schemata with one speech act being assigned a code in both. This is not controversial – the classification schemes were quite different.

What is more interesting is that there were plainly a set of 'fuzzy' speech acts. A respondent in one contribution to a conversation could begin talking about the present, swing to a recollection of the past and then project to the future. This speech act would be recorded as all of 'present', 'remembered past' and 'future'. Another coding principle applied to speech acts which referred to 'they' or 'them' where the pronouns indicated that the speaker was referring to powerful actors with some determinant capacity in relation to the development of events. This usage was identified by both researchers independently in the initial reading through of transcripts and then located specifically by a text search for the words, with only those acts where the pronouns were used in relation to power being coded as 'they–power'.

Yet another coding principle was that every speech act was coded to the person uttering it. We had a broad general description of each speaker based on a simple 'face sheet' questionnaire they had completed prior to the group discussion. This classified them in terms of age, sex, personal and familial connection with mining, and own occupational history. In addition most of the groups were pre-existing with quite distinctive characteristics, for example, a group of primarily older adult women in a women's health group, business studies students aged between 16 and 18 at a local FE college, a group of porters in a local hospital and so on. Every speech act thus had both an individual code and a group code, which code contained information about the individual uttering it and the group in which it was uttered. These codes were variate traces of the speakers and of the groups. In other words there was a connection between quantitative information about speakers and groups organized as two sets of case-variate trace data matrices, and the multidimensional and fuzzy qualitative classification of speech acts.

We were and are particularly interested in how people saw the future after the end of coal mining. That was our original stimulus for engaging in the research in the first place. The historical chronology of pre own time, remembered past, present and future certainly emerged from the texts but was also in a sense 'pre-existing'. We, ourselves, could locate the images along that time line. The issue of injury and disease was by no means surprising, although none of the images contained any referent to this aspect of mining. The use of 'they' and 'them' to stand for often anonymized powerful actors was not something we had anticipated although it made perfect sense to us when we read it – both researchers live in the same cultural milieu as the respondents and have family connections with mining and with South Shields.

Note that our process of classifying was really very simple. We read the transcripts separately and devised a scheme of classification and classified, discussing at each stage. Since one researcher did most of the classificatory work he largely confirmed it by discussion with the other. We did use 'memos' to annotate this process, as stipulated by Glaser and Strauss, but, whilst aware of grounded theory, were not working to grounded theory schemata in this process.

The transcripts from this project have now been lodged with the UK Economic and Social Research Council's QUALIDATA archiving system and are available for secondary analysis. We mention this because it raises the possibility of others working through these texts and dealing with them differently. In other words, it raises the issue of the validity of our classificatory scheme. Will others classify in the same way as us? Does it matter if they do not? Subsequent researchers might have different issues in mind when reviewing the transcripts. Their classificatory schemata will reflect those interests, which is not an issue in relation to the validity of a classificatory scheme constructed for our purposes. It seems difficult to conceive of a 'platonically real' classification which might be imposed as measurement on textual data of this kind. Instead we must rely on process and triangulation for the establishment of validity.

The first argument advanced for the use of computer based processes in qualitative research by both Dey (1993) and Fielding and Lee (1998) is that this makes the management of data much easier. Crucial to this process are the tasks of scanning, searching, coding and retrieving. Scanning refers to the initial coding of transcripts by researchers who read through them and on the basis of a preliminary construction of theory – based on both disciplinary (in the case of the South Shields study interdisciplinary drawing on history, sociology and cultural studies) and in vivo concepts – assign codes to elements. Searching refers to the use of text search facilities in which elements containing appropriate text are called up and coded if the context of the text corresponds to the coding principle – as with the 'they–power' coding in the South Shields study. Typically the coding process is organized in the form of a 'tree' of 'nodes' in which more refined categories are included as subsets of more complex categories. The current state (December 2000) of part of the node tree for the South Shields study is indicated in Figure 9.2. The nodes at each level have many more sub-nodes than are illustrated here.[3]

The coding process is always undertaken with a view to retrieving the segments of text thus coded so that they can be called up for the graphical part of the ethnographic process – the writing up. When thinking about and writing up a study we can call up the pieces of text which jog our memory and stimulate our thinking and which can serve to illustrate our argument. Qualitative writing is almost always based on validation by reference to examples, to chunks of appropriate 'in vivo' data.

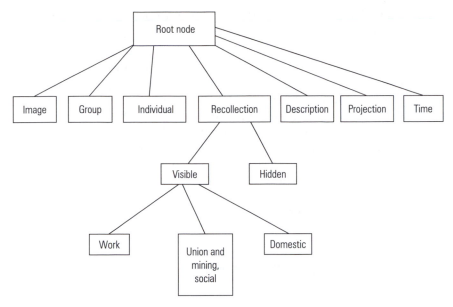

Figure 9.2 *Node tree for landscape study*

Let us go back to the implications of having variate traces of cases and groups as well as coded text items. Again the example can illustrate. We found very different responses to a series of images showing the construction, operation, demolition and vacant site of the Crown Tower, the huge winding gear of Westoe Colliery which dominated the South Shields skyline for some thirty years. All the individuals in all the groups apart from that of the young business studies students could identify this structure and its function and could associate it with mining recollections. The business studies students literally did not know what it was. They thought it was a factory chimney, not unreasonably given its form. Whereas the older groups and individuals, including people in their late twenties who were just ten years older than the business studies students, knew and related to the Crown Tower, the business studies students didn't know it and regarded it as something representing a past which they were glad to be rid of.

Why did they have these views? We can, and did, pick over their discussion and identify a theme of 'the desirability of postindustrialism' which lends meaning to their position. We can also note that they were the only group who had not spent some adult life 'in the shadow of the Crown Tower', not in the sense that it was quite so enormous as to overshadow a large town, but rather in that it represented an industrial 'way of life'. So we could relate the new meanings to age cohort. But, these were business studies students – that is to say they were not just young but were involved in a process of education which was about the transmission of discourses of business rationality, a rationality that is often inherently hostile to the labourist industrialism represented by mining and its images. Was it age which generated the new meaning set? Was it exposure to the discourses of business rationality? Was it both in combination?

Of course that set of questions predicates an extension of theoretical sampling. We should have set up a group of older adults with a business background and got them to talk to the images. Typically in a project with limited funding and a tight time scale we weren't able to do this, but that would be the way to go. And it would be the way to go because we are interested in causes, in the complex contextual and non-linear processes that structure meaning as meaning structures action. In other words, we are interested in the generative consequences of being young in a postindustrial society whilst being exposed to the discourses of business rationality. This is a causal story about complex systems and complex causes. Can we investigate it in an any more systematic way?

Qualitative Comparative Analysis (QCA) – a Boolean approach

Those of us who used SPSS pre Windows, when you had to write command lines as opposed to simply dragging and dropping, are familiar with Boolean logic through the use of the IF statement, imported direct from Fortran.[4] The IF statement is the basis of the construction of new variate traces based on specification of conditions thus:

IF (NO EMPLOYED WORKERS GT 1) AND (TENURE = OWNOCC)
THEN TENWK = 1
ELSE = 2

If the household contained more than one employed worker and its tenure was owner occupation then on a variate trace combining work relation and tenure it had a value of one to specify that it was both of these things. Otherwise it was coded as different – something else. This sort of Boolean approach is the basis of what Ragin (1987) called 'Qualitative Comparative Analysis' (QCA) and Huber and Garcia (1991) called 'Qualitative Configuration Analysis'. Fielding and Lee describe this as 'a simple, compact, if somewhat restricted, way of analysing patterns of causation in a small to moderate number of cases' (1998: 157). The procedure involves coding aspects of each case into categories but the causal reasoning is different from that of traditional variable analyses. Fielding and Lee put it like this:

> Unlike the data matrix in quantitative research, where the analytic focus is on variables displayed in the *columns* of the table, it is the *rows* which are important here. What is being examined for each row is the *configuration* of causes associated with the presence or absence of an outcome for the case. (1998: 158)

The procedure is basically a stepwise approach in which elements are eliminated through comparison of cases so as to identify the most parsimonious instance of causation. Ragin (1994: 12) considers that this approach follows an experimental logic of reduction with the stepwise elimination being analogous to direct control. It must be said that there may be multiple 'prime implicants' – in other words the most parsimonious representation of cause may include more than one cause. This is plainly different from the controlled experiment which deals in single causes. In QCA the actual causation is understood, at least implicitly, in terms of a combination of factors in interaction. There is explicit recognition of 'causal complexity' (Coverdill et al., 1994: 57). Of particular significance is the recognition that a particular outcome might result from different combinations of conditions and that single factors might combine with different other factors to produce different outcomes. In other words, by recognizing interaction the procedure recognizes contingency and complexity.

Hicks (1994) notes that QCA seems to work in the same way as 'neo-analytic induction', a description of analytic induction as practised when comparisons are made not only with cases with positive outcomes but with those with negative outcomes, comparisons are made on a multiple case basis rather than successive pairwise comparisons of single cases, and there is an acceptance of the limited and local character of theoretical description. Again this is essentially compatible with a complex realist account.

There are practical difficulties in the use of QCA. It requires input in the form of dichotomous variables – binary attributes in which a condition is absent or present. This is the same requirement as that of cluster analysis procedures when working with nominal level data. Recoding quantitative nominal or ordinal variables into binary attributes is a relatively straightforward, if somewhat laborious, task and can easily be done in SPSS. When dealing with ratio scale measures there must be a preliminary ordering undertaken which has some sort of theoretical foundation and which reflects the actual patterning of the continuous data.

Binarizing text elements is rather more complicated. By implication classification allows a text element to be measured at a nominal level and even the fuzziness of such classifications does not pose a problem if the representation is as binary attributes. Take the example of statements referring to past, present and future in the South Shields study which we fuzzily coded to all three time levels. This becomes a positive code on three separate binary attributes. Actually this approach really does seem to allow for the multidimensional and complex character of qualitative meanings. We might expect QCA to differentiate among respondents who do link over time and those who don't. Technically we do not have a problem.

Conceptually there is more to argue about. A text element is an expression, a component of a document,[5] rather than a measured variate trace. Classifying a text element is a process of measuring the output of a system at a particular instance. If we refer back to Bateson's discussion of the difference between 'facts' and 'values' in Chapter 4, we might think that text elements are always 'values' in the sense that they are not constant across time, even across the local time which is within our boundary of possible explanation. However, we cannot think of them as purely 'caused' products of the systems that generate them. When people generate a meaning in a conversation, that actually feeds back, along with their appreciation of the responses of others, into the way they understand the world and the way they will act in it and on it. This is a very action centred version of symbolic interactionism; if you like, symbolic interactionism squared. The essential thing to remember is the recursivity of social action and consciousness. However, given that we bear this in mind, then exploratory classification for input to QCA seems allowable.

QCA is plainly an interesting procedure that straddles quantitative and qualitative approaches. Many might certainly worry about its basis for making any kind of generalization beyond the contexts in which it is applied but Complexity Theory's insistence on the local character of knowledge means that it is not an issue for us. More seriously, we have to consider the criticism that might be mounted by a frequentist statistician as to the validity of the accounts generated even in a local context. If we regard our data as generated by a sample from a local universe, then any relationships of cause may be artefacts of that sample rather than descriptions of the local universe. This is precisely the same problem as we encountered in our discussion of Cluster Analyses in Chapter 6. Again, I would argue that we have to turn to process and triangulation methods of validation because we have no account of sampling distributions which would enable us to construct probabilistic knowledge. QCA is really a determinist story, which is not surprising given its close resemblance to analytic induction. In this respect its potential in relation to establishing something like 'single case probabilities' in a Popperian sense has already been noted in Chapter 5. There might seem to be a contradiction between describing the procedure as inherently deterministic and then going on to suggest a probabilistic use, but in many respects we might consider single case probability to really be an account of complex and specific determination.

From a complex realism perspective we will always be somewhat wary of any approach that includes the word 'analysis' in its title. It is interesting that proponents of QCA do assert that it is holistic but it does seek to reach into cases in order to identify patterns of causes. I do think that this approach is a potential route to the understanding of control parameters, provided of course that it is always employed in exploratory mode. In other words, we are not confirming hypotheses here but are engaged in a constant iterative engagement with social reality in a programme founded on integrative method. The iterative and provisional character of the methods of qualitative 'analysis' is of the utmost importance.

There are a number of other computer based approaches to qualitative interpretation which involve the use of expert systems. These are fully described in Fielding and Lee (1998) and are plainly interesting. However, conceptually they are simply aids to processes of interpretation in something very close to a grounded theory tradition. In contrast, hypertext methods do seem to be about thick description and, thereby, the programme of cultural interpretation. We should not dismiss hypertext approaches and the modelling potential they incorporate may well be useful to us, but they are not part of a programme for exploring cause.

Iconic modelling

Qualitative data packages typically now incorporate features that allow researchers to 'model'. The idea of a model is very important to us so any sight, sound or scent of it ought to attract our attention. At first impression we might conclude that there is not really much relationship between quantitative and qualitative modelling. Richards gives us an account of the processes underlying the latter version using the language of the important package NVIVO:

> Qualitative researchers often wish to draw, diagram or represent visually ideas, hunches, perceived patterns or relationships between parts of their projects, discoveries in their data, ideas in their literature and so on. Some of the ingredients of such models are project documents or nodes, or their sets or attributes, some are not. Ideas change and links become more tentative, or more confident, diagrams build cumulatively in layers as understanding accumulates. Nvivo provides a modeler designed for such a qualitative modeling. (1999: 143)

There is absolutely no mathematical formalism here and if formal representation is the essence of a quantitative model, then qualitative models are definitely something else. But is formal mathematical representation the essence of the quantitative model? If we think of models as exploratory tools then mathematical representation is a means to exploration, not an end in itself. When we move from the elegant, but often useless because not isomorphic with reality, linear models to quantitative exploration of the non-linear, we generally have to abandon analytical formalism and turn to crude numerical iteration. That word iteration again – we keep pegging away until we get something that seems to fit. This seems to be exactly what Richards is saying about qualitative modelling – it is iterative and moves towards something that seems to fit.

There is another basis on which we might see some rather strong resemblances between quantitative and qualitative modelling. If it looks like a duck, walks like a duck and quacks like a duck then it is a duck – a rather neat vernacular expression of prototypical classification. On a prototypical basis qualitative modelling not only iterates – it walks like quantitative modelling – it also generates pictorial representations of causal links – it looks like quantitative modelling. Since both are aids to the production of causal accounts we might conclude that they also quack in the same register. The looking alike is very important.

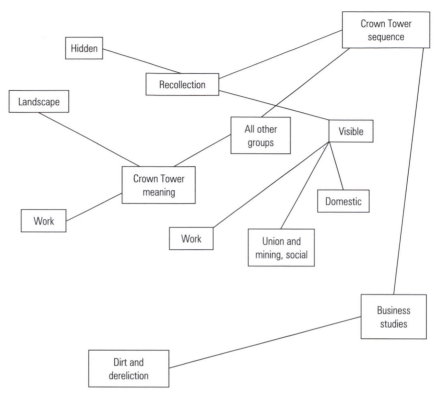

Figure 9.3   *Meanings of the Crown Tower sequence*

Models are pictures of relationships. Figure 9.3 shows, as a single layer, a model of 'meanings of Crown Tower sequence' constructed from the South Shields data. It is multi-layer in its virtual form but can only be represented as a single layer on a printed page. The model shows that for all groups except the business studies students, the images were correctly identified. The business studies students identified the tower with 'dirt and dereliction' and nothing else of significance. For other groups it called up very varied memories and led to comments on the significance of cultural change.

What was going on in causal terms here? At one level the images caused the expression of meanings by the groups but the images were, in the sense of Orthodox religiosity, icons. They stood for the thing and contained something of its essence. Actually, given that for the Crown Tower the images were a sequence, a very slow movie in four frames of the whole existence of the structure, they were an iconic representation of a dynamic process. For the business studies students process didn't seem important but for the other groups it did. For the business studies students any causal connection was one way. The Crown Tower images 'stimulated' reference to dirt and dereliction. For the other groups the cultural causal flows were inherently recursive.

Although the exercise looks like the ultimate in quantitative trivialization, we might have carried out a survey in South Shields in which people were shown the Crown Tower sequence and then asked to identify the structure yielding a bivariate response of correct or other (incorrect and don't know), asked to say they had very positive, positive, neither positive nor negative, negative or very negative views of it (a Lickert scale), and asked to give typical face sheet information about their age, gender etc. We could then have constructed a causal model of attitudes to the Crown Tower understood (by us as researchers at least) as a proxy for views on the industrial past. This would have none of the richness or depth of the qualitative materials, which enable us to turn to language and contextualize people's expression of meaning for them, and it certainly would not have permitted emergent categories, but it might well have yielded a model looking very like Figure 9.3. However, it would not have allowed us to add in things which we did not measure – which we did not specify in advance. There would be no in vivo coding possible.

We do model with qualitative materials and, mostly, we (which collective pronoun here includes those of us who engage in qualitative representations of the real) model in causal terms. This is an essential part of any integrative method. Let us consider the very important implications of that term considered in relation to Freire's conception of 'participatory research'.

Integrative method

The term 'integrative method' in this sense is due to Lemon and Seaton (1999) who are writing explicitly in a complexity frame of reference and derive their programme from Newby's (1992) argument that social science must be an integral and not marginal part of the processes of understanding the role of scientific and technological activities and understandings in social and economic development. Consequently they define the term with an emphasis on the way in which models can generate information that is relevant to policy. Lemon and Seaton argue for interdisciplinarity and the modelling is central to their discussion. In particular, and this theoretical assertion is reflected in the actual research practice of their team, they assert the relevance of 'models generated by semi-structured social enquiry techniques' (1999: 23).

In summarizing the whole project, Lemon and Oxley (1999: 237) note that complex systems are subject to multiple interpretations and that any model which makes sense of local environmental issues must include representation of the interpretations of all local actors. If local actors' views are incorporated then an iterative process can be initiated in which the model is taken back to local actors who respond to it and refined in the light of those responses. As they say: 'This view of integrative method immediately questions the role of science as an objective observer and analyst and recognizes the reflexive nature of the process whereby the scientist is inseparable from the focus of the study' (1999: 239). This is not a problem for complex realists! Let us consider an explicitly political version of the same sort of practice.

> Participatory research is an approach to social change – a process used by and for people who are exploited and oppressed. The approach challenges the way knowledge is produced with conventional social science methods and disseminated by dominant educational institutions. Through alternate methods, it puts the production of knowledge back into the hand of the people where it can infuse their struggles for social equality, and for the elimination of dependency and its symptoms: poverty, illiteracy, malnutrition etc. (Heaney, 1995: 11)

The role of those with expertise in this can only be collegiate participation in empowerment, 'a consequence of liberatory learning. Power is not given, but created within the emerging praxis in which co-learners are engaged' (Heaney, 1995: 10). The method must be dialogical: 'The dialogical approach to learning is characterised by co-operation and acceptance of interchangeability and mutuality in the roles of teacher and learner. In this method, all teach and all learn' (1995: 10).

I have often thought that the gestures made by social scientists towards meaning are largely token. Workers in the tradition of Hermeneutics I are realists concerned with the elaboration of complex causal systems. Practitioners of pomo are concerned in principle – because their whole approach denies the possibility of anything else – with the meaning for they themselves alone. The first is a legitimate enterprise. The second, I suppose, keeps its practitioners off the streets and can be considered to contribute to public tidiness. Pomos will never be a threat to public order.

However, Hermeneutics I, and indeed any kind of science, is not legitimate either as contemplation or as practice when that practice is only in the interests of existing power systems. It does seem to me that dialogic iterative research – the return to the subjects and engagement with them first in establishing the validity, however temporary, of account, and then in dialogue about the role of the account in processes of social change, is what matters. There is a name for this sort of thing – action research. That will be the subject of the final section of the Conclusion of this book.

Conclusion

The purpose of this chapter has been to consider the convergence between quantitative and qualitative approaches to causal reasoning. The key link between the two is the focus on the case rather than some abstraction from the case reified and regarded as a variable. The idea of causal reasoning by constant comparison is by no means new but the IT resources make it much more available to us. We can handle far more cases and reconstruct far more trajectories. This is likely to be a crucial part of the evidence base of social and related scientific practice and has enormous potential for both understanding and social action.

Notes

1 The decline of religion accounts for a lot. Most writers on hermeneutics have plainly never been to a bible class or yeshivah or koranic school. Those who have include the spoiled priest Heidegger, so perhaps a religious upbringing guarantees nothing.

2 Valuable as Crotty's *The Foundations of Social Research* (1998) is as a lucid and coherent account of philosophical concerns in relation to research practice, his dismissal of the significance of ontology is misconceived. It is worth noting that the word cause does not appear in the index of this important text.

3 Many users of qualitative packages who adhere to a more or less grounded theory approach worry about the way in which a node tree becomes rather firm and fixed and thereby makes the reformulation essential to the practice of grounded theory substantively more difficult. Trees are not absolutely fixed and can be restructured but they do stiffen with use.

4 It is still much easier to construct IF statements in SPSS by writing command lines than by using the menu system.

5 Actually the component may not be textual. It could be an element in a pictorial representation. However, text elements are by far the most common 'instances'.

Conclusion

The conclusion to this book has two components. The first will reiterate the essential arguments of the text by specifying what the book is arguing against *and* what it is arguing for. The second will pick up the theme of research as critical practice and argue that not only is a critical quantitative social science possible, but that any useful critical social science must make use of quantitative exploration and of quantitative modelling.

Down with:

- Analysis – the analytical programme which asserts that real complex systems can be understood in terms of their component parts and that the task of science is explanation based on the description of these component parts and specification of the causal relations among them.
- Variables – the abstraction and reification of aspects of real complex systems from those systems and the consequent treatment of these reified abstractions as having real and independent causal powers.
- Universalism – the project of establishing laws of social relations which hold always and everywhere.
- Linearity – the assertion that the trajectories of real complex systems follow paths in which change is incremental and can be described by mathematical formalisms based on linear equations.
- Mathematical formalism – the effort to write descriptions of the social world in terms of specific sets of equations, whether linear or non-linear.
- Derivation of the complex from simple rules – related to mathematical formalism as above, but involving the specification of rule governed behaviour rather than the construction of equations; typified by game theory and rational choice approaches.
- Relativism – the postmodern abandonment of any criterion of judgement as to the accuracy of even local representations of the world.
- Assertive innumeracy – the postmodern and, in some but by no means all versions, feminist assertion that the quantitative description and exploration of the world is simultaneously invalid and oppressive.
- Hypothesis fetishism – the belief that statements tested on the basis of frequentist conceptions of probability can generate adequate descriptions of the nature and potential trajectories of real complex systems.
- Contemplation – the belief that knowledge can ever be separated from social action and thereby from social consequences.

Up with:

- Complexity – understanding of the character of real complex systems in terms of wholes, parts, interaction of parts with parts, parts with wholes, and of systems with other systems in their environment, within which they are embedded, and which they contain.
- Non-linearity – recognition that the interesting and significant shifts in the trajectories and hence characters of complex systems are those that involve radical shifts of kind.
- Localism – the recognition that knowledge is inherently contextual and that a crucial component of the specification of any item or system of things and relations known is the delimitation of the spatial and temporal boundaries within which that knowledge might hold good.
- Categorization – the specification of kinds – stamp collecting – as a central activity of science since understanding of significant processes is based on knowing when and how transformations of kind occur and classification is an essential preliminary to the mapping of such transformations.
- Exploration – the use of measurements in the construction of patterns that offer clues as to the nature of complex systems and their trajectories both as specific systems and as ensembles of systems.
- Modelling – the iterative and reflexive development of models based on both quantitative and qualitative descriptions of real complex systems which we can use both as aids to thinking about those systems and as delimiters of the range of possible future trajectories of those systems.
- Connectionism – the recognition that any useful description of real complex systems must itself be complex. This does not preclude the representation being less complex but it must incorporate some element of complexity, for example in the form of explicit interaction, within itself.
- Action research – the recognition that knowledge is always used in the reconstitution of the social world and that we must take specific account of this in our research processes and practices.

Crotty (1998: 78) remarks that: 'The phenomenological movement was launched under the battle cry of "Back to the things themselves".' We can scarcely argue that the kind of peering into the entrails of complex systems through the use of computer based extensions of our cognitive range is equivalent to the phenomenological programme of dealing with things as they present themselves to us as conscious human beings. Or rather, we might argue exactly that. Hayles (1999), in arguing that our interaction with machines makes us 'posthuman', points out that this proposition implies both terrors and pleasures. We might add capacities to that set. I would argue that the data manipulation and image generating capacities of computer based technologies of investigation can be understood, at least in part, as extensions of our ability to perceive the complex world. To say this is to beg a whole debate on perception and instrumentation, but we do see things through the machine management of lots of numbers. We see phenomena and we see them as whole systems, not as analysed parts. Perhaps what is becoming possible is a synthesis of the analytical and phenomenological modes – a synthesis of understanding through breaking up with understanding the whole thing. It is, at least, a thought.

Action theories imply action

> The Philosophers have described the world – the point however is to change it. (Karl Marx, *Thesis XI on Feuerbach*)

My older daughter when aged six read this aloud from the inscription on Marx's tomb in Highgate Cemetery as 'The Philosophers have described the world – the point however is to chance it.' I have always thought she hit on a profound truth – one which we might consider particularly seriously when reviewing a field engaged in considerable part with arguments about probability. The essence of chancing it is to have a go, and if you don't have a go you change nothing. A critical theory is not just a description, not even just a normative description which judges what it describes. It is a prescription for and guide to action. Crotty puts it like this: it is making

> ... a contrast between a research that seeks merely to understand and a research that challenges ... between a research that reads the situation in terms of interaction and community and a research that reads it in terms of conflict and oppression ... between a research that accepts the status quo and a research that seeks to bring about change. (1998: 113)

Not the least of the virtues of Crotty's book is that he includes Freire as a key critical theorist of the twentieth century, and dares to point out that Freire developed *and implemented* a theory of engaged action based on dialogue with those in the situation of action well in advance of the supposed innovations of a uniquely feminist method. Freire's own approach was largely linguistic and literary, which befits a programme founded around the transmission of literacy as a tool for emancipation. I have always been a firm believer in the value of numeracy as another tool in this process.

This is not simply a matter of the role of quantitative description in defining the character and tendency of our social orders – the specific role of statistics as understood by both Williams and Desrosières. It is also to do with the range of possible futures.

> It is somewhat disquieting to realize that the model we are going to build will contain the behaviour of actors, which will depend in turn on the models available to them, including this one. That is why the aim of these models is not predicting the future. It is to help understand the past and the present and the mechanisms that underlie them, and to explore possible futures so that they can be discussed, and evaluated more clearly. The initial use of such models would

be to help set the agendas of the different actors: what would be a good or bad thing, and for whom? (Allen, 1997: 178)

We cannot know the character of the present complex social world unless we measure. We cannot know the possible range of futures unless we use those measures to construct models. The combination of qualitative and quantitative exploration of causal processes in complex social systems which has been proposed in this book does seem to offer us the possibility of at least exploring the potential consequences of our actions for us. Note that this is not a proposal for utilitarianism. Allen explicitly recognizes the potential for social conflict and social division. There is no universal or general social good, unless we resurrect, as I am perfectly willing to do, a universalism based on proletarian status.

Complex modelling is not an esoteric academic game. It is an important tool in business and financial decision making. We might consider that it has the potential for being a tool in social action as well since it helps us delimit the range of the possible. After all, as O'Connor pertinently put it, in the social world the future is 'not a matter of what will happen but what will be made to happen' (1982: 328).

Bibliography

Abbott, A. (1988) 'Transcending General Linear Reality', *Sociological Theory*, 6: 169–186.
Abbott, A. (1992) 'What Do Cases Do? Some Notes on Activity in Sociological Analysis', in Ragin, C.S. and Becker, H. (eds) *What Is a Case? Exploring the Foundations of Social Inquiry.* Cambridge: Cambridge University Press.
Abbott, A. (1998) 'The Causal Devolution', *Sociological Methods and Research*, 27 (2): 148–181.
ALCD (1997a) 'Methodology and software for computer-intensive analysis of complext longitudinal data', *ESRC Research Programme into the Analysis of Large and Complex Datasets.* Swindon: Economic and Social Research Council.
ALCD (1997b) 'Using multi-level models for the analysis of large and complex data sets', *ESRC Research Programme into the Analysis of Large and Complex Datasets.* Swindon: Economic and Social Research Council.
Allen, P.M. (1997) *Cities and Regions as Self-Organizing Systems.* Amsterdam: Gordon and Breach.
Archer, M. (1998) 'Realism and Morphogenesis', in Archer, M., Bhaskar, R., Collier, A., Lawson, T. and Norrie, A. (eds), *Critical Realism – Essential Readings.* London: Routledge. pp. 356–382.
Archer, M., Bhaskar, R., Collier, A., Lawson, T. and Norrie, A. (eds) (1998) *Critical Realism – Essential Readings.* London: Routledge.
Bachman, J.G., O'Malley, P.M. and Johnston, J. (1978) *Youth in Transition*, vol. 6: *Adolesence to Adulthood.* Ann Arbor: Institute for Social Research.
Bailey, K.D. (1994) *Typologies and Taxonomies. Quantitative Applications in the Social Sciences 102.* London: Sage.
Banai, R. (1995) 'Critical Realism in Urban and Regional Studies', *Planning and Design (Environment and Planning B)*, 22 (3): 563–580.
Bateson, N. (1984) *Data Construction in Social Surveys.* London: Allen and Unwin.
Bhaskar, R. (1979) *A Realist Theory of Science.* Brighton: Harvester.
Black, T.R. (1999) *Doing Quantitative Research in the Social Sciences.* London: Sage.
Blackman, T. (1995) *Urban Policy and Practice.* London: Routledge.
Blaikie, N. (1993) *Approaches to Social Enquiry.* Cambridge: Polity.
Blalock, H.M. (1979) *Social Statistics.* London: McGraw Hill.
Blalock, H.M. (1982) *Conceptualization and Measurement in the Social Sciences.* London: Sage.
Booth, T. (1988) *Developing Policy Research.* Aldershot: Avebury.
Bowker, G.C. and Star, S.C. (1999) *Sorting Things Out.* Cambridge, MA: MIT Press.
Bradbury, F.C.S. (1933) *Causal Factors in Tuberculosis.* London: National Association for the Prevention of Tuberculosis.
Bradley, W.J. and Schaefer, K.C. (1998) *The Uses and Misuses of Data and Models.* London: Sage.
Brown, C. (1995) *Chaos and Catastrophe Theories. Quantitative Applications in the Social Science 107.* London: Sage.
Brown, G. and Harris, T. (1978) *The Social Origins of Depression.* London: Tavistock.
Bryman, A. (1988) *Quantity and Quality in Social Research.* London: Unwin Hyman.
Bynner, J. (1994) 'Analyzing Change Over Time Using LISREL', in Dale, A. and Davies, R.B. (eds) *Analyzing Social and Political Change.* London: Sage. pp. 98–117.
Byrne, D.S. (1989) *Beyond the Inner City.* Milton Keynes: Open University Press.
Byrne, D.S. (1997) 'Chaotic Places or Complex Places: Cities in a Post-industrial Era', in Westwood, S. and Williams, J. (eds), *Imagining Cities.* London: Routledge. pp. 50–72.
Byrne, D.S. (1998) *Complexity Theory and the Social Sciences.* London: Routledge.
Byrne, D.S. (1999) *Social Exclusion.* Buckingham: Open University Press.
Byrne, D.S. (2001) *Understanding the Urban.* London: Macmillan.

Byrne, D.S. and Doyle, A. (1997) 'Transformed landscape – culture and visual imagery in a town built on coal', R0002221969 Economic and Social Research Council Final Report.

Byrne, D.S., Harrison, S., Keithely, J. and McCarthy, P. (1985) *Housing and Health*. Aldershot: Gower.

Byrne, D.S., Williamson, W. and Fletcher, B. (1975) *The Poverty of Education*. Oxford: Martin Robertson.

Carley, M. (1981) *Social Measurement and Social Indicators*. London: Allen and Unwin.

Carlisle, E. (1972) 'The Conceptual Structure of Social Indicators', in Shonfield, A. and Shaw, S. (eds), *Social Indicators and Social Policy*. London: Heinemann. pp. 23–32.

Carter, R. (forthcoming) Review of Pleasants, N., *Wittgenstein and the Idea of a Critical Social Science: A Critique of Giddens, Habermas and Bhaskar*, London: Routledge (1999), in *Culture, Pedagogy and Society*.

Cicourel, A.V. (1964) *Method and Measurement in Sociology*. New York: Free Press.

Cilliers, P. (1998) *Complexity and Postmodernism*. London: Routledge.

Cilliers, P. (forthcoming) 'Boundaries, Hierarchies and Networks in Complex Systems', *Journal for Innovation Management*.

Clifford, H.T. and Stephenson, W. (1975) *An Introduction to Numerical Taxonomy*. London: Academic Press.

Coffey, A., Holbrook, B. and Atkinson, P. (1996) 'Qualitative Data Analysis: Technologies and Representations', *Sociological Research OnLine*, 1 (1): http://www.socresonline.org.uk/1/1/4.html.

Coverdill, J.E., Finlay, W. and Martin, J.K. (1994) 'Labour Management in the Southern Textile Industry: Comparing Qualitative, Quantitative and Qualitative Comparative Analysis', *Sociological Methods and Research*, 23: 54–85.

Crotty, M. (1998) *The Foundations of Social Research*. London: Sage.

Crutchfield, J.P. (1992) 'Knowledge and Meaning: Chaos and Complexity', in Lam, L. and Naroditsky, V. (eds), *Modelling Complex Phenomena*. New York: Springer-Verlag.

Cullen, M.J. (1975) *The Statistical Movement in Early Victorian Britain*. Hassocks: Harvester Press.

Dale, A. and Davies, R.B. (1994) *Analyzing Social and Political Change*. London: Sage.

Dale, A., Arber, S. and Proctor, M. (1988) *Doing Secondary Analysis*. London: Unwin Hyman.

Dale, A., Fieldhouse, E. and Holdsworth, C. (2000) *Analyzing Census Data*. London: Arnold.

Daston, L. (2000) 'Review of Desrosières (1998)', *London Review of Books*, 22 (8): 2000.

Davies, B. (1968) *Social Needs and Resources in Local Services*. London: Michael Joseph.

Davies, R.B. and Dale, A. (1994) 'Introduction' in Dale, A. and Davies, R.B. (eds) *Analyzing Social and Political Change*. London: Sage. pp. 1–19.

Davis, J.A. (1984) 'Foreword' to Hellevik, O., *Introduction to Causal Analysis*. London: Allen and Unwin. pp. xv–xviii.

Desrosières, A. (1998) *The Politics of Large Numbers*. Cambridge, MA: Harvard University Press.

De Vaus, D.A. (1991) *Surveys in Social Research*. London: UCL Press.

Dewey, J. and Bentley, A.F. (1949) *Knowing and the Known*. Boston: Beacon Press.

Dey, I. (1993) *Qualitative Data Analysis*. London: Routledge.

Doran, J. and Palmer, M. (1995) 'The EOS Project: Integrating Two Models of Palaeolithic Social Change' in Gilbert, N. and Conte, R. (eds) *Artificial Societies*. London: UCL Press. pp. 103–125.

Doran, J., Palmer, M., Gilbert, N. and Mellars, P. (1994) 'The EOS Project: Modelling Upper-Palaeolithic Social Change', in Gilbert, N. and Doran, J. (eds), *Simulating Societies*. London: UCL Press. pp. 195–222.

Dorling, D. and Simpson, S. (eds) (1999) *Statistics in Society*. London: Arnold.

Douglas, M. and Hull, D. (eds) (1992) *How Classification Works*. Edinburgh: Edinburgh University Press.

Draper, D. (1996) 'Discussion of Goldstein and Spiegelhalter (1996), *Journal of the Royal Statistical Society – Series A*, 3: 416–418.

Drogoul, A. and Ferber, J. (1994) 'Multi-agent Simulation as a Tool for Studying Emergent Processes in Societies', in Gilbert, N. and Doran, J. (eds), *Simulating Societies*. London: UCL Press. pp. 127–142.

Ekstrom, M. (1992) 'Causal Explanation of Social Action', *Acta Sociologica*, 35: 107–122.

Elliott, J. (1999) 'Models Are Stories Are Not Real Life' in Dorling, D. and Simpson, S. (eds), *Statistics in Society*. London: Arnold. pp. 95–102.

Emirbayer, M. (1997) 'Manifesto for a Relational Sociology', *American Journal of Sociology*, 103 (2): 281–317.

Encyclopedia of Statistical Sciences 1999 (eds-in-chief S. Kotz, N.L. Johnson) New York: Wiley.

Erikson, B. and Nosanchuk, T.A. (1992) *Understanding Data*. Buckingham: Open University Press.

Everitt, B.S. (1993) *Cluster Analysis*. London: Edward Arnold.

Everitt, B.S. and Dunn, G. (1983) *Advanced Methods of Data Exploration*. London: Heinemann.

Fabian Society (2000) *Paying for Progress: A New Politics of Tax for Public Spending*. London: Fabian Society.

Fielding, N.G. and Lee, R.M. (1998) *Computer Analysis and Qualitative Research*. London: Sage.

Frankenberg, R. (1966) *Communities in Britain*. London: Penguin.

Freire, P. (1998) *Pedagogy of Hope*. New York: Continuum.

Garson, G.D. (1998) *Neural Networks*. London: Sage.

Geertz, C. (1973) *The Interpretation of Cultures*. New York: Basic Books.

Gernet, D. (1998) 'Classifications and Predictions by Neural Networks and their Social Implications', in Liebrand, W.B.G., Nowak, A. and Hegselmann, R. (eds), *Computer Modeling of Social Processes*. London: Sage. pp. 85–96.

Gilbert, N. (1993) *Analyzing Tabular Data*. London: UCL Press.

Gilbert, N. (1995) 'Emergence in Social Simulation' in Gilbert, N. and Conte, R. (eds), *Artifical Societies*. London: UCL Press. pp. 144–156.

Gilbert, N. and Conte, R. (eds) (1995) *Artificial Societies*. London: UCL Press.

Gilbert, N. and Doran, J. (eds) (1994) *Simulating Societies*. London: UCL Press.

Gilbert, N. and Troitzsch, K.G. (1999) *Simulation for the Social Scientist*. Buckingham: Open University Press.

Glaser, B.G. and Strauss, A.L. (1967) *The Discovery of Grounded Theory Analysis*. Mill Valley, CA: Sociology Press.

Goldstein, H. (1995) *Multilevel Statistical Models*. London: Edward Arnold.

Goldstein, H. and Spiegelhalter, D.J. (1996) 'League Tables and Their Limitations', *Journal of the Royal Statistical Society – Series A*, 159 (3): 385–443.

Gould, S.J. (1991) *Wonderful Life*. London: Penguin.

Hacking, I. (1992) 'World Making by Kind Making: Child Abuse as an Example', in Douglas, M. and Hull, D. (eds), *How Classification Works*. Edinburgh: Edinburgh University Press. pp. 181–238.

Hage, J. and Meeker, B.F. (1988) *Social Causality*. London: Unwin Hyman.

Hakim, C. (1982) *Secondary Analysis in Social Research*. London: Allen and Unwin.

Halfpenny, P. (1997) 'Situating Simulation in Sociology', *Sociological Research Online: http://www.socresonline.org.uk/socresonline/2/3/9.html*.

Hanneman, R. and Patrick, S. (1997) 'On the Uses of Computer-Assisted Simulation Modeling in the Social Sciences', *Sociological Research Online*, 2 (2): *http://www.socresonline.org.uk/socresonline/ 2/2/5.html*.

Harré, R. (1976) 'The Constructive Role of Models', in Collins, L. (ed.), *The Use of Models in the Social Sciences*. London: Tavistock, pp. 16–43.

Harvey, D.L. and Reed, M.H. (1994) 'The Evolution of Dissipative Social Systems', *Journal of Social and Evolutionary Systems*, 17 (4): 371–411.

Hayles, K. (1999) *How We Became Posthuman*. Chicago: University of Chicago Press.

Heaney, T. (1995) *Issues in Freirean Pedagogy. http://nlu.nl.edu/ace/Resources/FreireIssues.html*.

Hellevik, O. (1984) *Introduction to Causal Analysis*. London: Allen and Unwin.

Hicks, A. (1994) 'Qualitative Comparative Analysis and Analytic Induction', *Sociological Methods and Research*, 23: 86–113.

Holland, J.H. (1998) *Emergence*. Reading MA: Addison–Wesley.

Huber, G.L. and Garcia, C.M. (1991) 'Computer Assistance for Testing Hypotheses about Qualitative Data', *Qualitative Sociology*, 14: 325–348.

Hull, D. (1992) 'Biological Species' in Douglas, M. and Hull, D. (eds) *How Classification Works*. Edinburgh: Edinburgh University Press. pp. 50–79.

Irvine, J., Miles, I. and Evans, J. (eds) (1979) *Demystifying Social Statistics*. London: Pluto.

Jeffrey, P., Seaton, R. and Lemon, M. (1999) 'Complexity, Systems and Models', in Lemon, M. (ed.) *Exploring Environmental Change Using an Integrative Method*. Amsterdam: Gordon and Breach. pp. 71–82.

Khalil, E.L. (1996) 'Social Theory and Naturalism', in Khalil, E.L. and Boulding, K., *Evolution, Order and Complexity*. London: Routledge. pp. 1–39.

Khalil, E.L. and Boulding, K. (1996) *Evolution, Order and Complexity*. London: Routledge.

Kritzer, H.M. (1996) 'The Data Puzzle: The Nature of Interpretation in Quantitative Research', *American Journal of Political Science*, 40 (1): 1–32.

Krzanowski, W. (1998) *An Introduction to Statistical Modelling*. London: Edward Arnold.

Lakoff, G. and Johnson, M. (1999) *Philosophy in the Flesh*. New York: Basic Books.

Land, K.C. and Felson, M. (1976) 'A General Framework for Building Dynamic Macro Social Indicator Models', *American Journal of Sociology*, 82: 565–604.

Langeheine, R. and van de Pol, F. (1994) 'Discrete-Time Mixed Markov Latent Class Models', in Dale, A. and Davies, R.B. (eds), *Analysing Social and Political Change*. London: Sage. pp. 167–197.

Lee, R.M. and Fielding, N. (1996) 'Qualitative Data Analysis: Representations of a Technology – a Comment on Coffey, Holbrook, and Atkinson', *Sociological Research OnLine*, 1 (4): *http://www.socresonline.org.uk/1/4/if.html*.

Lemon, M. (ed.) (1999) *Exploring Environmental Change Using an Integrative Method*. Amsterdam: Gordon and Breach.

Lemon, M. and Oxley, T. (1999) 'Where to From Here?', in Lemon, M. (ed.), *Exploring Environmental Change Using an Integrative Method*. Amsterdam: Gordon and Breach. pp. 231–240.

Lemon, M. and Seaton, R. (1999) 'Towards an Integrative Method', in Lemon, M. (ed.) *Exploring Environmental Change Using an Integrative Method*. Amsterdam: Gordon and Breach. pp. 17–26.

Levitas, R. (1996) 'The Legacy of Rayner', in Levitas, R. and Guy, W. (eds) *Interpreting Official Statistics*. London: Routledge. pp. 7–25.

Levitas, R. and Guy, W. (1996) *Interpreting Official Statistics*. London: Routledge.

Liebrand, W.B.G., Nowak, A. and Hegselmann, R. (eds) (1998) *Computer Modeling of Social Processes*. London: Sage.

Losee, J. (1993) *A Historical Introduction to the Philosophy of Science*. Oxford: Oxford University Press.

MacKenzie, D. (1979) 'Eugenics and the Rise of Mathematical Statistics in Britain', in Irvine, J., Miles, I. and Evans, J. (eds), *Demystifying Social Statistics*. London: Pluto. pp. 39–50.

Marsh, C. (1982) *The Survey Method*. London: Allen and Unwin.

Martinotti, G. (1999) 'A City for Whom? Transients and Public Life in the Second-Generation Metropolis' in Beauregard, R.A. and Body-Gendrot, S. (eds), *The Urban Moment*. London: Sage. pp. 155–184.

Mills, C.W. (1959) *The Sociological Imagination*. Oxford: Oxford University Press.

Newby, H. (1992) 'Join Forces in a Modern Marriage', *Times Higher Educational Supplement*, 17 January, p. 20.

Oakley, A. (2000) *Experiments in Knowing*. Cambridge: Polity.

O'Connor, J. (1982) 'The Meaning of Crisis', *International Journal of Urban and Regional Research*, 5: 301–328.

Ostrom, T. (1988) 'Computer Simulation: the Third Symbol System', *Journal of Experimental Psychology*, 24: 381–392.

Pawson, R. (1989) *A Measure for Measures: A Manifesto for Empirical Sociology*. London: Routledge.

Pawson, R. and Tilley, N. (1997) *Realistic Evaluation*. London: Sage.

Phillips, D. (1995) 'Correspondence Analysis', *Social Research Update* 7: *http://www.soc.surrey. ac.uk/stu/SRU7.html*.

Pleasant, N. (1999) *Wittgenstein and the Idea of a Critical Social Science: A Critique of Giddens, Habermas and Bhaskar*. London: Routledge.

Plewis, I. (1994) 'Longitudinal Multilevel Models', in Dale, A. and Davies, R.B. (eds), *Analysing Social and Political Change*. London: Sage. pp. 118–135.

Prior, L. (1989) *The Social Organisation of Death*. Basingstoke: Macmillan.

Ragin, C.C. (1987) *The Comparative Method: Moving beyond Qualitative and Quantitative Strategies*. Berkeley, CA: University of California Press.

Ragin, C.C. (1994) *Constructing Social Research*. Thousand Oaks, CA: Pine Forge Press.

Reed, M. and Harvey, D.L. (1992) 'The New Science and the Old: Complexity and Realism in the Social Sciences', *Journal for the Theory of Social Behaviour*, 22: 356–379.

Reed, M. and Harvey, D.L. (1996) 'Social Science as the study of Complex Systems', in Kiel, L.D. and Elliott, E. (eds), *Chaos Theory in the Social Sciences*. Ann Arbor, MI: University of Michigan Press. pp. 295–324.

Richards, L. (1999) *Using Nvivo in Qualitative Research*. London: Sage.

Rivlin, A. (1971) *Systematic Thinking for Social Action*. Washington, DC: The Brookings Institution.

Robinson, W.S. (1950) 'Ecological Correlations and the Behavior of Individuals', *American Sociological Review*, 15: 351–357.

Rose, D. and O'Reilly, K. (1997) *Constructing Classes*. Swindon: ESRC/ONS.

Rosen, R. (1987) 'Some Epistemological Issues in Physics and Biology', in Hiley, B.J. and Peat, F.D. (eds), *Quantum Implications: Essays in Honour of David Bohm*. London: Routledge. pp. 314–327.

Ruelle, D. (1991) *Chance and Chaos*. London: Penguin.

Sayer, A. (1992) *Method in Social Science*. London: Routledge.

Sayer, A. (2000) *Realism and Social Science*. London: Sage.

Shaw, M. and Miles, I. (1979) 'The Social Roots of Statistical Knowledge', in Irivine, J., Miles, I. and Evans, J. (eds), *Demystifying Social Statistics*. London: Pluto. pp. 27–38.

Sneath, P.H.A. and Sokal, R.R. (1973) *Numerical Taxonomy*. San Francisco: Freeman.

Thompson, E.P. (1978) *The Poverty of Theory*. London: Merlin.

Troitzsch, K.G. (1998) 'Multilevel Process Modeling in the Social Sciences', in Liebrand, W.B.G., Nowak, A. and Hegselmann, R. (eds), *Computer Modeling of Social Processes*. London: Sage. pp. 20–36.

Tukey, J.W. (1977) *Exploratory Data Analysis*. Reading, MA: Addison–Wesley.

Two Crows (1999) *Introduction to Data Mining and Knowledge Discovery*. Potomac, MD: Two Crows Corporation.

Ulanowicz, R.E. (1996) 'The Propensities of Evolving Systems', In Khalil, E.L. and Boulding, K. (eds), *Evolution, Order and Complexity*. London: Routledge. pp. 217–233.

Valentine, C. (1970) *Culture and Poverty*. Chicago: University of Chicago Press.

Williams, M. (1999) 'Single Case Probabilities in the Social World', *Journal for the Theory of Social Behaviour*, 29 (2): 187–201.

Williams, M. (2000) *Science and Social Science*. London: Routledge.

Williams, M. and May, T. (1996) *Introduction to the Philosophy of Social Research*. London: UCL Press.

Williams, R. (1965) *The Long Revolution*. London: Penguin.

Williams, R. (1979) *Politics and Letters*. London: Verso.

Znaniecki, F. (1934) *The Method of Sociology*. New York: Farrar and Rinehart.

Index